GARMENT
OF D

GARMENT OF DESTINY

A Surgeon's Global Quest for Identity and the Ties that Bind

DR. ABDALLAH DAAR

BARLOW BOOKS
fine books for enterprising authors

Library and Archives Canada Cataloguing in Publication data available upon request.

978-1-988025-34-6 (paperback)
978-1-988025-35-3 (ebook)

Printed in Canada

TO ORDER IN CANADA:
Georgetown Publications
34 Armstrong Avenue, Georgetown, ON L7G 4R9

TO ORDER IN THE U.S.A.:
Midpoint Book Sales & Distribution
27 West 20th Street, Suite 1102, New York, NY 10011

Publisher: Sarah Scott
Book producer: Tracy Bordian/At Large Editorial Services
Cover design: Paul Hodgson
Interior design and layout: Rob Scanlan/First Image
Copy editing: Wendy Thomas
Proofreading: Eleanor Gaspark
Indexing: Wendy Thomas
Marketing & publicity: Debby de Groot/MDG Associates

For more information, visit **www.barlowbooks.com**

BARLOW BOOKS

Barlow Book Publishing Inc.
96 Elm Avenue, Toronto, ON
Canada M4W 1P2

In memory of my parents, Jamila and Salim, and for Shahina, the ultimate of life companions, and Ajmal, the greatest of friends. For the future generation, Xara, Azlan, Ayla, and Leyna, and their parents, Lamees, Tarik, Nadia, and Kyle; and their uncle, Marwan. And for Africa, home of the next Einstein.

As a surgeon and global health specialist, I have always found solace, direction, and guidance in the words of Dr. Martin Luther King Jr.:

> *In a real sense all life is inter-related. All men are caught in an inescapable network of mutuality, tied in a single garment of destiny. Whatever affects one directly, affects all indirectly. I can never be what I ought to be until you are what you ought to be, and you can never be what you ought to be until I am what I ought to be ... This is the inter-related structure of reality.*

For me, these words are not just aspirational. They are a prescription for survival. Hailing from Africa with mixed ancestry, I am labelled a "visible minority"; to some, I am "the other." But I know King's words can be understood by, and empower, people *everywhere,* despite the rising tide of polarization that plagues our world. I know that wherever we may have been born, we all have a dream to be one thing: equal members of the human community.

I wrote this book because of a disturbing trend: Despite the enormous progress being made globally in areas like poverty, health, and improved nutrition, every day we see alarming indications that our unique human fabric is unravelling.

This is a book of hope. In a small and humble way, it is my effort to renew Dr. King's dream, and the dreams of many others. We *can* make the world a better place. Each of us is a unique thread, and we must take *personal* responsibility for what becomes of our shared human inheritance—our future—our garment of destiny.

Dr. Abdallah Daar
August 2018

Contents

An Introduction

Who Are You?

My name is Abdallah Daar.

If you ask me, "Who are you?" I will tell you that I am a doctor—that I am a Canadian. I am an immigrant and I went to university in England. Or I might say that I am a husband and father of three, or that I live in Toronto. You might say, "Well, there are a lot of doctors, and a lot of people who are Canadian; lots of people are fathers too."

And I would say, "That is true." With all these people I have much in common. What I say about myself—how I conceive of my own identity—easily could be said of others. If you asked what else, I might mention that I enjoy reading books about history or talking philosophy. I could tell you about my love of good food or that I can speak several languages fluently, including Swahili! "Really?" you might say. "Why in the world do you speak Swahili?"

And that is how we start. Our stories are the keys to who we are and what we become. A door opens where before we might not even have seen one. Before I was the blank. Now I am "that Canadian guy who speaks Swahili." I have an identity. Identity is like a lifeline. What if someone asked, however, "Who is he?" *He looks foreign. He seems dark. He sounds like a Muslim.* These things, too, I am, but not in the same way that I am those other things.

* * *

There is no one in this world that I know better than myself. Or at least that is what I—we—often want to believe about ourselves. Our self. But who is that person we think we know? What is my identity? And is my identity really mine or merely a perspective that I borrow on a temporary journey that we call life? Do I even know myself or am I merely a being who is known by others for reasons that may or may not have anything to do with who I actually am?

Identity might be like a snowflake: no two are alike. I think we all want to believe that we are unique as individuals. And we are. Few of us, however, are completely at home only in our self. We need others, if only to be reminded periodically of the fact that we are seen. After all, few of us trust or even recognize the face that confronts us daily in the mirror; often we need others to tell us who we are. So identity also might be like the shadow we carry around with us wherever we go—a projection that only hints in broad lines and angles.

It has been said that a human life is a book in which we set out to write one story and end up writing another. It is true, but not just of life. In my case, it is true also of the book itself. As a result, the stories follow a non-linear path, moving back and forth in time and place, because so many of the stories and memories are interconnected, often serendipitously. The past and the present are connected, of course—easier to separate oneself from one's own shadow than from the past! The farther along I travel this path of life, too, the more I believe that beginnings and ends are illusions. Who I am is the summary of all I have been and of who I have encountered and who has had an influence on me. The past keeps shaping the present. Furthermore, even though I write about myself, this book is not a typical autobiography. I hope that it ends up being less about me than about people *like me* who make up this wonderful garment of destiny we call life. "There is no such thing as history," wrote Emerson, "only biography." I love telling stories because, as the great South African author Athol Fugard said, "the only safe place is inside a story."

I tell stories about who I am and about others who directly or indirectly have had an impact on who I am, and about why you and I are the same. People like my friend Dr. Izzeldin Abuelaish, author of *I Shall Not Hate: A Gaza Doctor's Journey on the Road to Peace and Human Dignity*; Nobel Prize for Physics winner Abdus Salam; pioneering South African physician and human rights advocate Bill Hoffenberg; my mother and father; my Circassian great-grandmother; my best friend; new friends; and many others.

"Every life converges," wrote Emily Dickinson, "to some center." It is a rich and tantalizing thought; I take it to mean not necessarily that we at some point achieve perfected identity—an otherness and autonomy we confuse with the *self*—but, rather, that in our relations with other people we are always finding the *centredness* of our shared humanity, the convergence to what philosopher Alasdair MacIntyre called the "virtues of acknowledged dependence." In short, we are all in this together; we cannot do it alone.

We all need mentors in our lives; one never knows who that mentor will be or where he or she will be found. It could be a parent, a neighbour, a teacher, or a complete stranger encountered in a book. "A poet," wrote Gandhi in his autobiography, The Story of My Experiments with Truth, "is one who can call forth the good latent in the human breast." For the young Gandhi, the "poet" was the quintessential Victorian art critic and social thinker John Ruskin. Gandhi believed he had discovered some of his deepest convictions reflected in Ruskin's Unto This Last, a passionate but controversial polemic against industrialism and unregulated capitalism. A friend had given Gandhi a copy of the book in 1904, and it transformed his life. "I determined to change my life in accordance with the ideals of the book," he wrote. "I arose with the dawn, ready to reduce [Ruskin's ideals] into practise." It is hard to imagine two individuals less alike and more widely separated culturally than Gandhi and Ruskin. The book is out of print today and was out of date by the time Gandhi read it; only the tedium of a long and boring train ride induced the young man to read it, but it came alive and consumed his heart like fire! It is remarkable to me still that Gandhi could have had such a powerful awakening from a book that came under his attentive gaze purely by accident. I think about the power of serendipity. Is it such? Or is it that we are intersecting all the time, but for reasons both practical and abstract we fail, or simply neglect, to be attentive?

Powerful influences can reach us not only one to another but also through time and space—across the ages. We don't know who and we don't what or when. Only the wind knows where the seed will find fertile soil! What I have found—what has been and continues to be true for me—is that our lives intersect in mysterious but powerful and meaningful ways. "Out of timber so crooked as that from which man is made," wrote Immanuel Kant, "nothing straight can be built." This quote is a favourite of mine because it so powerfully summarizes what I believe to be so wonderful about our human diversity. It became—in paraphrase—the title of a book by Isaiah Berlin, the philosopher of ideas who also happened to be the founder of Wolfson College at Oxford, my alma mater.

Always intersections! This book is in large part a record of those mysterious intersections. I did not know the importance of many of those encounters at the time; perhaps I should say that often I had not the perspective or objectivity to appreciate the significance of what I experienced, but that, too, is the way of things. What is wisdom, after all, but comprehending finally what we only thought we understood before? But a caveat: emphasizing our shared humanity—the reality of our ultimate oneness—is not to deny our claim of individuality and originality. As human beings it is our diversity that unites us. The garment of destiny is not of one colour or texture but many; it is, however, one garment.

We should pay attention to what Herodotus discovered more than two thousand years ago: "The past does not exist. There are only infinite renderings of it." That ought to make us appreciate each other's stories. I believe that there is no clash of civilizations because we have one human civilization.

Who am I? I am everything you see. And nothing you see. And so are you. I am Abdallah Daar: human being.

Preamble

Holy Peacock: We Are All Displaced Persons

In the social jungle of human existence, there is no feeling of being alive without a sense of identity.

— Erik Erikson

I have been intrigued by the idea of displacement all my life. It could be voluntary or compulsory. It amuses me no end, for instance, that every fall for one day millions of North Americans pile into cars or airplanes for long trips to celebrate and give thanks for the blessings of "family," only to pile back into cars and airplanes for long trips home—which for most of us is usually some place we were not born or grew up in.

The Thanksgiving holiday, which celebrates the 1621 Pilgrims' first harvest shared with the Wampanoag Indians, is homage to the home of our roots; where we tend to live is the home where we have put down *new* roots. It is, however, still home.

Others, of course, have no choice but to accommodate their exile, and the roots of displacement—exile—go back as far as humanity itself. Adam and Eve are perhaps the most famous of the original exiles. For his part, Satan paid for his ambition by being expelled from heaven, but Milton had his Satan in *Paradise Lost* say, "Better to reign in Hell than serve in Heav'n" (an observation, by the way, about the seduction of power that, for me, has interesting explanatory applications to our current state of affairs). One of the most famous sculptures by Bernini portrays the exiled Trojan hero Aeneas lugging his son, father, and their household gods from the smouldering rubble of Troy on a nomadic voyage that—according to legend—will lead to the founding of Rome.

Or as Aeneas would have called it, *home*. In other words, all homes are to some extent built upon the rubble of old homes. None of us are original, we are all wanderers—we all carry with us some version of our "household gods"—in search of . . . a place of belonging and permanence: a room of one's own, perhaps.

Gibran Kahlil Gibran was in a way the prophet of exile, a man who lived as an adult in the West but longed profoundly for his beloved Lebanon, from which he felt he had been uprooted. "I am a stranger in this world, and there is a severe solitude and painful lonesomeness in my exile," he wrote, but then he added, "Mankind only exiles the one whose large spirit rebels against injustice and tyranny. He who does not prefer exile to servility is not free in the true and necessary sense of freedom."

Can we separate physical from spiritual exile? Aren't they equally painful? Rumi writes that the "sweetness and delights of the resting-place are in proportion to the pain endured on the Journey. Only when you suffer the pangs and tribulations of exile will you truly enjoy your homecoming."

The great social observer Marshall McLuhan wrote that Canada "is the only country that knows how to live without an identity." As a person with mixed ancestral origins, I am not sure that is true. Can anyone—any of us—truly live without an identity? Isn't McLuhan's lack of identity—albeit expressed in the negative—itself a kind of identity?

I have a dear friend, Terry, who happens to be McLuhan's daughter. When I first met her, she had just completed making a film called *The Frontier Gandhi,* which is about a close friend of Gandhi named Badshah Khan, who co-developed with Gandhi the methods of nonviolent resistance that were later adopted by Martin Luther King Jr. It took Terry nineteen years to get the documentary right. With her unerring and profound eye, Terry had also once compiled and annotated a wonderful book of Indian sayings called *Touch the Earth: A Self-Portrait of Indian Existence.* She quotes Geronimo, the great Apache chief (called Goyahkla by his people), whose lands had been appropriated by the American government: "It is my land, my home, my father's land, to which I now ask to be allowed to return. I want to spend my last days there and be buried amongst those mountains. If this could be I might die in peace, feeling that my people, placed in the native homes, would increase in numbers rather than diminish as at present, and that our name would not become extinct."

This beautiful but haunting observation makes me think about Aeneas and his journey, but in reverse. In a sense, *to be* is to be *at home* somewhere. This need is not cultural or racial; it is a fundamental human need. Even in the harshest of circumstances, human dignity always matters to those who suffer. To have a name is to have an identity that is linked to dignity. No one wants to have his name made extinct. To be in exile is to lose your original identity. For some, it is to lose your identity, period.

Identity has had—continues to have—a powerful influence on me. I write in this book often of having been lucky in my life. I have been; many people I grew up with in Tanzania were not lucky and I think identity is part of the reason. I am lucky to "be" who I am and to have had a rich share of success and privilege and honours, but I can't help believing that luck played a huge part in helping me become *who I am*. Cervantes wrote that "to be lucky in the beginning is everything." It was absolutely true for me.

I was lucky to have been born in circumstances that allowed me to get a good basic education; then an incredible stroke of luck got me into high school, where I did well enough to be among the tiniest number of students selected to go to medical school in Uganda; there I survived the identity politics and violence of the murderous Idi Amin regime and became a displaced person, finishing medical school in London. Another set of auspicious academic circumstances got me into the University of Oxford in 1975, and by the time I left Oxford a decade or so later I was a transplant surgeon and was headhunted to go to help build medical schools in the United Arab Emirates and Oman, where I was professor of surgery from 1988 to 2000. But the biggest stroke of luck that was later to change my career occurred in Bangkok in 1994, when I met the director-general of the World Health Organization, and, again without any specific planning on my part, I was pulled into global health a few years later, an event triggered by the unnecessary death of my eldest sister from malaria (mosquitoes kill more people every day than do sharks in one century). In a very happy coincidence this triggered my meeting Peter Singer in Toronto in 1998.

Those lucky breaks have led me to a truly international life in global health. Since that propitious day in 1998, Peter and I have worked together on a variety of global health issues. It's been our honour to work with Bill and Melinda Gates to fulfill their profound conviction that every life has equal value. Working with the Gates Foundation and our own programs in Toronto, we have sought to change the health and social circumstances brought on by poverty and discriminatory colonial policies in developing countries, particularly in African countries like Tanzania, where I was born.

Peter and I started working with the Bill and Melinda Gates Foundation in 2003, initially helping to establish its Grand Challenges in Global Health research and innovation funding program. A grand challenge was defined as a specific critical barrier that if removed would help to solve an important problem in delivering health care to the developing world. We then brought the Grand Challenges idea to Canada. In 2010 we co-founded Grand Challenges Canada (GCC), an organization, I'm proud to report, that has contributed in a significant way to a real improvement in global health (you'll read about it later in this book).

It's been very fulfilling to work on a global mission, and yet I am often reminded that, at heart, I am a person who lives far from my homeland where a significant part of my identity was formed. This fact was driven home in vivid fashion in 2016, when Peter and I launched the Humanitarian Grand Challenges initiative. Our long-term aim with this initiative is to work with partners in the humanitarian community to transform humanitarian responses by making them more effective and efficient.

Peter and I set up a meeting in Toronto to kick off our work. We sat around a rectangular table, and microphones were set on the table and some were built into the ceiling. Some of our staff sat on chairs next to the white painted walls. Some participants called in from as far as Australia, using BlueJeans, our videoconferencing platform.

In the room that day we had a group of about twenty participants from governments, NGOs (Doctors Without Borders, the Red Cross, Save the Children, Care International, World Vision, and so on), philanthropic organizations, and others interested in identifying and funding innovative methods to make humanitarian action more efficient and effective in the long term. These are people whose organizations like to be prepared to save lives, alleviate suffering, and maintain and protect human dignity during and in the aftermath of man-made crises and natural disasters.

The agenda was packed so we started early in the morning. To put matters in perspective for all participants, we had invited a Syrian refugee couple, Mahfouza and Bachir Brimo, to set the tone and lend some realism to the discussions that would follow. Mahfouza is a dignified, thoughtful, attractive woman who appeared to be in her late forties. Bachir is handsome, too, sombre, and probably about fifty. They had been in Canada for about five months and were just learning to speak English. We had looked for a Kurdish-speaking translator but could find only an Arabic speaker. Luckily the Brimos spoke both languages. The translator, however, had got lost in Toronto traffic, and we had to make a start because of the day's busy agenda.

Peter looked to me expectantly. We had been in similar situations in our many travels together over the past nineteen years, and I had used my excellent Swahili to facilitate meetings in East Africa. I now foolishly agreed to translate, knowing that my Arabic is much poorer than my Swahili. Nevertheless, we managed to get a good conversation going. We learned from Mahfouza and Bachir that they belonged to the ancient Yazidi community, whose ancestral home is near their sacred Sinjan Mountain that spans northern Iraq and Syria. The Iraqi side is close to Nineveh, once the largest city in the known world. It is mentioned in Genesis in the Tanakh (Hebrew Bible).

The Yazidis, while being monotheistic, are not Muslim, Christian, or adherents of the Jewish faith. Their poorly understood gnostic religion has a belief in a benevolent peacock angel, which some of their enemies have interpreted to be a form of Satan worship. It is a largely endogamous community that mostly keeps to itself. Over many centuries it has been persecuted by many of its neighbours, but in the recent past it has been a particular target of the so-called Islamic State (ISIS). At least twenty-nine Yazidi mass graves were uncovered during the military campaign to take back Mosul from ISIS, and more have been found since then in other areas. Tens of thousands of Yazidis have been pursued, captured, tortured, raped, sold, and resold into slavery and the women forced into service as sex slaves. Thousands more have been killed or compelled to convert. The United Nations has formally recognized these atrocities as genocide. But it goes beyond the technical definition of genocide. In my experience as a global health specialist who has seen much poverty and suffering in many ravaged communities, I have come to accept that *every time we deny the humanity of another we are committing genocide.*

The Brimos and their five children were lucky. Bachir had made a modest living as a cobbler in Afrin, their village in northern Syria near the Turkish border. Its official symbol is the olive tree, reminding us of the olive branch of peace and reconciliation. At the beginning of the Syrian war in March 2011, the Brimos were internally displaced near Damascus. When hostilities ceased and life seemed to return to normal, the family moved back to Afrin. It was, it turns out, a huge mistake. The ceasefire fell apart shortly after their return and ISIS attacked the village with its characteristic murderous zeal. The Brimo family just managed to escape and ended up as refugees in Lebanon. Life for Syrian refugees at the camps was extremely tough, but at least they were safe. Most Syrian refugees in Lebanon are not in camps and instead have been forced to survive as best they can: finding shelter wherever possible, eating whatever and whenever they can, begging, and hoping.

The Brimos were registered with the UN and were lucky enough to be selected to immigrate to Canada, except for their eldest daughter who, being over eighteen, was considered an adult. She was registered separately and was then still in Lebanon.

Peter Singer, his wife, Heather, and her local church had sponsored this family of six, and the Singers took them into their home when they first arrived in April 2016. The children are now in school, the family is settled in Toronto, and they are happy and grateful to Canada. Their major concern and worry now is about their daughter, who is still a refugee in Lebanon with her two children and a husband who suffers from bad asthma.

The interpreter eventually did find her way into the meeting. We concluded our conversation with the Brimos, they left, and we continued with the rest of our agenda. All day we discussed humanitarian crises under various conditions: natural disasters like earthquakes, cyclones, floods, and droughts; and man-made disasters including civil strife, wars, and other violent situations. We talked about refugees, displaced persons, and large-scale migrations. We talked about what the various organizations and governments were doing and thinking of doing in the future, focusing on innovations. The meeting was intense, fast moving, and very fruitful.

We also did a quick consensus-building (Delphi) study to identify and rank what this group would consider to be the kinds of innovations that might constitute a grand challenge. I found it fascinating that among the top five, three were focused on identity. The first innovation on the list of twelve established a rapid, on-the-ground method of creating and implementing a personal digital identity for all those affected by the humanitarian crisis situation—for example, refugees. This would be very useful for registries and databases, for disbursement of funds, for heath care and follow-up, and so on. The second, linked to the first, would establish a reliable, accessible digital safe box where those affected could deposit copies of their vital documents like birth certificates, identity cards, and passports. The third covered gender and made suggestions for strengthening women's leadership roles in planning to reduce the risk of disasters and improving humanitarian responses. We also heard from Jeffrey Cyr, an Indigenous Canadian, who reminded us of the principle of "nothing about us without us" and that "wealth is to be shared, not hoarded." He also told us about the Moose Hide Campaign, in which men wear small, tanned squares of moose hide on their lapels to stimulate conversations about how they should deal with violence against Indigenous women and girls.

At the end of the day's agenda, we went around the table, asking each participant to briefly summarize their impressions of the work we did that day. When it came to my turn, I paused for a long time and then said: "The things we discussed today resonate deeply with me at a personal level. You see, I was myself once a displaced person."

Chapter 1

Ghosts of Aggrey Street

There is nothing like returning to a place that remains unchanged to find the ways in which you yourself have altered.

— Nelson Mandela

Some things will never change. Some things will always be the same. . . . I have to see a thing a thousand times before I see it once.

— Thomas Wolfe, *You Can't Go Home Again*

In 2009 my colleague Peter Singer and I were on a research trip to Tanzania, the result of a unique global health program we had developed focusing on the intersection of biosciences, innovation, global health, and bioethics. The trip to Tanzania was to study its innovation system, which for us meant studying in detail the links, if any, among its educational, industrial, technological, intellectual property, and other areas that are needed for socio-economic and health innovation. We would then work with the government to build up such institutional capacity and link them to improve that kind of innovation. (We did this kind of work in several other countries in the developing world.)

Peter and I are great friends as well as esteemed colleagues, and he knew that I was born in Tanzania, but as far as I can recall, I never really expressed any compelling desire to him to revisit any ancestral sites. So when one morning in Dar es Salaam, the capital, I broached the subject of me taking a stroll down memory lane, he was curious but not surprised. In fact he was quite supportive. "Do you want me to go with you?"

What I had not told Peter was that I had more on my mind than casual nostalgia. Since stepping foot back in Tanzania after so many years I could not help thinking of the death of a beloved sister, an experience that haunts me to this day. Her death, in fact, was a major reason I was on this trip. Anyway, I said yes to Peter. I was anxious about what I would find, and I figured I might need the company.

We stepped outside the hotel and into the bright sun. It was a hot morning already and we decided to take a taxi. As we wound and wove our way through the hot and crowded streets, I leaned my face out the open window and did the best I could to link the memories I had of my childhood with the Dar es Salaam that presented itself to me. On the hot and dusty breeze I could still detect the fragrance of the sea, but the city was much bigger and far more bustling and cosmopolitan than I remember it as a boy. The food stalls and the cozy cafés, however, with their rich milky sweet tea looked the same. The taxi pulled to the side of the road. I was surprised. *Why are we stopping?* I wondered. After a time, the driver turned his head around and, impatient, shot me a puzzled look.

"Aggrey Street?" he barked in Swahili.

"Yes," I answered.

He raised his hands—palms up—and shrugged. *We are here,* the gesture communicated. We climbed out of the cab and back into the hot sun. The American writer Thomas Wolfe wrote a novel in the twenties about the futility of returning to the past. *You Can't Go Home Again,* he titled the book. He was right. The home in Aggrey Street that I had lived in for so many years as a child was gone, as was my grandmother's house in Mahiwa Street. In their place stood snazzy boutique hotels. In fact, much of the old neighbourhoods had changed completely. Oddly, the fact that the physical remnants of my past had disappeared and been replaced by completely modern structures seemed only to crystallize my memories and make them both more vivid and distinct. I could see my house in my mind's eye as if it were only yesterday. Of course, when I opened my eyes it was gone.

I had a far more disturbing experience when—on the same research trip—I decided to visit another childhood town. When I was between the ages of four and seven our family lived in the very tiny town of Dodoma, about 400 kilometres (250 miles) from Dar es Salaam in central Tanzania. Not only was our house still standing, but it also hadn't seemed to age one bit. It was like I had travelled back in time. Much later Peter asked me how my trips down memory lane had been. "Was it worth it?" I felt as if I had suddenly been brought face to face with two completely different fates! What if I had stayed? What if I were like so many friends I remember who—for reasons of poverty or lack of opportunity or poor education or who were just plain unlucky—fell into that hopeless downward spiral of poverty and despair that afflicts so many in our world? *Was I that special? Why me? What about them?* I told Peter I wasn't sure. "I don't know," I said. "I'll let you know when I'm done." I am still working on it.

Chapter 2

In Search of Lost Time

Kusadikika ni nchi ambayo kuweko kwake hufikirika kwa mawazo tu.
(Kusadikika is a country that only exists in our imagination.)

Kusadikika, Shaaban Robert,
the father of Kiswahili literature

"Home," he mocked gently.
"Yes, what else but home?
It all depends on what you mean by home. . . ."
"Home is the place where, when you have to go there,
They have to take you in."
— Robert Frost, *"The Death of the Hired Man"*

I was born in the capital town Dar es Salaam in 1948 in what was then Tanganyika in East Africa. After a revolution in 1964 Tanganyika and neighbouring Zanzibar merged into a country called Tanzania. Tanganyika had been under German rule until that country's defeat in World War One, when the British took over. At the time I was born it was under British control. Most of my youthful years were spent in Dar es Salaam, but because of my father's business partnership with his elder brother Ali, we also lived for short periods in Morogoro and Dodoma.

I began life in what can be described as an Arab household, but my mother tongue was Kiswahili (Swahili). When I think of my childhood I cannot help but be reminded of the wonderful thing I know as Swahili culture. But who are the Swahili? It is not an easy question to answer. There are historical, cultural, linguistic, geographic, economic, and other aspects bearing on the subject. Scholars like Al Ameen Mazrui and Ibrahim Shareef trace the origins further back in history than those, like Jan Knappert, who emphasize a more recent mingling of the majority African with other cultures. The complex discussion continues, as noted by Aijaz Ahmad: "Among the African peoples, the Swahili are unique in at least one respect, for it is about them more than any other people, that the question is perennially asked: who are the Swahili?"

There is some merit in Knappert's argument that "the Swahili are neither African nor Asian, but sui generis, an open society, tolerant and free." It is these elements of openness, tolerance, and freedom that I value most. This East African coastal, largely Muslim, culture is for me an intrinsic, perhaps the dominant, part of my several identities. With roots in Lamu, Mombasa, and Zanzibar, the culture has evolved as it continued its coastal trajectory south to Dar es Salaam, Kilwa, Mafia, and beyond. These coastal areas have thus had some Arab, mostly Omani, influences and share a rich culture underpinned by the Swahili language. It has a tradition of cultural production in music and poetry, of living together in peace, and of respecting all. A lot of intermarriages have taken place in these coastal areas of East Africa, between the various Bantu African tribes themselves, and between them and the Arab traders. East African Indians have married Africans to a much lesser extent.

The Swahili language is thus made up primarily of Bantu and Arabic words, with a much smaller contribution from other immigrant languages like Hindustani. To this day a preponderance of nouns in Swahili are of Arabic origin. Indeed, the name "Swahili" itself is derived from the Arabic word for "coastal."

I grew up speaking Swahili. It was the language we spoke at home and is the language I still speak when I am with my brothers and sisters. It is now the lingua franca of the whole of East Africa and beyond. As such it has become a very powerful language for political communication, administration, social interaction, and trade.

Common Swahili cultural elements include men's and women's dresses. Men often wear a *kanzu* (a robe, usually white) and a "Zanzibari" hat, with sandals. Women wear colourful dresses and cover themselves with even more colourful *kangas*, colourful fabrics on which are written poems or excerpts from a Swahili traditional musical style called Tarab, which I am very fond of. The verses have an apparent surface meaning but have two or three different layers of deeper meaning, with a lot of double entendres. A kanga that I possess has written on it in Swahili, "Let's love each other sincerely and don't waste each other's time."

For me it is a sublime, peaceful, enchanting, accepting, respecting, tolerant, syncretic, and mature culture. It is a culture that was close to me when I was a kid growing up in Dar es Salaam and I grew up to love it, to feel comfortable within it, and to a large extent to identify with it. I view this culture a bit romantically, but what is wrong with being romantic about something that I value so much?

The country I was born in was under the control of the British Empire. My birth certificate says that I was born on August 30, 1948, but the date seems disputable. My father worked very hard all his life and was so busy that small details often escaped his attention. Neither my younger sister Latifa nor I had been officially registered at birth. One day, having finally tired of my mother's nagging, my father went to the registration office but could not remember who had been born when and decided to write in August 30 for both of us! So who really knows! I feel much younger!

During the first few years of my life, we lived in Morogoro, about 190 kilometres (120 miles) west of Dar es Salaam. It was so small that it had no proper medical facilities, and people who required treatment were essentially on their own. There were no hospitals or obstetricians for delivering babies, for instance. Expectant mothers who could afford it had to be driven to Dar es Salaam where there was a small hospital and a Goan obstetrician named Dr. (Mrs.) Pais, who assisted with most of the nine children that my mother delivered. That in delivering nine children my mother never suffered a loss is a miracle.

In Morogoro, a sleepy, poor, rural town with a population of less than fifty thousand, poor people who were sick relied only on folk remedies. Infant mortality rates were very high and very few children grew up having regular medical check-ups of any kind. Simple infections that are easily cured today with inexpensive medications often would kill children back then. I remember many children my age growing up who showed unmistakeable signs of malnutrition, or underdevelopment, or diseases related to poor hygiene and tainted water. Of course, today we are intimately aware of the link between poor nutrition and brain development. Most of Morogoro's poor families—and many were dirt poor—suffered unnecessarily and in helpless silence. To whom or to what could anyone in need turn for help?

My family was lucky. My father and uncle had a butchery business. The brothers' two families grew up together in a large house by the river.

My father bought the cattle while my uncle Ali supervised the slaughter and marketing of the meat in Morogoro. This entailed my father travelling almost continuously, so in the end he decided to move us to live in Dodoma, an even smaller and more desolate town, to reduce travelling back and forth. Dodoma was our version of the Chicago stockyards: cattle breeders and buyers met to buy and sell cattle that then were transported by train to Morogoro for slaughtering. By the time we moved to Dodoma, I had an elder brother, Said (eleven months older than me), a sister Ghaniya (a year younger than me), and a younger sister Latifa.

My earliest substantial memories were of events in Dodoma. I was about three or four years old when we went to live in Dodoma for about three years. Dodoma is in the centre of Tanzania (which is why it is now the political capital), about 450 kilometres (280 miles) west of Dar es Salaam. The Germans had established it in 1907 when they were building a railway line. It was a poor town, dusty, hot, and dry, and full of flies. There was little vegetation and no paved roads. I don't recall if we had a refrigerator; we certainly did not have a television or a telephone. We were by no means well off but we were better off than most. When we lived in Dodoma, I think we did have electricity, but that was not the case for the majority of people. We had indoor plumbing but no centrally piped water, perhaps because Dodoma was such a dry place. So we bought water from roving tankers, and it was then pumped to a tank on the roof. There was just one toilet (of the pit latrine type, where you did your stuff sitting over an open, smelly fly- and cockroach-infested pit) for all of us, so sanitary conditions were not that good and got worse when the pit was full.

Because Dodoma was so small, we could walk everywhere quite easily. There was a small but neat well-built church not far from our home. I think it was an Anglican church. A Greek family lived nearby. The majority of Africans mostly lived outside the main centre of the town. Farmers with cattle or produce came into town to sell their merchandise and spend their money on market days. The farms were small and grew mostly vegetables, like cassava and maize. For most poor families, the main diet was a meal made from maize. Today it is very much the same. Those better off had a little store that might sell groceries to bring in a small income. For our family, poverty was relative. All six of us lived in a small rented house at the periphery of the town. The house, which had concrete floors, was rather dark inside. It had two small bedrooms and a sitting room and a small concrete yard at the back.

My most vivid early memory of childhood is watching my sister Fareeda being born. We were too far from Dar es Salaam for my mother to deliver at a proper hospital and no facilities existed locally so Fareeda had to be born in Dodoma, without a doctor or a birth attendant. There were no maternity clinics, no antenatal care, and if there were trained midwives, my mother did not know about them. Only a friend of my mother's, Barkah, was there to help as a doula. God knows what would have happened if there were complications. I have a vivid memory of watching in the night with my younger sister Ghaniya from outside the house through a window as my little sister was born, and I am embarrassed to admit that it was not a joyful experience. All my later life, I have been wondering why it is that human life should be brought into the world in such a messy, bloody, painful way. Is there an evolutionary perspective for what has been called the Curse of Eve? I would hate to fall back on Scripture for an answer. I find no enlightenment in Genesis 3:16, where it says, "Unto the woman He said, I will greatly multiply thy sorrow and thy conception; in sorrow thou shalt bring forth children," and as if that's not bad enough, it continues, "And thy desire shall be to thy husband, and he shall rule over thee." In those days the relationship of women to men was almost of this ancient, patriarchal type. I am surprised that this messy reality of parturition did not put me off medicine forever.

Another memory, however, had more significance and preoccupies me to this day. I would have been younger than five years old and I was walking along a main road in Dodoma. It was afternoon, and the air was hot and still and the flat road I was walking on suddenly sloped down. When I reached that point I had the most intense sensation that I had effortlessly lifted off the ground and was floating high above our neighbourhood. I could see people walking along the street and coming in and out of houses or shops and just going about their day, completely oblivious to this small boy floating in the sky above them like a bird.

I didn't call out to anyone or make my presence known. I was not afraid or surprised at floating above the village. I never thought to myself, Well, this is odd. It all seemed so normal. I remember only being very keen to watch and observe. It was like the world below was a giant living map that I could comprehend all at once. And then that vision started appearing in my dreams all the while we lived in Dodoma, but not only in my dreams.

It was not uncommon for me to be walking along that same road in broad daylight and have the same sensation of suddenly being lifted skyward. I should have been at least modestly curious about why this was happening; I was, after all, born with a very healthy curiosity. It never occurred to me, however, to subject the experience to interrogation. It is just what happened, and I was far more interested in having the experience and exploring its possibilities and boundaries than I was in questioning its existence. Nor did I understand what it meant. What I do recall vividly was that the sensation was pleasant and not at all disorienting; in fact, it had quite the opposite effect: somehow the world seemed more ordered and made more sense to me. I was not at all superstitious and had not yet come across the work of Freud. I have come to understand my strange experience not so much as a subconscious wish for escape, for instance, but more as a way I developed to understand and structure the world. When I see what is around me, I need to find a perspective that is at a more objective remove; this technique of objectifying the subjective—of broadening and deepening a perspective, of trying to understand everything and everyone on any question or conflict that I encounter—has become as normal and natural to me as breathing.

Anyway, this odd experience continued to occur at least up until the time I was in medical school. Thinking back on it, I realize I never discussed the experiences with anyone; on the other hand, I never felt as if it were something that needed mentioning. It wasn't that I felt special in any meaningful way. It's possible I suspected the same thing—or the same kind of thing—was happening to other people. I never asked and they never said.

"Myself effusing and fluid—a phantom curiously floating," wrote Walt Whitman in one of his poems.

Until today, for some odd reason, I associate the smell and colour of reddish-yellow ochre with Dodoma. Ochre among Tanzanian tribes is associated with the Maasai, especially the young Maasai moran who paints himself with the red ochre during dance ceremonies.

I met the Maasai frequently as a teenager because they, too, reared and sold cattle, and when one or more of them were on a bus, you knew immediately because of the fragrance of ochre. Nowadays many Maasais work in the tourist industry, usually as guards at hotels and resorts. But why do I associate ochre with Dodoma? Were some Maasais there? Had the local Wagogo tribe adopted Maasai traditions? I remember Maasais used to come to sell their cattle in Dodoma. In any case, I am not sure of the reason. I recall a funny story we often retold about my cousin Abdulrab (a famous boxer in Tanzania). Abdulrab was on a bus and, as was his habit, he was talking very loudly to his friend sitting next to him. All at once there was a sharp tap on his shoulder.

"Will you please lower your voice?" It was a polished English voice coming from the seat behind him. "You're disturbing your fellow passengers!"

Abdulrab had a hot temper and loved getting into fights. He jumped up from his seat, ready to confront the man but was completely taken aback to see a mature Maasai in full traditional dress complacently gazing at him.

"Did you just speak to me in English?" Abdulrab asked, too astonished to be angry.

"I did," answered the man.

Abdulrab asked: "But how?" He had never before heard a Maasai speak English—forget about the King's English! The Maasai lived a pastoral life in rural areas, raised their cattle, hunted lions, and lived a very traditional life. For a Maasai to speak English was incredibly rare.

"I am a graduate of London University," the Maasai gentleman replied to Abdulrab matter-of-factly. After that they continued with a very friendly conversation.

Many years later while running a course on genomics and global health in Kenya, I met another Maasai, one with a remarkable history. His name was Onesmo Ole-MoiYoi. He was born in Loliondo, Northern Tanzania, in 1943. The Maasai moved easily between countries and he went to school in both Kenya and Tanzania. At some point, his brilliance was recognized and he was admitted to Harvard University, where he was an Aga Khan Scholar between 1964 and 1968. He graduated from Harvard with a BA cum laude in chemistry in 1968, immediately entered Harvard Medical School, and graduated in 1972 with a medical degree.

Ole-MoiYoi proved so capable and bright he was accepted straightaway into Harvard's residency program at Brigham Hospital, after which he started teaching at Harvard and was appointed to the position of a research scientist. He became a Capps Scholar in molecular endocrinology while he did research and taught at Harvard until 1982. He then returned to Kenya to work as a senior scientist at the International Laboratory for Research on Animal Diseases (ILRAD), where his research was focused on diseases like trypanosomiasis (sleeping sickness), before going on to become a founding director of the Institute for Molecular and Cell Biology–Africa and then chairman of the Kenyatta University Council. More recently he became a senior consultant for the Aga Khan University Faculty of Arts and Science, which I have also been helping in various ways.

In Dodoma there was a Hindu temple nearby, but I don't recall there being a mosque near our house or anywhere else we frequented as kids. However, there was a Jamatkhana (a combination of mosque and community centre) for the Ismailis. On our dust-covered street, some of our neighbours were small-time shopkeepers. These were Indians, mostly, and a few Arabs. I recall no Africans who owned a shop at that time.

In Dodoma the majority of kids my age did not go to school, as it was not compulsory. Today this would be considered wasteful of young lives, perhaps even illegal, but we got good physical exercise and fresh air and nurtured our friendships. Some helped their parents at home or on farms or in shops; some were taught by their parents or by teachers at home; most just played in the neighbourhood. I recall, for example, walking some distance from town to a sandy, dry riverbed spanned by a bridge with iron railings. My elder brother, Said, and I would swing from the railings and then let go so we would drop the 7.5 metres (25 feet) or so on to the cushion of hot sand underneath. It was a thrilling sensation and we would do this over and over until our feet began to hurt. We valued the serenity. It was quiet, apart from the occasional sound of a bird. There were bushes around, mostly thorny bushes, and we would often get superficial cuts on our arms as we walked through them to the bridge. *Were we really wasting our lives at that tender age, or going through the early school of life?*

No doubt I am romanticizing childhood freedom in a Huckleberry Finn manner. The liability of the distanced perspective is that I have the luxury of indulging a "backward glance." The reality is that many—in fact, most—of the children I grew up with never progressed much beyond the limited subsistence levels characteristic of their parents' lives. What I have learned about poverty is that there are often too many rungs to climb on the ladder of life. Often we need help.

In any case, there could only have been the rare government school, and that would have been of poor quality (this was years before independence). I was not yet six, the age children traditionally started school, but I don't recall being registered in any school before we moved back to Morogoro. Dodoma was hot, dry, and dusty, and the swarming flies were the bane of our existence. Today, where I live mostly in Toronto, one fly in a restaurant would be a catastrophic breach of hygiene. In Dodoma they were a health risk, among others, transmitting a bacterial infection that causes trachoma, a disease associated with poverty and poor sanitation. It affects the conjunctival covering of the eye, the cornea, and the eyelids. The common picture is of small children squatting in the dirt while feasting flies crawl over their eyes and eyelids, repeatedly infecting their eyes. About eighty million people living in the tropics—the huge majority of whom are children—have active trachoma. Untreated, the disease can cause loss of vision or blindness by scarring the eyelids so that they turn inwards and the eyelashes continuously rub on and damage the cornea.

Years later when I was professor of surgery in Oman, my colleagues and I performed a controlled, randomized clinical trial of various surgical procedures to correct trachmatous scarring of the upper eyelid; in my research laboratory we studied immune systems of Omanis with blinding trachoma to look for markers of disease susceptibility and resistance. We pushed the boundaries of knowledge and produced evidence to improve the lives of patients, and the resulting papers were published in major scientific journals. But with all our knowledge, because we have not addressed the social determinants of health, trachoma and many other diseases of poverty have not been eradicated.

Time and time again in my professional life as a doctor and global health professional, I have become frustrated at the difficulties of finding ways to bridge the formidable gap between knowledge and solutions and their implementation and application on a scale large enough to make a real difference. We often have the means but cannot summon the will. Thankfully, working with organizations like the World Health Organization, the Bill and Melinda Gates Foundation, Grand Challenges Canada, and the African Academy of Sciences, I see doors being opened to real and sustainable progress. But much more needs to be done. In fact, Morogoro features prominently in my mind for what is one of the most painful memories of my life.

In December 1997, when my family and I were living in Oman, my teenage daughter Nadia took a phone call from someone she didn't know; the person was very agitated and was speaking rapidly over a poor phone connection. When I returned home that evening, Nadia told me the caller had spoken rapidly in a mixture of Arabic and Swahili. She had concluded from the call that it was my brother-in-law Nasser, calling us about the death of my sister Alwiya.

Death. My body froze. I immediately called Nasser in Morogoro. He was in tears. "Alwiya has just died, Abdallah."

I remember feeling as if I had turned inside out; the sudden shock and the pain buckled my knees. I was a doctor; I saw death every day. But this was like a part of me that had died.

"What happened?" I asked.

"Malaria."

Unfortunately, malaria was a familiar disease in that area of the world. Alwiya had contracted that common parasitic disease; the next day she was drenched in sweat with a high fever and complained that her whole body was aching—that her bones were hurting. She was taken to a local outpatient clinic where she was prescribed chloroquine, a frankly antiquated drug to which the malaria parasite in Tanzania had become resistant; nevertheless, the practitioner at the clinic (I am not even sure to this day the person was a trained physician) assured Alwiya she would get better soon and sent her home.

Of course, she did not get better, only worse. The medication had no remedial effect on her condition at all. She had become weak and could barely stand on her own; Nasser said she was like a rag doll. Two days later she was admitted to a nearby hospital that had originally been built for South African freedom fighters based in Tanzania. There they put her on a glucose drip. It grieves me to tell this story and even now it makes me so angry. Alwiya was a diabetic and this intervention most likely elevated her blood sugar to dangerous levels. She died the next day.

I reacted very badly. I was apoplectic with outrage: *her death was absolutely and unequivocally unnecessary*. Had she been transferred to a hospital in Dar es Salaam, for instance, staffed with competent experienced physicians, she almost certainly would have survived. I was overwhelmed with guilt, anger, frustration, and, most of all, impotence.

I was professor of surgery in Oman at the time this happened. It was to become my life's Rubicon moment; nothing would ever be the same. A question turned endlessly in my mind: *What am I doing with my life?* Here I was, a doctor working at one of the most advanced hospitals and medical schools in Oman—one of the best facilities in the world—having recently performed a world-record-breaking transplant operation—living a good life, but my sister who lived only five hours away by air had just died from an easily treatable infection.

The majority of Tanzanians I grew up with suffered either directly or indirectly from poor health, inadequate nutrition, and lack of access to medical care. In my time as a medical student in Uganda, the story was much the same. And I would see similar deprivation as a young doctor treating the less fortunate in London. And yet, it all seemed somehow at a distance from me. I was here and the bigger problems were . . . *out there*. It was a profound reckoning. I took a step back and said to myself: "I have to do something about this. I have to change from treating a few relatively well-to-do patients and find a way to attend to the health needs of many, many more people in need in the developing world, where the majority of people live." I decided I would dedicate my life to the issue of global health. It would not bring back my sister, of course, but I hoped that I might help save others.

It took a while to find my way into global health.

Of course, I grew up conditioned to relative privation: we were taught by our parents never to leave a tap running and to always switch lights off. Conserving resources became an obsession with me, and when I was at high school, I would leave the dorm before bedtime and go to the library and central hall to switch off each light that had been left on there. My friends thought I was totally mad! But that frugal attitude was why, in later life in my efforts on behalf of global health, I was always looking for low-cost models of health care delivery. This led to some work my Toronto colleagues and I did to identify and study such frugal models in the developing world and examine them for the potential to be brought to the rich developed world. We called this "reverse innovation." One of the low-cost systems we studied was India's Aravind Eye Care System. I had had the opportunity to visit India to study this system, and what I found in southern India reminded me very much of the Tanzania of my childhood, when blindness was a very common condition, especially among adults and the elderly, but also in children. I myself remember many cases of blindness as a child in Dar es Salaam, Morogoro, and Dodoma. Cataracts are a common condition worldwide and often the treatment is routine and remarkably successful. Back then, however, no treatment was available to the majority in Tanzania. I remember vividly the father of one of my African friends in Dar es Salaam. I would visit him in his village on the outskirts of town and see him holding his father's hand, leading him to the outhouse or for a short walk.

The saddest memory for me, however, is recalling how common it was for children with poor vision who ended up fully or partially blind only because they did not have access to or could not afford simple eyeglasses. Nowadays in my wanders around Toronto, I often have passed "dollar stores" where eyeglasses are piled like apples and oranges in bins out front, not quite but essentially a dime a dozen. It makes me crazy that what is so abundant in one country can be a thing of priceless and precious value in another. As I note later, introducing the efficiencies of the Aravind system to Tanzania would bring huge benefits.

As I said, I had a profound reckoning after my sister's death that put me on a journey of transformation. It was an overpowering psychological shock that became the trigger for changing my life and profession. In 1998 I decided I would take a sabbatical leave to give me some time to recover and reflect on what I really wanted to do, while doing some teaching and research at another university. Stanford University invited me to spend my sabbatical there, and within about a month of arriving in Palo Alto, I received a call, totally out of the blue, from the director-general of the World Health Organization, Dr. Nakajima, asking me to do some research and write a long report on medical genetics, biotechnology, and global health. This was to be yet another life-altering event that I remember well to this day. The work I performed for WHO opened my eyes to a particular set of gaps in the application of biotechnology to improve global health, and I made that my entry point into global health when I decided I would resign from my comfortable position in Oman and move to the University of Toronto in the year 2000.

Of course, all that was in the future. What I realize today is that my passion for change had its beginning in my beginnings . . . in childhood . . . in the rich red soil of Dodoma and Morogoro and Dar es Salaam.

Chapter 3

A Dar es Salaam Childhood: Of John Wayne, a Slaughterhouse, Snakes, and Bullets

We define our identity always in dialogue with, sometimes in struggle against, the things our significant others want to see in us. Even after we outgrow some of these others—our parents, for instance—and they disappear from our lives, the conversation with them continues within us as long as we live.

— Charles Taylor, *Multiculturalism*

I cannot even begin to imagine who I am without first recalling who my mother and father were or the impact they had on me. American poet Anne Sexton wrote that it doesn't matter who her father was, what mattered was "how she remembered who he was." I disagree. It matters very much to me who my father was, because that is what made him the man I remember.

My mother and my father did not have an easy life. They loved and deeply respected one another, even though their marriage had been arranged (as was customary at the time). It was my father's second, my mother's first (and only). The age difference was significant: seventeen years. My relationship with my mother was—by far—the most important and the most positive for me in my life. My relationship with my father—as any son will admit—was more complicated. Sons often become more like their fathers than they want to admit, and often in ways that they cannot, or will not, acknowledge. This may be so because we do not know it is happening.

My father worked himself to death and died at a relatively young age. I vowed never to do the same. I would be different. In many ways I was; in some I was the same. The influence of my mother was more positive.

My father, Salim, was born in 1916 in what had been German East Africa. After Germany was defeated in the First World War, however, the land fell under the control of the British Empire and it became known as Tanganyika. It did not achieve independence until 1961. My father died in 1969, so essentially he spent his entire life in a country of majority black Africans ruled by white Europeans. He grew up in a family that was culturally and ethnically Yemeni Arab, but in a wider environment of African, Swahili culture. He spoke both Swahili and Arabic well.

My father's father, Said, was born in Hadhramout in Yemen, served as a soldier in India in the 1890s, and then moved to Tanganyika where he became a businessman, establishing a cattle-trading and butchery business. Even now I do not know why he chose this line of work. I never met my paternal grandfather, whose legacy, especially through the butchery and cattle business, has affected my father's and my generation. He was a ferocious, bigger-than-life person, and it was said that he had slain a lion with his own hands (possibly a family myth). He had left Yemen as a teenager to work in the army of the Nizam of Hyderabad in India. The princely and wealthy Nizams had intermarried with Yemeni royalty ruling Hadhramout, which makes up a large part of Yemen. Hadhramout is very beautiful, with many long sandy beaches facing the Indian Ocean, a large plateau, and mountains not far from the coastal areas. Between the mountains there are fertile, breathtaking *wadis* (valleys). The largest of these is Wadi Hadhramout, wherein lies the walled city of Shibam, the oldest skyscraper city in the world, fancifully named "the Manhattan of the Middle East." Shibam was built on a rocky spur high above the *wadi* itself as one of the earliest examples of town planning based on vertical construction. Beginning in the sixteenth century the skyscrapers were built of mud and are still in use today. It is now a UNESCO World Heritage site.

A royal family that originated in the Yafe'i Mountains of Yemen, the Qaetis, ruled a large part of Hadhramout with British protection, until ferocious Yemeni fighters kicked out the British in 1967. My paternal ancestry is Yafe'i. The Yafe'i are renowned for their bravery, entrepreneurship, and worldwide migration. You will find them in Sheffield and Wales in the United Kingdom and in New York, Michigan, and around Chicago, Illinois, in the United States. Together with many people from Hadhramout, they travelled extensively in Asia to Malaysia, Indonesia (where many modern-day politicians and civic leaders hail from Hadhramout, including a former foreign minister of Indonesia, Ali al Attas, and the former prime minister of Malaysia, Abdullah Badawi), and as far as China. They also travelled down the East African coast, following the trade winds that changed direction every six months, facilitating trade across these parts of the world. Because of the ties between the Yemeni and Indian royal families, it was not uncommon to find Yemenis in Hyderabad.

There is an origin story in my family that a distant ancestor on my father's side was one of six brothers who had killed a member of another family, who had dared to speak in public to one of the female members of our ancestral family. The event occurred at a well high up in the Yafe'i Mountains of Yemen. People in that part of the world lived by the law of vengeance or retaliation, Qisas, which decreed that a life has to be taken to avenge another. Qisas in the legal sense is part of Sharia, as indeed it is in many Western legal systems that still practise the execution of first-degree murderers, but in our context here it was more like a blood feud perpetuated by tribal customs, sometimes lasting years if not generations. The apparent upshot was that the six brothers had to escape to other parts of Yemen, where each started a clan of his own. One of these led to the line of my paternal grandfather, Said.

Yemenis from Hadhramout divide themselves into three tribal categories: Seyyids, the religious elite claiming to be direct descendants of the Prophet, who valued education, especially religious education—part of their power was exercised through their control of knowledge; Qabili, the brave fighting ones that my Yemeni forebears belonged to—their clan leaders are called Sheikhs—who were more interested in arms and military affairs and totally underemphasized education; and the merchant class, who went under different names. As a child I recall hearing that my father would prefer a poor Qabili rather than a wealthy merchant to marry one of my sisters. When communists took over South Yemen after the British left in the late 1960s and called it the People's Democratic Republic of Yemen, they tried to abolish all these distinctions. These outdated concepts and practices have disappeared in most families but still persist to some extent in South Yemen after the overthrow of the communist regime.

My father had no formal schooling but later in life he could read and write Swahili—not well—mostly for his work. Success for him and most Arabs and Indians of his generation was measured by success in business. He began working in his father's business when he was very young and that was essentially all he knew professionally for his entire life.

When I was four years old in Dodoma, I began to be aware of him as a father, although even at that time he seemed away at work a lot. He was always up early and returned home late. So he was a bit of a stranger to us until later in life, when we moved to Dar es Salaam. In Dar es Salaam my father could on occasion be talkative when totally relaxed, but most of the time he was not much of a conversationalist, except when he was with my mother. When he met his few friends—this did not happen often—he was gregarious and all smiles. He was very popular with them. Most days he would return home from work around eight or nine at night and he was always exhausted—barely able to keep awake. Mother would greet him and they would talk for a bit and he would sit down on the couch and immediately fall asleep. Only rarely would he be in a state where my sisters would run to him to welcome him home. He had worked hard as a child but I also got the impression from stories he told that he had been a rather wild boy. He had enjoyed hunting with friends. He had liked a good time and might have been a bit fond of alcohol as a young man. He did drink at home but I never saw him drink to excess. He kept a small bottle of brandy handy for "medicinal purposes." Mother did not seem to mind; she herself never drank.

From the few studio photos we have of my father, he appears a handsome man who reminded many people of the young John Wayne. Being so good-looking he certainly could have attracted the attention of other women if he had wanted to, but he never sought such diversions. He loved to spend time with his daughters, especially the younger ones. He did not read to us and we had no games at home to play with him. I doubt he would have wanted to play games anyway. In retrospect, I did miss not having long, heart-to-heart conversations with him. In my own life with my children, what I missed most was not spending quality time with them when they were young. It still makes me tearful to think about that.

Even as hard as he worked on his business in Dar es Salaam, my father was barely making ends meet, so the money my mother received from renting her house was a huge help. Never do I recall my mother complaining or begrudging my father anything she had. Like my father, to whom would she have turned for relief? At the time much was expected of wives in their support for the husband. But my mother was more than just an ordinary wife. She was a rock for my father, a respected advisor, as much his partner as his wife. As a grown man now, I wonder how she managed to survive those years with so many children to take care of plus the emotionally draining burden of my father's constant financial worries and setbacks. Between them they must have developed a resilience system that functioned well and protected us children from the worries they were dealing with.

At about the age of twelve, I started to work in the family butchery business and I saw more of my father. He didn't actually own the abattoir where we butchered the meat. It was owned by the municipality and was shared with other butchery owners who sent their cattle to be slaughtered early in the morning. Municipal employees did the actual slaughtering at the abattoir and the butchery owners paid a fee for all the services.

When I was working for my father, my routine was to wake up around three every morning. The driver would pick me up and we would arrive at the abattoir at about 3:30. I usually worked there for about three hours. I hated having to get up that early and never much enjoyed the work, but my father needed help, and I was his son and I just wanted to help him. I recall often feeling deep sympathy for how hard he worked and how exhausted he was when he came home. Working in an abattoir was a rough and unsentimental introduction to the brutal realities of our relationship to other animals. I started in the abattoir at a very early age, and today I cannot recall exactly how I felt but there must have been—at least at the very beginning—feelings of shock or outrage or repulsion. At first, it was not easy watching the slaughter. I will never forget the huge expressive eyes of the cattle as they were tripped to the floor and put to death under the blade of a huge knife. They would bellow with terror as their blood drained, splashing to the floor, and their lively bulging eyes glistening with tears suddenly darkening to lifelessness. I watched as the carcass was skinned and cut up. It was horrible at first, but after some time I became accustomed to the process and was able to distance myself from the drama of death. My father mostly wanted me around to ensure the meat was dealt with in a hygienic manner and none was diverted. I remember having to put up with hostile glances directed at me by the slaughterers, who were angered by my monitoring presence.

"Look! The young inspector!" they grumbled to each other as they flashed their knives.

My brother Said also helped at the abattoir in the beginning but at some point he left Tanzania for Aden, and later went to the United States in search of better opportunities. I am not sure that my father ever actually believed I would take over from him in the butchery business. He was always too consumed in the moment, for one thing. The future, in a sense, did not really exist for him. And for me, I went along because it was what it was, and for the moment, I was reasonably happy.

The cattle were penned on my mother's small farm. On the way to the pen I would always stop at a small street-side tea stall run by a woman wearing a colourful *kanga* that always had a special poetic message written on it. For ten cents I would buy a special kind of dilute sugary ginger tea that was served with mandazi, an African sweet cake with an outer shell of cooked flour and an empty inside: the combination was divine. Of course, the work I was doing for my father was hazardous and completely unsuitable for a boy my age. But times were different back then! I remember when I was about thirteen I was sent by my father to collect a cow that had fallen sick and could not walk. It might have had African trypanosomiasis (called sleeping sickness in humans). Standing around the cow, surrounded by bushes that reached knee high, getting ready to lift the cow into the van, I felt a sharp tug against my right shin. I was wearing shapeless, loose trousers; when I looked down I saw a snake slither away. Luckily for me, the venom had mostly been wasted on the fabric of my trousers; the snake's fangs had missed puncturing my skin. The snake was absolutely of the poisonous variety and I had avoided being bitten by a hair's breadth. Otherwise I am reasonably certain I would have died.

My brother Said also narrowly escaped death. One day, he and the driver came back early from the abattoir without the cargo of meat. The van was riddled with bullets. This was one week after the Zanzibar Revolution of January 12, 1964. The soldiers in the mainland Tanganyikan army had become dangerously restive about a whole series of conditions: low salaries, subpar accommodation and lousy food, lack of promotion opportunities, and the humiliation of continued leadership by British officers. So they mutinied, arrested their British officers, and rampaged and terrorized people in Dar es Salaam, shooting and breaking shop windows and looting. They even broke into our house in Aggrey Street, terrorizing my mother and the kids, looking for weapons; my father handed them his ancient double-barrelled shotgun that he used for birds and small antelopes on his trips to Dodoma and back.

Said and the driver, it turned out, had been shot at from the side of the road as they neared the abattoir area. Luckily for them, the weapons the soldiers had were mostly antique hand-me-downs and the soldiers themselves were not well trained in marksmanship. Bullet holes peppered the front doors of the van but had not the force to penetrate the metal. Said and the driver could easily have been killed that morning.

About three afternoons a week, after working in the mornings at the abattoir and going to and returning from school, I would drive my father around town on business and other errands. We would occasionally talk about the future of my siblings, although this was in general terms, focusing on school and who might marry my sisters; after Said had left home, my father would ask about him and how he was doing. We never talked about politics; he listened to the radio if he got home early (which was rare) but had no interest in politics at all except to the extent it might affect the business. He owed money to the bank and we talked about that and about his plans to earn more profit to pay off those debts. He empowered me to sign cheques and deal with the bank and he would ask me for updates on the bank accounts. There was never talk of any of us leaving Tanzania: his world was Tanzania. He was born there and he would die there. My parents knew I did well at school and wanted me to become a doctor; it was a huge ambition at that time for them to formulate, since no member of our family had ever even reached secondary school.

My father was a family man, devoted and caring to his children, even though he was not always overtly demonstrative of his feelings. He was very protective, especially of my sisters. It was how he showed his love for us—by protecting us. His favourite family activity was to take us out for ice cream and snacks followed by a trip to the beach. This happened about once a week and always on a weekend. We would all pile into the car and he would drive us to Cosy Café, where they served ice cream, kebabs, samosas, and cutlets. After that we would drive to the beach, and he would park. My mother and my father would walk on the sandy beach and she would sit down on a bench and he would pace up and down the beach, until finally she would convince him that it was time to go home. He used to smoke cigarettes and then later a pipe—his favourite pipe tobacco being Erinmore Flake, which had an amazingly deep and beautiful fragrance.

My father had a reputation as a rather kind and charming man. In fact, he had a rather ridiculous nickname: Bob! I recall once I was with him in the car and we were driving down Kichwele Street when a friend of his, Ahmed Yahya, shouted, "Bob!" My father impulsively slammed on the brakes to wave and the car behind hit us and damaged our car. I think I was more shocked about my father being called "Bob" in public like that than I was scared at being in an accident.

For some reason my father absolutely adored my best friend, Ajmal. He treated him as if he were his own son. When my father's health was in decline and he was admitted to the hospital, I would visit every day.

"Where is Ajmal?" he would ask.

"Well," I said, "he is at school," or wherever he might have been.

"Make sure you bring him next time."

The funny thing is, I would tell this to Ajmal, and he would always get a worried look on his face like he was twelve years old and had been summoned by the principal to the office. "Why does he want to see me, Abdallah?" Ajmal would ask, terrified. But he was a good friend and came with me to visit my father whenever he could, and we would sit and talk and later I would ask Ajmal if he could remember what my father had said to him, and he would say something like "I have no idea!" and we would both laugh.

Once, Said and I bought a car together when he was about fourteen and I was thirteen. Our maternal grandmother, bi Ghaniya, had given us some money for something useful but instead we bought a second-hand red Volkswagen. Neither of us had a driving licence. In the evenings we would park the red VW in front of our house.

Father had no idea whose it was. When he went to a Somali mechanic to repair his own car, the mechanic said, "I repaired your kids' car last week." Father marched back home and, oh, he was angry! We got a good thrashing. He took the car and put it in our yard. We couldn't drive it any more. After a while we needed money so we opened the back of the VW and took out the engine and sold it. Later, when Father wanted to move the car, he discovered there was no engine and we got a second thrashing.

Father was stern and he didn't let my brother and me get away with anything when we were kids. He would sometimes chase us in the house with a stick and we would run away and climb tables and jump over beds until Mother would intervene to cool down the situation. He could be stubborn. For instance, when Ghaniya, my younger sister, finished secondary school in Dar es Salaam, she was selected to go to a high school in Tabora, far in the interior. Father abruptly and without thinking said no.

My mother was very devoted and respectful of my father, but she had her own mind and when it was important she put her foot down. Education was one of those issues. "She must go," my mother said. "I trust my daughter. It is a boarding school and they will take care of her." My mother then came to me and said, "Go and talk to your father. Your sister wants to go to school. It is the right thing. He knows it too but he won't admit it. You talk to him. He will listen to you."

I had my doubts. I pleaded with him for two hours. It was never my mother's way to object or interrupt or put down her foot. She never lost her temper or reproached or scolded. She had a gift for guiding my father to the right decision. When my mother felt strongly about something, she would get her way but always in a very gentle and persistent manner. "Salim," she would say, "no, that is not right. Salim, let us think about this a bit more." Anyway, in the end Ghaniya went to Tabora. And she ended up as a graduate student in Oxford! (Oxford somehow attracted members of my family: my sister Ghaniya went to St. Catherine's College; her husband, Abdulkhalique, studied international relations at Oxford; and Tarik al Said, who was later to marry my daughter Lamees, went to Pembroke College.)

A very odd thing occurred before my father died. The butcheries had been sold off by this time and he was not working. His health was bad and he knew it. One day he announced in the morning that he had invited several of his friends for lunch. Mother scrambled to cook *pilau* and indeed several people turned up. The next day the same thing happened and more people turned up for lunch. This went on for a month! Every day he would invite people home for a feast; some of them were friends, some were colleagues or business acquaintances or neighbours, but some were people he had met that day! No one could figure it out. It was as if he knew his time was running out and he had to make up as best he could for all the time he had lost.

My father died at the age of fifty-three in 1969. He and my mother had been on a short holiday staying with a friend of the family called Said Turki, who managed a sisal estate in Tanga. When my father collapsed at Turki's home, my mother called my brother Said in Dar es Salaam. Said asked Ajmal to drive him and my cousin Jabir to Tanga. When they arrived, my father was dying. It was a blessing that he died in my mother's arms, surrounded by at least a few of the people he loved.

It saddened me enormously that I was not with him in his last moments. I also felt a terrible wave of guilt. I should have done more. I was at medical school in Kampala at the time, and I caught a flight in time for the burial, which, according to generally accepted Muslim custom, must take place the same day. For all of us in the family, this was the end of an era. For me personally it was the beginning of a whole set of new responsibilities.

Eerily, something happened many years later that put the death of my father in a strange parallel context with the death of Ajmal's mother. Ajmal and I were living in Toronto at the time, and one day—literally for no reason—I had a sudden but overpowering impulse and picked up the phone.

"Ajmal, I need to see your mum this evening."

"Why? You never visit my mother except on special occasions. Why now?"

"I don't know," I said. "I just have this feeling that I must see her today."

"But Abdallah, it is not convenient today."

I insisted, he relented, and that evening Ajmal and his sisters and I gathered around their mother in her apartment. All her children were puzzled about why I had insisted on seeing their mother that day, and I shrugged and admitted that I really did not know why either.

"I just had this feeling I needed to be here."

She teased me a great deal and we all laughed a lot. On the way out, she hugged me tight and told me to take care of myself. Later that night I caught the red-eye flight to Los Angeles for some work. The flight arrived at about six the next morning and as the airplane was taxiing on the runway to the terminal, I received a text from Arzina, Ajmal's sister.

"How did you know my mother would die last night?"

I know my father loved us very much, and all of us have fond memories of him. The love outshone his shortcomings. He did all that he could for us. And no one can expect anything more from a father.

Chapter 4

From Circassia to Zanzibar: A Portrait of Two Quietly Powerful Women

One good mother is worth a hundred schoolmasters.

— George Herbert

A man came to the Prophet and said, "O Messenger of God! Who among the people is the most worthy of my good companionship?" The Prophet (PBUH) said: "Your mother." The man said, "Then who?" The Prophet said: "Then your mother." The man further asked, "Then who?" The Prophet said: "Then your mother." The man asked again, "Then who?" The Prophet said: "Then your father."

— The Hadith

Most of us do not need to reach very far down to find that our roots often stretch quite far and in quite exotic directions. For me that is especially true, but even I am surprised at times with how far the backward-casting shadow can fall. For instance, Swahili culture has been an immensely important shaper of my life. In ways that are less direct and obvious, however—far less tangible but just as meaningful—I follow family roots on my maternal side back to the rugged regions of the Caucasus Mountains. Located between the Black Sea and the Caspian Sea, the area straddles Europe and Asia. I speak of the Circassians.

That part of my identity has fascinated me for years. Like the Russians, the Magyars (Hungarians who had emigrated from the Ural Mountains 2,000 kilometres (1,243 miles) northeast of the Caucasus Mountains) and others in that part of the world have been considered by scholars to be both European and Asian, raising intriguing questions about identity: How do people lay claim to an identity? I suspect the Circassians would choose neither, remaining just "Circassians." What if we all decided to choose "none of the above"? Who would we be? The Georgians, the close southeastern neighbours of the Circassians in the Caucasus Mountains, have claimed to be Europeans because they were among the very earliest of Christian communities, but would the Ethiopians also claim to be European because they were among the earliest Christian communities in Africa? Or the Iraqis in the Middle East? And who really decides where Europe ends and Asia starts? The answer is that someone one day made an arbitrary decision. Turkey straddles both; it is a short ferry ride from one to the other!

Growing up, I recall distinctly my great-grandmother, Bakhtiyar, known to us children as Bibi Kubwa (Kubwa as used here is Swahili for a big or elderly relative). She must have been about seventy-five at the time. She was tall, I remember, and beautiful, elegant, and very fair-skinned. She had exotic, penetrating greenish eyes and long lustrous hair that was combed daily into two braids by my sister Fawzia.

She spoke to us in broken Swahili, which I did not think about much at the time. Every now and again, however, she would welcome a visitor, Said Turki, and they would speak fluently in a strange language I assumed was Turkish. (Sadly, it was in the house of the same Said Turki in Tanga that in 1969 my father fell ill and died.)

My great-grandmother was born Bakhtiyar bint Yusuf *(bint* denoting *daughter of*). A Circassian, about whose family background we know nothing, she had been abducted from the garden of her home when she was eight, along with her twelve-year-old sister, Sayara bint Yusuf. The kidnapping almost certainly took place in Istanbul, the capital of the Ottoman Empire, in the year 1884. The kidnapped girls were forced onto a ship owned by the Austrian Lloyd shipping line bound to Jeddah (a part of what is now Saudi Arabia, in the region of Hejaz). In Jeddah they were transferred to a waiting steamship—the *Malacca*—which was owned by Seyyid Barghash, the then–Sultan of Zanzibar. Barghash's father, Seyyid Said Bib Sultan, had moved his court from Oman to Zanzibar in 1840 and from there he ruled both countries. There were ten Circassian girls, as well as nine castrated boys (eunuchs), on the *Malacca*; they had been bought by Seyyid Barghash's agents and were being taken to his court in Zanzibar.

I found much of this important information at the British National Archives at Kew near London, where the official letters of John Kirk, the then–British Consul in Zanzibar, are kept. In correspondence towards the end of 1884 with the British Foreign Minister, Earl Granville, Kirk reports this particular shipment of enslaved girls and eunuchs arriving in Zanzibar on the ship *Malacca*. That was almost certainly the last ship to bring slaves to Zanzibar from Jeddah or anywhere else in the Ottoman Empire. Under British influence, by the 1880s the slave trade in Zanzibar was winding down rapidly. Sultan Barghash himself died in 1888 and in 1890 Zanzibar became a British Protectorate, after which there appear to have been no further shipments of slaves to Zanzibar from anywhere. The notorious Zanzibar slave market was shut down. It would, therefore, appear that my great-grandmother Bakhtiyar was among the last—perhaps *the* last—contingent of slaves to be taken to Zanzibar.

The Circassians have a long and interesting history. They are from the northwest Caucasian Mountains, now in the Russian Federation. They were farmers, with a long tradition and culture of their own, which included a monotheistic religious philosophy called Habze, which co-existed with both Christianity, which was brought in by the Byzantines beginning in the fourth century AD, and Islam, which was brought in about a thousand years later. Since the sixteenth century Circassians have been Muslims. They (and their neighbours the Georgians) were considered by anthropologists to be the purest (unmingled) of human "races" and were placed at the top of the racial hierarchy—they were called Caucasians. (Today, obviously, the term *Caucasian* is loosely reserved for white people of European descent.)

Circassian men were renowned for their bravery and military skills, much in demand for hundreds of years in the armies of the Ottomans and in North Africa during the Mamluk period and afterwards, when they rose to prominent political and military positions. They had fought incredibly bravely for decades against the Russians, who were expanding southwards to the Black Sea, ethnically cleansing the Circassians and annexing their lands. The Circassians were finally defeated around 1865 at their last stronghold and capital, Sochi (the spa town that hosted the 2014 Winter Olympic Games), where the remains of thousands of Circassians are buried. Like the exiled Aeneas putting behind him the smoking ruins of Troy, as many as a million defeated Circassian survivors took to an armada of rickety boats across the Black Sea to a new home in the Ottoman Empire.

Even at seventy-five, my great-grandmother was a beautiful woman, empirical evidence of the legend of Circassian women being the most beautiful in the world! Of course, the tribute proved a terrible curse as Circassian women were in high demand as concubines, including in Ottoman and Zanzibari royal harems. In fact, P.T. Barnum, the infamous American promoter of "The Greatest Show on Earth," featured a Circassian beauty in one of his circus shows. It cost a penny to view the woman, and a flourishing trade existed for cosmetics that supposedly revealed the secret of Circassian beauty. By the mid-nineteenth century, a Circassian girl could be purchased for about £100 in Istanbul, a considerable sum at the time. However, after the Circassians were forced into exile following their disastrous defeat by the Russians, huge numbers of displaced Circassian girls faced hunger, homelessness, poverty, and destitution; not surprising, then, that in Istanbul Circassian girls could be bought as slaves or concubines for as little as £5.

Bakhtiyar's sister Sayara was married for a while to Ali, the sultan's son. Bakhtiyar herself was to marry a man she fell in love with at the palace. He was called Mohammed Hejazi and was working at the palace as a coppersmith. He must have come to the royal court from the region of Hejaz, which includes Mecca, the traditional pilgrimage destination for Muslim worshippers. Bakhtiyar and Mohammed eventually moved from Zanzibar to Dar es Salaam, probably in the early 1900s. They had three daughters, one of whom was my grandmother Ghaniya, and a very handsome son, Abdulhameed, who later moved to Kenya to join the British army, probably to fight during the Mau Mau uprising.

It should come as no surprise that my great-grandmother—like anyone who has suffered a great trauma—was reluctant and unforthcoming about details. I guess it was a kind of post-traumatic stress disorder. As a child I don't remember her talking about her experiences. Most of what I know about her later life I heard from my mother and other family members.

In any case, my mother, Jamila, was born to Ghaniya in Dar es Salaam in 1932. Jamila, meaning "the beautiful one," was a modest person, yet so many people outside the family knew her or of her. Recently someone I hardly knew stopped me in the street in Muscat and said, "Last night I dreamt about your mother. She was a great human being." Among my generation of siblings, if we meet a person with almost perfect behaviour and personality, when talking about that person afterwards we would say, "*Utafikiri kalelewa na Bi Jamila.*" It's Swahili for "You would think she was brought up by Bi Jamila." "Bi" is a Swahili honorific term for a respected woman.

My mother grew up in Kigogo, not far from Dar es Salaam, on a coconut farm that belonged to her father, a man of the same Yemeni ancestry as my paternal grandfather. By the standards of the time my mother's parents were relatively well-to-do, but that was not to last long, for much of their farm was taken over by the British to build a road to Morogoro; many years later what remained was nationalized by the Tanzanian government.

Growing up in Kigogo, my mother had a constant companion and friend, a slender African girl, whose parents likely lived in the neighbourhood, perhaps working either at home or on the farm. I have a lovely photograph of the two girls: Mother, wearing a surprisingly short and trendy dress, looks about seven years old, and the African girl, also dressed well with a nice necklace and large earrings, looks about ten. From the vegetation and building in the background, I guess it was taken on the farm. Mother kept in touch with that girl as they both grew up, and I recall her coming to visit us at home in Dar es Salaam when we were kids.

The influence of growing up with an African girl as a constant friend must have been formative for my mother; it would certainly have contributed to how very accepting she was of other people all her life. Mother was given an abandoned calf as a pet and this calf followed her everywhere, even into the bathroom! I don't know how or why, but at some point in her childhood she developed a very strong moral compass that was the defining feature of her life and of ours. Somehow that compass developed in her a very enlightened and confident sense of self.

There were no schools and my mother never had a formal education. Even if she had gone to school, she would have had to stop when, through an arranged marriage, she married my father in 1946. She was about thirteen years old and my father was about thirty. By the standards of the time, the age difference was not unusual and was totally acceptable. It is very likely that my mother saw my father for the first time on their wedding day. Luckily he was a good-looking fellow! By 1946 her father had already passed away, so the marriage proposal would have come to her mother, who had by then moved from Kigogo to live in a house she bought in Mahiwa Street, in the more "African" part of Dar es Salaam, next to a house owned by her other two sisters. It was in Mahiwa Street that I first met Bakhtiyar.

Our mother was beautiful (of course!) with a roundish face, black hair, and hazel-brownish eyes. She resembled somewhat the Egyptian actress Faten Hamama, who was married at one time to Omar Sharif. She was relatively short and had a very fair complexion and spotless skin. She had a beautiful soul. None of us children had ever seen her angry. She was always gentle, calming our father during his occasional fits of anger.

My mother's father died when she was very young and she never talked much about him; I do not expect he had much of an influence on her overall. I do recall one story, however, that must have been very traumatic to her. Her father had a partner and they jointly owned the farm at Kigogo. The partner had grown up as a castrated slave in Zanzibar. By the time he was a grown man, that black eunuch kid had been assimilated into the Arab/Swahili culture of Zanzibar. He had a sister with whom he lived and they had moved to Kigogo together.

The two partners had a major falling-out that resulted in a long and harrowing court case that went on for years. My grandfather eventually won the case but his partner took the news so badly that he committed suicide by ingesting a powerful poison. My mother was young at the time but the incident touched her deeply. She could hardly comprehend how two people who were so close to each other that they built houses next door to each other and spent most of the day together could suddenly become such bitter foes. I know that it touched her so much that she could hardly talk about it to us. It would bring tears to her eyes when she talked about the sister of the person who committed suicide. That lady had been entrusted with bringing up one of the young princes of Zanzibar, Khalid Qais al Said, and she brought the prince with her to Kigogo, where he grew up with my mother for a while. Khalid became a famous soccer player and later Oman's ambassador to South Korea and other countries. I met him in the 1990s when I was professor of surgery at Sultan Qaboos University in Muscat, where he was a patient of mine briefly. He would describe to me his childhood and his pranks when he was growing up in the same extended household as my mother in Kigogo.

As a child I remember that my mother seemed always to be pregnant. In total she bore nine children: three sons and six daughters. I was the second after my brother Said. The next seven (one of whom was my younger brother, Mohammed) after me came at intervals of about two years. She also had a few miscarriages. My father had been married before he married my mother. When he was still in his early twenties, his first wife died, leaving behind two young girls, Alwiya (Sluma) and Mluka, and when we were born we considered them to be our full sisters. Later, my second cousin Fawzia came to stay with us, and she, too, simply became a full sister to all of us. So there were twelve of us in all: three brothers and nine sisters. Alwiya, Mluka, and Fawzia were themselves to have arranged marriages and were very happy, which is not a very politically correct admission to make nowadays. If you asked them, they would freely admit they had not married for love; on the other hand, though the marriages were arranged, in no way had they been coerced or pressured to marry against their wishes. They did not fall in love but grew into love over time. It is not always the case, of course.

My grandmother on my paternal side, for instance, was an interesting woman. Far'e was born in Yemen of a Habashi mother and Arab father. Habashi in Arabic translates as Abyssinian, which refers to Ethiopians and Eritreans, many of whom lived in Yemen and may have become Yemenized. They are considered as fair, peaceful people, highly honoured by the Prophet, who advised his persecuted people in the early days of Islam to go to Abyssinia "for the king of Abyssinia does not tolerate injustice and it is a friendly country, until such time as Allah shall relieve you from your distress."

Far'e migrated to Tanganyika as a girl. Before she married my grandfather, Said, she had been married to a drunken and abusive man in Bagamoyo, not far from Dar es Salaam. She could not tolerate the man and one day in desperation and resolve to end his abuse, she set fire to the house with him inside. He managed to escape and soon after they were divorced.

Said and Far'e had a wonderful marriage and were blessed with two sons, Ali and my father Salim, and a daughter, Muzne. Besides her incredible iron will, there are two things that I remember especially about my grandmother: she was blind and she had supernatural powers. Far'e was normally sighted until she developed cataracts in her fifties. An operation on one eye by a traditional healer was badly botched; she developed a severe infection in that eye, which she lost. The other eye was not operated on, and so the cataract in it continued to deteriorate until she became totally blind in that eye also. Cataract surgery today is common and the incidence of complications has been reduced to a minimum. Back then, however, treatment was not commonly available. And if it was, the likelihood that the surgeon had the requisite skills to perform the surgery successfully was remote.

To her credit, she never lost her basic cheerfulness and vitality. She never felt sorry for herself and we loved her and pampered her in any way we could. I did not know until my teen years about the abuse she had suffered at the hands of her first husband, but as I grew older I came to admire greatly her courage and resilience. As far as I know, my grandfather Said was a very good man and they were happy together. It bothers me even today, however, that she became totally blind basically for no reason other than inadequate medical care. She suffered just like so many people in so many parts of the world—our world today—suffer unnecessarily. To me, as a kid, it all seemed terribly unfair.

As children we believed that our grandmother Far'e possessed supernatural powers. Whenever there was an unusual or stressful situation, she would fall to the ground, stretch her limbs rigidly, and lose consciousness for a period. When she came to, she would talk about things happening in places far away or predict events that later came to pass. Her voice changed during this period, as if someone with a different voice were speaking from inside her body.

She herself would remember none of this. However, at that time all of us believed without doubt, and some in our family still believe, that she possessed unseen angelic forms (spirits) that came to talk to us when she had one of those fits. Those spirits were there to protect her, and the tradition is that they can be inherited by members of the next generation. Maybe one of my sisters has them now!

To me—as a child—it was impressive. And at that time supernatural explanations were not that uncommon. People need to have an explanation for the observations they make and the things that happen to them. Those explanations are based on what they have been told or taught, or have heard of. In scientifically developed societies, the first recourse is the laws of physics, chemistry, biology, and so on; in more traditional societies, the explanations cannot be based on scientific thinking. However, even in the developed world, scientific explanations can be way off course. We see this in the area of mental health, for example, when explanations of symptoms of, say, autism and schizophrenia have been based on the wrong theories for a very long time—and only now are we beginning to ask questions based on what is actually taking place in the brain, in terms of chemistry and circuits.

What came before could well be termed primitive thinking. In a way I was lucky when I was growing up for I was surrounded by a mixture of rational thinking and the superstitions and mythologies of all the cultures around me: African, Arab, Swahili, and Indian. It was just part of life. I think that mythology and supernaturalistic thinking helped me to understand people better and to ask deeper questions.

I often wonder if my own experiences of being on that road in Dodoma and "floating up" were somehow influenced by, or related to, my grandmother's supernatural "flights" into the unknown. As a scientist and medical professional, I have been trained to filter the world and all that happens in it through a rigorously rationalist lens. We know so much today, but what we need often is not so much an explanation as a sense of meaning. We also need to be better listeners. Back then the world seemed far more open to the reality of the supernatural and what today we would dismiss as silly superstitions or myth. In retrospect, as a physician, I could argue that my paternal grandmother was simply suffering from epileptic fits (or even a mild form of multiple personality disorder) every now and then. It was not uncommon for people to believe that spirits of the departed could still interact with them and affect their lives and destinies. Many believed in witchcraft and the existence of people among them who had powers beyond the normal, and that such powers could be directed at others for good or bad outcomes.

Most people when asked would say their mothers had been very loving and they loved their mothers in turn. Fewer would say their mothers were the greatest influence in their lives. When I reflect on the many influences on my life and I ask what most shaped my identity, personality, and values, there is little doubt it was my mother. I can honestly say that there has never been anyone in my life whom I respected and admired more. She taught us that you didn't do things that would hurt people's feelings, that you should treat others as you would want them to treat you. She lived that ancient philosophy every waking moment. She was very sensitive all her life to the pain of others, especially when it was the consequence of an injustice—real or imaginary. The idea that our actions—even what seem insignificant actions—have consequences for others was another of the many important early lessons I learned from her.

Her unshakeable belief in the basic goodness of humanity is always on my mind when I find myself in situations where I have doubts. After US president Trump's 2017 executive order banning people from six Muslim majority countries, I began, for a while, to imagine people seeing me not as who I am or what I am but only as what they see: in this case one of those people—*a Muslim*. Is this what it had come to? Asking not what it means to be an American but who is qualified to be an American? Not only did this engender in me powerful feelings of alienation, insecurity, and humiliation, but real anger and frustration. I was furious! I remember, however, thinking of my mother and her powerful but quiet indomitable strength. She lived her beliefs without fanfare or display. She had a way of engaging with truth that never felt confrontational, and not a day has gone by that I don't find myself attempting to emulate her. My mother was more than my mother: she was my most profound teacher.

My mother was a conventional Muslim, though not in the sense it is usually conceived of in the West today. Her Muslim beliefs were important to her; she prayed and performed her devotions regularly. She honoured the principles and spirit of Islam, if not always the secular requirements. She would not have expressed it this way, but I believe she had an instinct for what was of value in a spiritual sense and what was merely dogmatic. Treat every human being with respect. Be kind and compassionate to the less fortunate. These are not values exclusive to Islam; nor are they Christian, Jewish, Hindu, or Buddhist monopolies. For my mother to dishonour another human being—no matter who—was to dishonour and offend Allah. If she was subversive in any way—and I think in this respect she may have been—it was in understanding intuitively the difference between universal human values and the secular rules of behaviour that subjugated women to men. There are God's rules and there are men's rules and she knew which mattered. In her case, of course, man-made rules were not a euphemism but a quite literal description of social life at the time. She was a wonderful example to me of the power of doing what's right.

She was devout but she never forced religion on us. She never compelled us to pray. Her approach was always to lead by example, and that behaviour had a profound impact on me. She lived what she internalized and she practised what she embraced, always gently, but not—I must admit—with indifference. She could be—she was—uncompromising when it mattered. Her moral and ethical compass never wavered from the true.

I recall fondly that my mother would read the Qur'an and quite often would discuss with us what she had read but in a way that always seemed less doctrinaire than instructive and exploratory. The mind in the process of discovery is a habit that I joyfully inherited from my mother. Her belief was of the kind that opened one's eyes to the best in human nature. She never lapsed into stale orthodoxy and was always turning words and lessons over in her mind, refreshing and renewing. When I hear people talking about faith today in the sense of black-and-white obedience to a set of rules or principles, it makes me think of my mother's creative approach to faith. Her open-mindedness and her abiding faith was a gift to us. It was never *This is what you must do.* It was *What is it right to do?* It has been astonishing to me in my life—it still is—how seldom this simple and straightforward dictum emerges as the guiding principle behind our actions (including but not limited to politics). Not *Can it be done?* or *How much will it cost?* or *What will it benefit me*? No. *What is the right thing to do?*

What I learned from my mother, too, was humility. I wish we all could acknowledge more the value of humility in our lives. Living by example, for instance, is to me the most beautiful kind of humility. When I hear politicians nowadays talking about perceived threats from "this group" or "that group," I always think of my mother and how she drilled into us how important it was not to judge people by superficialities like their religion or wealth.

When we lived in Dar es Salaam, there were some Indian ladies in our neighbourhood she enjoyed chatting with, and a small distance away she had some Arab and African friends. But with so many children at home and with my father requiring so much attention, my mother did not have the luxury of free time. The most anticipated occasions for serious socializing would have been at weddings; in Swahili culture, there was a tradition that women going to a wedding all wore a dress sewn from the same material. I remember many times my mother getting together with other women to sew dresses for weddings; it was a wonderful time to exchange news and just talk. Religious holidays were times for family and communal gatherings as well.

My mother did not spend much on herself. She sewed most of her and her daughters' clothes herself and hardly wore any perfume or put on make-up. However, she had one particular perfume that she absolutely loved, was faithful to, and used very sparingly because of the cost. It is a well-known brand that has been around for ages, a classic that came in a beautiful square glass bottle with faceted corners and a fairly large octagonal stopper. It is Chanel No. 5: a classic, just like my mother.

With Mother there was always a door open for communication. No matter how outlandish the subject, she would listen, sympathize, and support, unless some third party was going to be harmed. At the age of about fourteen, I had decided on a whim that I wanted to travel around the whole of East Africa. I often had such urges. I went to inform my mother of my decision. My passport was tucked in my trouser waistband. I lifted my shirt and showed her the passport. Her eyes opened wide in surprise.

"Why are you carrying a passport?" she asked.

"I want to travel round East Africa on my own."

"Why?"

Now, this in a nutshell was the difference between my father and my mother. My father would have responded to my decision with a flat and final no. My mother wanted to know *why*. She had the authority to say "Absolutely not" and send me to my room. I probably would have run away anyway, and I think she knew that. She must have trusted me—even at fourteen. It might also have been true that secretly she envied the freedom I possessed by virtue of being born male—an entitlement that culturally and socially she had been denied. I explained that I had a wish to travel and learn about the three countries that made up East Africa. "I wish to meet people, and grow up a bit." I told her my plans; she listened carefully. She asked a few questions and wondered if I would manage. I assured her I would. She nodded her head.

"I am going to be really worried until you return. Okay, go now," she said. I didn't tell my father—he would have stopped me.

I think the whole trip took less than ten days. I lost weight and was exhausted but also exhilarated! It had been a wonderful adventure. Of course, my father must have asked where I was and my mother would have told him. Interestingly, he never asked me about my trip. I imagine my mother told him it was something I needed to do, and "that is what he must do."

I think of Bi Jemi, as we fondly called Mother, often. She spent the last fourteen years of her life in Muscat, Oman, where we had built a house. Shahina, my wife, had designed and supervised every step of the house's construction, and since I was based in Toronto and was on the road most of the year, Mother lived with Shahina in Muscat. Shahina and I were in Shanghai when Mother died on October 10, 2010. The date 10/10/10 is very auspicious among the Chinese. I remember Shahina and I walking along the crowded streets of Shanghai, buildings festooned with celebratory bunting, music playing loudly from shops and markets, when the phone call came from my sister Latifa.

My mother died very much as she lived. She was staying with my sister Latifa while we were in Shanghai. It was late afternoon, and Mother had invited some members of the family over for tea. She was sitting comfortably on a sofa chatting with them when, without a gasp or expression of pain or discomfort, her head slid sideways onto her shoulder, and she stopped talking. Peaceful. No melodrama. Surrounded by loved ones, during an act of generosity.

Chapter 5

Dodoma to Morogoro: Ya Qaharaa

We all carry within us our places of exile . . .
— Albert Camus

It was during our time in Morogoro that my father became ill with what seemed severe depression. We had moved to Morogoro from Dodoma in 1955. I would have been about six. We all lived together with my uncle's large family in one immense rambling house. There must have been about thirty of us altogether in that house, which had two wings, one for each family, but we nevertheless lived, ate, and socialized in that one house. We loved our cousins, especially the ones who were roughly of our ages: Samira, Talal, Munir, and later Majda.

The house was built near a river and that meant we had rather easy access to fresh water, which turned out to be quite a luxury as there was no piped water in the early days. I don't remember what preceded my father's sudden turn to a state of depression. It was like one minute the lights are on and everything is fine and the next the switch is flipped and it's complete darkness. But it could not have been that simple. Today I would diagnose his ailment as a form of reactive depression, with elements of anger, regret, and anxiety. Of course, we all knew how cranky and ill tempered my father could be when exhausted, and so at first we kids assumed this was nothing more than fatigue from overworking. In any case, this was one of the most unpleasant memories of my childhood.

What brought on the illness was a mystery. Mother was elliptical in her explanation and alluded only vaguely to some disagreement my father had had with my uncle Ali (his older brother and business partner). My father had had an incredibly respectful—and we assumed a close—relationship with his older brother, so much so that I do not believe my father felt comfortable—capable, even—of broaching any subject likely to cause a rift between them.

Whatever happened between them, my father soon moved into, and remained in, his bedroom for nine months. I don't recall seeing him come out of that room during those nine months. We would occasionally see him through an open door, pacing up and down the room, unshaven, thin, and sometimes muttering to himself. I recall him repeating *"Ya qaharaa,"* an Arabic term that is difficult to translate but means something like "oh cruel"; when I grew up and my father used this term, it was in the context of cruel fate, lost opportunity, regret. We kids were too young to help in any way and did not go to his room often. Usually only Mother went in to be with him. She would take him his food, but he would rarely eat without my mother's patient, repetitive cajoling. She tried hard to console him but I am not sure that even my mother understood everything about the situation. She didn't know the true nature of his illness either, and that meant we kids were also in the dark. Her instincts would have been to diagnose some form of bewitchment or possession and to bring in a religious scholar to read the Qur'an in front of my father and build an amulet for him. But my father would not contemplate that and would have refused to wear an amulet, considering such stuff to be mumbo-jumbo and ridiculous. No one would have diagnosed depression but even if they had, there were no doctors to consult, and there were certainly no psychiatrists around. My father absolutely refused to go to Dar es Salaam for any treatment. To him, the problem was not medical, anyway. So my mother resorted to prayers. The only other person who would try to visit my depressed father was his mother, Far'e bint Suleiman.

Just as suddenly as my father's depression came upon him, it lifted. One morning my father woke up, showered, dressed, came out of the bedroom, and announced that he was driving his son-in-law Nasser to hospital for minor surgery.

What was this? We all were stunned at the sudden return of our father from self-imposed internal exile. He looked fresh and rested and appeared completely nonchalant, as if nine long months of depression and monastic seclusion had been nothing but a short dream. When he returned home from the hospital, he announced to his brother that he had made a decision to dissolve the partnership immediately and permanently; he recommended the business dissolution be conducted by arbitration mediated by community elders they both trusted.

And that was that. We were moving to Dar es Salaam! My mother welcomed the news as she had not been happy in Morogoro and was completely supportive of my father's decision. The cash settlement my father received from arbitration was not nearly enough to establish a new business and my mother contributed a significant amount from her own inheritance to establish his new enterprise.

After we moved to Dar es Salaam—it was around 1956—my father never looked back to his partnership days with his brother; he never spoke ill of him and continued to respect him and, as far as we could tell, to love him. When my uncle came from

Morogoro to visit us in Dar es Salaam, he would stay with us and there did not seem to be any anger or awkwardness between the two brothers.

I said my mother was not happy in Morogoro. We never actually talked about it, but I suspect after nine months of taking care of my father—essentially an invalid—had convinced her that we all needed a change of scenery.

I loved Dar es Salaam. It was located on the coast and it was hot and humid compared to Morogoro. But for me it was my first proper exposure to a big city and it was thrilling. For one thing, it was the first house we had that was equipped with efficient electricity and a centrally supplied water system. Even better, it had a Western-style indoor toilet. What a luxurious novelty! I remember feeling like a king. It was wonderful. What a miracle. Imagine!

My father owned a second-hand car, which was quite unusual among the Arabs and marked us as fairly well to do. We had a radio at home; television (black and white) arrived more than a decade later but we could never afford one. My father started business with one butchery and over the years expanded to owning three. By today's supermarket standards, his outlets were very small, but back then his business would have been considered modestly successful. The main one, Aswan Butchery, was fairly big but the others were very small and inside permanent covered market stalls.

Life for the majority of Tanzanians was characterized by a terrible lack of certainty: about how to feed a family or where to find safe supplies of water, about poor housing, subpar hygiene, about getting and keeping a low-wage job, about how and where to find medical treatment when children or loved ones were sick, and often about what they could do to make God favour and not punish them. They were caught in a poverty trap. In this sense, if someone asked me if our family were poor, I would say no, we were not. But the scale is relative.

During my earlier years as a child in Dodoma and Morogoro, I don't recall coming across any Africans who owned substantial businesses—virtually nothing providing anything much beyond a subsistence income. Some owned fruit and vegetable stalls and stores where they sold tea and cakes and cooked porridge. I always thought it odd: the Africans were outcasts—outsiders in their own home. In Dar es Salaam, however, the larger population must have created more opportunities for the majority Africans. A few in our general area owned and operated small shops where they peddled what we would now call "convenience store" items; others had small garages where they fixed tires and repaired cars (but mostly bicycles). Some owned small food stores. None that I knew ever achieved much beyond blue-collar work. Not too long ago I came across an interesting reference to my hometown in *Going Solo,* an autobiography by the famous English author Roald Dahl, who had been stationed in Dar es Salaam in the late thirties as a young employee of the Shell Petroleum Company. Not surprisingly, he wrote glowingly of Dar es Salaam: "To me it was all wonderful, beautiful and exciting. And so it remained for the rest of my time in Tanganyika. I loved it all." Of course he did! Dahl was a young, privileged white Englishman living on an expense account in a country where the natives routinely were treated like servants at an enormous five-star hotel. For me the consequence of widespread injustice, poverty, malnutrition, lack of employment and educational opportunities, and overall uncertainty was very real and tangible and heartbreaking. In time, these societal inequities with their many vicious cycles became very salient in my mental life, almost to the point of obsession. I was angry and sad and determined to do something.

From Dar es Salaam my father made regular trips to Dodoma to the auction yards to buy the cattle, and then he would drive back home. The cattle would arrive a few days later and would be kept in a pen at what remained of my mother's farm in Kigogo. A small portion of the land was farmed for vegetables, and I recall a Chinese family who had rented another small part to grow fruits and vegetables.

When I was a kid, the population of Dar es Salaam could not have been more than a hundred thousand people, which is very small when I consider that the Greater Toronto Area is home to seven million. But it seemed enormous to me then. We lived near the central downtown commercial area, but I loved walking to the seaside because there the air was refreshingly fragrant and clean. The beaches were lined with coconut trees that swayed as if they were dancing in the breeze. Their branches came alive as noisy exotic birds took off, skimmed over the sea on the breeze, returned, and flew off again. It was a working area for fishermen and even now I can summon the pungent aroma of fish. Just inland from the harbour the streets were lined with beautiful casuarina and acacia trees, and further in we had large numbers of fruit trees. There was no shortage of mangoes, papaya, cashews, and citrus fruits like oranges, tangerines, lemons, and limes. People also grew African spinach; we called it *mchicha* and loved eating it at home. Other vegetables grown in or around Dar es Salaam were sweet potatoes, pumpkins, and cassava.

I loved swimming at Kinondoni beach with my friends. There was an inviting place maybe half a mile away and we would swim from our side to that headland. A ferry also ran across that stretch of sea.

The smells of the sea, of salt and seaweed, the shrill sounds of terns and gulls, and the accompanying sight of coconut palms on the beach very close to the water: these are some of my favourite childhood memories of Dar es Salaam. For me the city was truly appropriately named: the haven of peace. Of the memorable natural smells from my childhood I recall Indian jasmine and queen of the night. Both grew near our home there. Jasmine was my mother's favourite flower (Nadia, our daughter, and her husband, Kyle, have named their first daughter Ayla Yasmine in honour of my mother).

At our maternal grandmother's house in Mahiwa Street in Dar es Salaam there were two trees that I most vividly recall even today. One was an ylang ylang tree, a tropical tree originally from Indonesia: the fragrance of its thin, yellow flowers is heavenly. The other was a fruit tree we called zambarau. I have never come across zambarau anywhere else than Tanzania. It's a kind of plum, with its characteristic small, very dark purple fruit and an unusual taste. To this day I am also bewitched by the fragrant aroma of smouldering coal and dried wood; it reminds me of my childhood experiences of wonderful food being cooked over wood fires. It is an aroma that evokes the texture of Africa itself; in fact, it is still the first thing that hits you when you step out of an airplane in Kampala (Entebbe actually)—that and the vivid red colour of the topsoil.

As a child I would have been described as a quiet and shy boy. I was calm and unexcitable, rather different from my brother Said. He had a hot temper. If a boy teased Said, most likely he would receive a sock on the nose.

I thought of myself as solitary. Even at an early age, I had an appreciation for the value of my own company. At the same time, I was self-driven and calmly determined. I understood even then the idea of taking risks and knew early on that risk was linked to reward. I never felt bored being by myself. For one thing, I almost always had a book close at hand, and if I didn't have a book I had my mind and my imagination. Once, when I was seven, we were out with the family and I just slipped out of the car and walked away; it was hours later before they found me after an extensive search.

I was fine and could not understand why my cousin was so angry with me. "You cannot walk off. You will become lost!" I thought, "I am not lost. I know exactly where I am going." I have always loved exploring—this has been true as much with ideas and opinions as it has been with places. When I went around East Africa on my own as a young teenager, I knew I might run out of money and that I would go hungry. I had no idea what would happen or who I would meet or where I would sleep if I wasn't in a bus or train. It was risky but not reckless. I always believed somehow that I would manage. This was the beginning of my lifelong habit of pushing boundaries. Plus, I am sure it helped me that from a very young age I was expected to assume a lot of responsibility for myself and for others around me.

I was eleven years old when I decided I wanted to drive. It did not matter that boys at that age were not allowed to drive. Driving was something I wanted to do. I decided I would teach myself to drive. My father had in his employ at any given time a driver of our meat van. I often rode with him and watched very closely what he did until I had the whole process secure in my mind. Usually I would begin by begging the driver to let me hold the steering wheel. Later I would help shift the gears (no automatic gearshifts in those days!). Eventually the driver would be so fatigued from my constant badgering he would let me take the controls. The first time I took complete control was when we were out of town on roads with little or no traffic. However, a few months later, when I was about twelve, I was confident enough to sneak the van out in the evenings and drive with my friend Ajmal through town. It was great fun.

One of the drivers, Musa, was a drunkard and great womanizer whose family hailed from the Seychelles (we used to call them Sheli Sheli). On occasion he would pick up a woman and ask me to get out of the van and go stand outside while he entertained the lady in the van. The rocking of the van and the moans from within embarrassed me. I couldn't tell on him because he could blackmail me: if I told my father about his womanizing, he threatened to stop allowing me to drive the van. He was also threatening in other ways. When he picked me up at three in the morning, I could usually smell alcohol on his breath; I was never sure whether this was him starting to drink for the day or ending from the night before—or both. He drove erratically and would sometimes brood sullenly before exploding in dark violent rages. Luckily he would be drunk and his aim was sloppy and I learned to stay as far away from him as possible. In the end I did warn my father of Musa's behaviour and he was fired.

I did not have a driving licence until much later. When I was about thirteen—still too young to drive legally—I was late coming back from my maths tutorial. I was speeding in our meat van and ran a red light. The police stopped me and ordered me to go straight to the police station. I assume he thought I would drive away, so as a precaution his colleague accompanied me in the passenger seat of the van. In retrospect, it is rather hilarious to me that they did not ask me if I had a driving licence even though I clearly was underage; they must have assumed that if I could drive a van in the centre of the city, I must have one.

I asked him if I could briefly stop at my house, which was on the way. "I want to tell my father that I am in police custody." The officer refused and told me to keep silent. I insisted.

"Look, I really need to tell my father where I am. He will be furious! It is right on the way. Why won't you let me stop?" He barked at me to "keep [my] mouth shut and drive!" Our house was coming up and I thought this made no sense, and I muttered something to the effect of "to hell with you!" The officer shouted at me again and grabbed the steering wheel. We struggled; the van skidded this way and that, and I was afraid it might tip over when at the last second he let go and we roared down the street. I slammed to a stop in front of our house. At this point I think the officer next to me was too amazed at my behaviour to be angry. I tooted the horn and someone came to the balcony of our house.

"Tell my father I have been taken to the police station!" I yelled.

The policeman had regained his composure; he was furious. "Out of the car!" he screamed. "Out of the car!" He insisted he drive the rest of the way. I said, "Fine." At the police station, I was booked and forced to spend the night in jail. I was very, very frightened: there were several other prisoners, all much older than me, and I was terrified of what would happen if I fell asleep, so I stayed awake all night. Next day they let me go but I discovered that my father had come to the police station in the evening and told the officers to keep me in jail overnight to teach me a lesson! He could have bailed me out, but he believed in tough love!

I was very thin when I was a teenager, especially in my early teens. My mother tried every which way to fatten me up but failed. A belief was common in the community that the source of the problem was the tonsils, that somehow they drained the energy from the body and took away the appetite for food, and that a tonsillectomy would solve the problem. I don't think I had more than my usual share of tonsillitis, but I also became convinced that I should have my tonsils removed.

And so I went to the Aga Khan Hospital with my older cousin Abdulrab to book myself for the operation, on my own initiative and without my parents' knowledge. My mother was terrified of anyone in her family having surgery under general anaesthesia (my uncle Ali had died while under anaesthesia) and she would have overruled me. I was only twelve or thirteen at the time, so I dragged Abdulrab along to provide consent. Imagine! No way could such a thing occur today. It would be unthinkable! Anyway, the surgery went well and I was home the same day, but what I recall most was how delighted I was that I would be eating lots of ice cream during my recovery! My mother was very upset at first but was too grateful I was alive to continue fussing. Actually, since I'd had my tonsils removed, she was very pleased that I would soon be putting on more weight. I never did. And she never told my father. People who have heard this story cannot believe it. "I know," I tell them. "Incredible. But that is how it was back then!"

I loved the movies, and in the evenings I would attend as many as I could, either with my friends or by myself. Unfortunately, my sisters were never allowed to tag along, largely because my father did not like the idea of my sisters being out at night. He was that kind of father. How could he protect his family if his daughters were out and about? My father was not so much religiously conservative as he was paternally conservative—especially when it came to my sisters. Maybe he remembered what he was like himself as a teenage boy!

My sisters and I came up with a solution. We collected enough spare change for a single ticket and I would go to the cinema to watch the movie with the idea of memorizing as much as I could. I would return home and we would all gather on the big bed—ten of us or more!—and I would replay the movie from beginning to end; we usually had snacks and I would play all the parts and act out the dialogue in theatrical voices. It was hard at first, but after a while I got the hang of it and in many ways it was more fun than the movie itself. In fact, of all my memories of childhood, this is the one that I cherish the most. Sometimes my mother would join us and those times were the best. What I remember is how much we laughed. My sisters would pepper me with questions and pretend to be scared during tense scenes or burst out laughing at comic scenes and applaud uproariously when the hero triumphed. I always bowed deeply at the end. I only wish my father could have been a part of it too.

In Dar es Salaam I belonged to a tiny group of friends that used to wander around looking for mischief. I remember once going into a shop and stealing a book. I don't remember what the book was and I think my only reason for stealing it—in homage to the greatest of Christian theologians and philosophers, the African St. Augustine of Hippo, who at the age of eleven went around stealing fruit simply because it was forbidden!—was purely for the malicious thrill. I lingered over the book in question and suddenly lifted up my shirt, tucked the book into my waistband, and walked hurriedly out. I was mostly the "good" boy in the family but every now and then I delighted in being a bit naughty.

I loved to read. I often hung around bookstores, newsagents, and magazine kiosks to read copies of the American news magazines *Time* and *Newsweek*. I would read them from cover to cover until the clerk cottoned on to what was going on and chased me out. *Time* magazine in particular played a very important part in my life, from when I was eleven or twelve. We had no television and rarely listened to the cumbersome radio at home, so it gave me a view of the world that I would not otherwise have had (not that the perspective of *Time* magazine was always that objective!).

Most local radio was unimaginative and boring and not worth listening to. The only radio programs my friends and I listened to were "call in" request music stations. Unfortunately, none of us had a phone.

At the time, music on the radio was largely pop hits tracking the UK charts. My music tastes evolved but in the early 1960s we listened to songs by singers like Cliff Richard, Elvis Presley, Helen Shapiro, Bobby Darin, and Neil Sedaka. My own favourites were Dusty Springfield, Marianne Faithfull, and Jim Reeves (I listened to him all the time later at high school). And, of course, the Beatles and Rolling Stones became very big. However, having as many Indian friends as I had, one could not help but listen to Indian songs by the great Indian singers like Lata Mangeshkar, Asha Bhosle, Kishore Kumar, and Mukesh. At that time we had little access to Arabic music because it was not played much on the radio stations we were able to receive, but, nevertheless, you couldn't be alive and not have heard the songs of Farid al-Atrash, Mohammed Abdulwahab, Abdel Halim Hafez, and the greatest of them all, Umm Kulthum.

Sometimes I would go and stay overnight with my half-Circassian maternal grandmother, Ghaniya—we kids called her Bibi Kali (the "strict" or "fierce" grandmother). She lived alone but quite often one of us would sleep at her house to give her company. While kind and generous (she was the one who gave my brother and me the money we misspent on the red VW), she was not much of a conversationalist and in the evenings would sit in silence by a large window facing the street.

Here she would set up her *paan* paraphernalia. *Paan*, of which there are many varieties, is an Indian preparation that is usually chewed after dinner, partly for the taste but, depending on what you put into it, also for its mildly stimulant effect. She would make herself her *tambuu* (Swahili for *paan*), using betel leaf, areca nut, chalk, sometimes tobacco, and a sweet sticky paste that colours the whole thing a bright red, which also then is in the saliva. Bibi Kali chewed this every night after dinner, and for hours she would sit at that window, looking out, making new small triangular *paans* the size of small samosas as the time passed until she went to bed. This ritual and the smells of the different ingredients were also part of my childhood, as vivid today as when I was ten years old sleeping at my grandma's house.

If there was any lingering bad feeling between my father and his elder brother, Ali, it did not show. On the few occasions Uncle Ali came from Morogoro to Dar es Salaam, he would visit us and if his work required him to stay the night he would stay with us. On one occasion it turned out he required minor surgery, and he stayed with us for a few days awaiting his appointment at Muhimbili Hospital, the largest and most advanced medical facility in Tanzania.

Uncle Ali was a very healthy middle-aged man at the time. He had developed a hernia resulting from a localized weakening of the abdominal muscles; it's a common surgical condition throughout the world, affecting all ages and is easily treated surgically. The operation carries negligible risk of death.

In fact, many years later as a young doctor in England, I performed hundreds of such hernia operations. I was actually involved in a clinical trial in Oxford of an innovative technique that allowed us to perform abdominal hernia surgery using only local anaesthesia. In Tanzania in the 1960s, there were no surgical and anaesthetic facilities available in small towns and villages and if they did exist they were so crude as to be functionally useless. For the majority of Africans, particularly those living in villages, if they developed a hernia they most likely simply lived with the condition. That meant years of slowly increasing swelling and pain, and the possibility of eventual bowel strangulation, leading to death. My uncle was probably able to pay for a private room and arrange surgery with a busy surgeon who was allowed to use some of his time for private practice.

The family in Morogoro had called the hospital earlier to ask after his condition and were assured that the operation had been a complete success. I drove my father to the hospital to visit my uncle the evening after his surgery. When we arrived at the hospital, however, his bed was empty. The nurse on duty told us to collect his body in the mortuary. Uncle Ali had died from "complications of the general anaesthesia," we were told. It was all we were ever told.

I remember a few other tragic stories like this. My mother's cousin lived in Rwanda and had many children. They worked hard but struggled to make a living there or in neighbouring countries like Burundi and the Democratic Republic of Congo, where medical care, sanitation, education, public health measures, and other necessities we take for granted are very poor or nonexistent. Three of her adult sons—in the prime of their lives—died of malaria. One of my sisters, Fawzia, was adopted by my mother after her father died in his thirties. He was bitten by a poisonous snake but was alive when taken to a Morogoro hospital for medical treatment. There was nothing they could do. They had no snake anti-venom to combat the poison, and he died later the same day.

Fawzia had a younger brother. One day he was playing in the backyard of the house when he stepped on a rusty nail. He died a few days later of tetanus. He had not been given a tetanus vaccine. A safe and effective tetanus vaccine had been developed in the 1920s, and by the 1940s it was widely in use throughout the West.

It prevented tetanus, and if, for example, someone later stepped on a rusty nail, the vaccine was reinforced by an injection of anti-tetanus serum given on the spot. But when Fawzia's brother developed the painful spasms that indicate that tetanus had set in, there were no facilities or the medical expertise to care for him.

About a decade ago I was asked to do an external independent review of a global program called the Special Programme for Research and Training in Tropical Diseases (TDR), based at the World Health Organization (WHO). Its main focus was on what are known as "neglected tropical diseases," which are part of the larger group of "diseases of poverty." One of those is lymphatic filariasis, caused by small threadlike worms that are transmitted by mosquitoes. Of course, I could not help but recall my childhood in Tanzania, where I knew many people suffering from this condition, mainly presenting with hugely swollen lower limbs (sometimes described as elephantiasis). In men, the genitalia, especially the scrotum, grew to such huge sizes that the patient was unable to walk and sometimes had to resort to carrying the scrotum ahead of him in a wheelbarrow. If today, with all our medical and social developments, lymphatic filariasis is still officially designated by WHO as a *neglected* tropical disease, imagine how much more neglected it was in my childhood: it was *totally neglected.* The millions who suffered were exposed to that debilitating disease and others because of poor social conditions like inadequate sanitation. Of course, lymphatic filariasis was only one of many neglected diseases the poor are at greatest risk of getting, which include onchocerciasis (river blindness), visceral leishmaniasis (black fever), dengue fever, and Chagas disease (a parasitic disease).

One of the reasons I love living in Canada is because of the country's commitment to providing quality health care to every citizen regardless of income. In my travels—especially to the

United States—I hear people wondering aloud about Canadian health care. "But don't you have to stand in line for health care?" I suppose it is true that often wait times are inconvenient, but is that not a rather trivial concern compared to the much larger health care systems in the United States that are so expensive and to which access is essentially restricted to the wealthy and to those with good insurance coverage? What is the value of having the most state-of-the-art medical technology if no one can afford it? I hear critics say we need to do better. Well, I think we are doing better! Sure, there are always going to be problems. But those problems can be solved. Providing professional health care at a reasonable cost is—and must remain—a human right in the same way that free speech and free association are rights. We cannot have a viable and vibrant democracy if we base access to health care on hierarchies of income. Nor can we pretend that we have no responsibility to help others in poorer countries to improve their health care systems.

It breaks my heart to think about how many children in Third World countries are still dying or suffering from so many debilitating illnesses and diseases that have been all but eradicated in the modern industrialized countries of the world. We need to realize that there are not first worlds and second worlds or even third worlds. There is one world. "Man is a social animal," wrote the Roman Stoic philosopher Seneca (ironically of Spanish origin), "and born to live together so as to regard the world as one house. The society of man is like a vault of stones, which would fall if the stones did not rest on another; in this way it is sustained."

Chapter 6

Awakening: My First Political Hero

I am not a teacher, but an awakener.

— Robert Frost

In Tanganyika we believe that only evil, Godless men would make the colour of a man's skin the criteria for granting him civil rights.

— Julius Nyerere

It has been my experience that it is impossible to exaggerate the influence on a child of a positive role model. For me that early role model was Julius Nyerere, a pioneer in the cause of African independence and self-rule and the first president of independent Tanzania.

I grew up very close to the majority black African community. Of course, even before I went to high school I had worked with many Africans at my father's business and I had made friends with them. On the way to the abattoir at dawn, we would often stop at roadside eating places and eat beans and drink sweet ginger tea with mandazi. When I was eight or nine and my father was looking for me, he would sometimes find me playing marbles in an alley in Kariakoo with my African friends. At Aga Khan Secondary School in Dar es Salaam, there were only a handful of African students; the majority were Indians, and the majority of those were Ismailis.

However, when I got to Mkwawa High School in Iringa in the southern highlands, the majority of students were African and so the majority of my friends were African. In biology, physics, and chemistry classes, my laboratory bench partners were African. When we needed frogs to dissect in class, we would go with both my Indian and African friends to look for them in ponds near the school. The future minister of communications, science, and technology of Tanzania, Peter Msolla, was one of the students I came to know at Mkwawa, and when Peter Singer and I were doing research in Tanzania many years later, Msolla was one of our main contacts.

Later at Makerere University Medical School, again the majority of students were African and I had many friends among them. (In fact, Nyerere himself was a graduate of Makerere University.) I also made friends with Africans on my journeys on behalf of my father to Dodoma, Shinyanga, and other towns. In Dodoma, first as a child and later in my teens, I got to know well the main local tribe, the Wagogo, and learned a tiny bit of their language. Tanzania's prime minister from 1990 to 1994, John Malecela, was born in Dodoma. I don't think I ever met him personally, but for the past fifteen years or so I have worked closely with his accomplished daughter, Dr. Mwele Malecela, who is now on the board of directors of Grand Challenges Canada. Even when Mwele and I were surrounded by English-speaking folk at board meetings and at international conferences, we would take time to talk in Swahili, and that's how I learned of the remarkable story of how her father, as a teenager, had met an Indian shopkeeper in Dodoma who helped him financially to go to his first university in Bombay! (He later went to Cambridge for graduate studies.) While John Malecela served his country in many senior political positions, including as foreign minister and representative to the United Nations, his daughter Mwele became a renowned scientist and was, until 2017, the director of Tanzania's National Institute for Medical Research.

The point is, I firmly believe my early acquaintance with poor and working-class Africans (the majority) gave me an inside track, so to speak, into the systemic injustices—minor and major—that characterized the colonial system created and enforced by the British prior to independence and that non-African communities helped to perpetuate before and after independence.

I can't remember exactly the first time I heard of Julius Nyerere—probably it would have been a radio broadcast or from a newspaper—but I do vividly remember him having an increasing presence in my life because of his impassioned pleas of racial and social justice. Everyone was talking about him. For one thing, we often listened to the radio in the van to and from the abattoir or on errands, and I recall how our African drivers would suddenly snap to attention and turn up the volume if Nyerere was speaking. This was a man, their reverential silence seemed to suggest, who deserves our respect and attention.

Nyerere was the founder in the 1950s of the Tanganyika African National Union (TANU), the main political party fighting for independence. He was a wise, astute, broad-minded, modest statesman. He counted Gandhi as a hero and was influenced by the writings of the liberal English utilitarian philosopher John Stuart Mill. When later I came to know more about Gandhi and Mill, I could see why I had liked Nyerere immediately. I remember in those early days thinking, *What power knowledge has! Here is a man who has read great books by brilliant minds and is going to change the face of Africa!* It was intoxicating. Nyerere was a socialist, of course, and while I was not exactly sure at the time what that meant (I studied its doctrines later), I found its overt utopianism and idealism absolutely irresistible.

"All human beings are equal," Nyerere preached from his everyman pulpit. The right to freedom of expression, of religious belief, of association and movement must be guaranteed to all and not only to the privileged few. "Every individual has an equal claim to respect and dignity," he demanded. Moreover, the abundant resources of the country belonged not to one man or an elite but to all citizens regardless of religion or gender or ethnicity or class. Let me tell you, to a thirsty young man anxious to drink long and deep of the well of human knowledge, and intoxicated with the idea of perhaps having a role to play in the drama of revolution, Nyerere's gospel was preaching to the choir. I was hooked! Here was a man to emulate.

Nyerere was loved and revered and respected by the African peoples of Tanzania then and now; however, the admiration was less among the Asian community, at least in the early days after independence when he was treated with everything from mild suspicion to open hostility, mostly because Asians overall were comfortable and had become wealthy under the British. What Nyerere was proposing threatened to jeopardize a status quo that privileged them over the Africans, and that was unacceptable to them.

As a teenager I had not met many politicians but had heard a lot about corrupt African leaders. But I admired and respected Nyerere because I could see he was a deeply honest and principled man. I was impressed that Nyerere committed a considerable amount of time to travelling throughout Tanganyika in the years prior to independence to talk to people in villages about what was coming. And while in those villages he listened to the ordinary folk. He became a highly respected leader in Africa, always pushing for African unity, acting on the same large African stage as Kwame Nkrumah of Ghana, and was also a respected international statesman on the world stage during the Cold War. He was one of the founding leaders of the Organization of African Unity, which later became the African Union (I have served on two High-Level Panels of that organization: one on biotechnology, the other on emerging technologies for Africa's socio-economic development; both were co-chaired by the great Calestous Juma, a Kenyan who was a professor at Harvard until his death in late 2017). I admired Nyerere's personal integrity, looked up to him, saw him as a hero, and regarded his socialist policies at the time as a path to socio-economic development for the majority of Tanzanians.

My children kid me that I will cry at the drop of a hat. I can be very emotional and tend to be drawn to larger-than-life characters that inspire me to deep emotional responses. Nyerere did that to me. I know there are many Americans of a certain vintage who read *To Kill a Mockingbird* by Harper Lee as young people and decided that Atticus Finch—the fictional hero of the book—was everyone's ideal father. Was Nyerere a kind of father substitute for me? A political one?

My Asian friends, both Indians and Arabs, could not understand why I was so supportive of Nyerere's policies. In high school I sometimes took to the streets to demonstrate in support of Nyerere and his policies, especially as promulgated in the Arusha Declaration, TANU's political manifesto that provided the vision of *Ujamaa* (familyhood), Tanzania's brand of socialism and self-reliance. I believe that this was because I saw, often first-hand and through listening to their stories, the injustices suffered by Africans: the poverty, the exclusion from good education, the poor health and lack of access to good health care, the segregation in social circles and at work, and generally the absence of a level playing field.

This might seem a bit sentimental in retrospect, but from an early age I was deeply sensitized to acts of injustice. I am still that way today. For instance, I will never forget an episode at high school in Iringa when I had gone to a barbershop for a haircut. The shop was owned by a prosperous Indian who always dressed very ostentatiously—always the best and most expensive of everything. What I will never forget were his gold cufflinks. Imagine! Gold cufflinks worn by a barber in a poor town in Tanzania! It struck me as so ludicrous and inappropriate.

What did it mean? In and of itself such a thing was not that remarkable, but under the circumstances it was profoundly disorienting to me. I began to think about this episode very deeply. The barber probably had immigrated to Tanzania quite recently, I reasoned; his accent had the ring of the outsider. *But after only a short time, he is doing well enough to wear gold cufflinks!* He had a car, a nice home, and probably African servants to do his every bidding. Whereas looking around me I didn't see any African barber shops. I didn't see an African who owned a bicycle—much less a swanky car—or who wore gold cufflinks.

Anyway, in my adolescent mind I was convinced that somehow Julius Nyerere would create a Tanzania where Asian barbers did not wear gold cufflinks while poor Africans scrabbled in the dirt outside for food. It was not just Nyerere and African independence that captured my attention at the time. This was around the time of the Cuban Missile Crisis when the Cold War seemed very close to transitioning into a hot war. I recall listening to newsreaders from the BBC radio broadcasts speaking sombrely of a countdown to nuclear war. Unimaginable that that world over there, so far from here, had brought all of us so close to the edge of annihilation! It seemed real and unreal, believable and unbelievable. It was perhaps the first time I realized how utterly interconnected the world was, and how mighty was President Kennedy's power—and how much he was adored around the world. I recall very distinctly the moment when I heard Kennedy had been assassinated, on November 22, 1963. I was at the abattoir and had stopped working to have an early morning cup of tea. I switched on the car radio and heard the news that I, like most people, thought would change the world.

In those days my attitude to America was shaped almost entirely by what I read in magazines. It was the height of the Cold War and there was no doubt that, according to *Time* and *Newsweek* (the twin colossi of American opinion-making at the time), the United States was the Good Guy and the Soviet Union was the Bad Guy (a simplistic dualistic political reduction that—remarkably—we seem to be cycling back to today, albeit with a peculiar modern twist that both Donald Trump and Vladimir Putin seem to be chasing to the lowest common denominator). While my friends avidly followed football scores, I was obsessed with tracking political scores. Washington and the Kremlin seemed to me to be playing a huge and hugely elaborate game, like a chess match. Later on as I read more and more deeply, I developed a more balanced and nuanced appreciation for politics, and especially of what was happening in Africa. Tanzania itself was trying hard to adopt socialism of a type that was not communism, and the country became a member of the Non-Aligned Movement, neither affiliated with nor beholden to either the United States or the Soviet Union.

My brothers and sisters were interested in politics to varying extents but we all had opinions on everything: socialism, capitalism, African freedom fighters, South Africa, Palestine, and so on. No one was shy about expressing those opinions. It seemed normal for me growing up to have sisters who were confident to speak their mind, at a time when most traditional Muslim families were not like that at all. Girls were required to keep silent and obey their parents—their father especially. Again, I have to credit my mother's quiet subversion in regards to undermining in her own way this dominant social stereotype.

Mostly I discussed politics with my friends. I have mentioned that I was not much into sports, but for me politics was the rugby of intellectual sports. I loved roughing it up with my friends. My group of friends included my older brother Said, my best friend Ajmal, another friend Adam, and my cousin Abdulrab. We would meet many evenings to discuss current events. We would stand outside Khalid Restaurant (which was diagonally across from where we lived on Aggrey Street), enjoy its great tea and milky coffee, and talk and argue. There were quite a few times when the volume reached a critical point and the verbal debating threatened to turn physical!

Of course we talked a lot about escalating tensions in Palestine. As far as I knew, most everyone in the developing world was sympathetic to the Palestinian cause. Our conviction was that the Israelis had illegally expropriated land properly belonging to the Palestinians and that this was an unacceptable injustice that must be corrected.

I was in high school in 1967 when simmering tensions between Arabs and Israelis boiled over into hostilities in what became known as the Six-Day War. That was the first time international politics was concretized for me. I remember listening to the BBC World Service radio in my bed late at night; it was the best source of information. I had my own small portable radio by then and regularly listened to the World Service program.

At the outset of the Six-Day War, it appeared that the Arabs had the upper hand. But it was the Arabs who were routed. I can remember feeling ashamed at how badly and stupidly the Arabs had performed. This was the third war they had fought against the Israelis and the third war they had lost. It was humiliating.

I had never met a Jew. If there were any in Dar es Salaam, they would have been few in number and I am pretty sure there was no synagogue. However, I do recall during the Six-Day War broadcasts hearing some Arab men in tea shops or in the street uttering negative remarks about Jews. The general view was that the Arabs had lost the war so, of course, they were not happy.

Much to my regret, Julius Nyerere's utopian adventure in building a better world via an enlightened socialism ultimately ended in failure. Ironically, following independence the Nyerere government nationalized without compensation my mother's house in Dar es Salaam as well as what remained of her share of the small family farm in Kigogo. I should have been furious—I should have felt betrayed—but I continued to think well of Nyerere's socialist policies. No one else among my friends and family did. In fact it was largely because of the socialist policies and the deteriorating economy that many Asians decided to leave Tanzania. Tanzania was almost bankrupted when it later fought a bitter war with Idi Amin's army. It was a successful war inasmuch as it deposed Idi Amin, ushering in a new era for Uganda. In any case, it was because of my affection for Julius Nyerere and what he was trying to do that I was flirting seriously with the idea of a career in politics.

At the age of around fifteen I sent an exploratory letter of inquiry to Kuwait University with the intention of studying political science and hoping that one day I would follow in the footsteps of my hero, Julius Nyerere. To be honest, I was smugly overconfident of my chances and was more than a bit surprised that after a month I still had not had any reply from the university.

After about two months or so, I forgot about it. One day I was walking along Kichwele Street in Dar es Salaam when I heard my name being spoken. I stopped dead in my tracks. A shopkeeper was chatting with some customers in front of his shop.

"Why are you talking about me?" I demanded.

The shopkeeper had a letter in his hand. "Are you Abdallah Daar?"

"I am!"

The shopkeeper said he had a letter with my name on it!

Well, that is very strange. "May I have it?" It was a letter from Kuwait University mailed to me months before! I tore it open. The university, it informed me, would be delighted to consider an application if I sent one, and that it would also provide me with a scholarship if I were accepted. It's funny, because looking back on the trajectory of my life I can see that there were many serendipitous moments along the way where, having set my mind to go in one direction, I ended up going in another direction—fate! Had the letter from Kuwait arrived in a timely fashion, I expect I would have applied, and had I been accepted, who knows where I would be today. But as chance would have it, in my letter to Kuwait University, I had listed my home address incorrectly, and I ended up not applying!

In Robert Frost's famous poem he talks about two roads in a wood and of a "road less travelled." Like many readers I initially assumed the poet advocated taking the less-travelled path. But that isn't what the poem means at all. What he was really saying was much simpler (and more profound!). We make choices, and the choices we make close off alternatives. What we cannot do is stand at the fork in the road. We must choose. What I have learned—and what Frost did not mention—is that sometimes life has a way of intervening by nudging us a bit down one road as opposed to another. I took my error as a sign that despite Julius Nyerere and his incredible impact on me, a career in political science was not for me. I would travel the other road. In a sense, however, it was the same road. No matter where I went, I was never far from my past.

At high school in the southern highlands of Tanzania, I had many bright African friends. They came from all around the country and had fascinating stories about their childhoods and how they had excelled to get to this prestigious school. Most, of course, were from very poor backgrounds.

One day on my bed I found a handwritten note addressed to me from a friend in the same dormitory, a gaunt, quiet, handsome fellow. He was very apologetic. He used the term "beset" to describe his current poverty and his pressing need for a few shillings to buy items he needed desperately, and so he had borrowed some money from my desk, promising to return the money the following month. Our friendship continued and the incident was never mentioned.

Even today Julius Nyerere is very much a source of inspiration. His focus on injustices and inequities led me to question my own priorities. His efforts had me asking myself what I could do to make the world around me a better place. The majority Africans around us had very little or no schooling, no transportation, no easy access to the few health facilities the government provided, and if they were able to get a job, it would almost always be very low-wage labour. I knew this from my father's butchery business: many of my father's employees had to wake very early to walk to work; they laboured all day and had to repeat the long walk back to their homes, often not much more than a shack on the outskirts of Dar es Salaam; they never talked about their wives or children; and when they fell ill, they could not afford proper medical treatment.

Julius Nyerere was teaching us to do better. He tried. I believed in his message. This idea that I could strive for the improvement of society was for me a big driver in the choice I made to go to medical school. If you ask most people why they want to go to medical school, they will say, "Well, I want to help people." It was true for me as well. But what I learned in my career was that "helping people" meant—frustratingly for me, at least—helping people one patient at a time. It wasn't enough for me. I wanted to help as many people as I could all at once!

As with my roots in Tanzania, there is a part of Julius Nyerere that I will carry with me in my heart always. I think that is what a great role model can do, and it makes all the difference in the world.

Chapter 7

The Best of Friends

A man's growth is seen in the successive choirs of his friends.

—Ralph Waldo Emerson

My best friend growing up was Ajmal. In fact, he is still my best friend all these many years later.

In Dar es Salaam, after school ended at around three, I would drag myself home absolutely exhausted. I would fall down and sleep. In theory I had a small room that I was supposed to share with my brother Said at night, but there was no fixed arrangement during the day. You just slept where there was room, and some of my sisters actually decided to sleep under the bed so they would not be disturbed. For me, however, the working day was not yet over.

Often Ajmal would come and wake me up (he had to do the rounds looking for me in different rooms!) at around 5 p.m, and we would go to the butcheries to collect leftover meat that hadn't been sold, take it to the central one, and put it into a refrigerator. Ajmal would help me to lift the meat into and out of the van. Usually we made it back home by about seven and then started thinking about meeting up with more friends. Usually we would meet first at Khalid Restaurant near our house. Shoot the breeze. Drink tea or go to a movie.

In fact, I recently came across a cinema ticket stub from the Avalon Cinema from 1964, the year Tanzania was created.

The ticket cost ten shillings, which was probably about a dollar and a half. At that time a pound of the cheapest cut of meat with a fair amount of bones cost one shilling and fifteen cents at Aswan Butchery. Africans, who were the main customers at Aswan Butchery, could afford even this least expensive meat only on the day they received their monthly salary, which gives an indication of just how little the majority earned in Tanzania at around that time, and how little access they had to good protein.

Anyway, some of the movies I recall seeing with Ajmal in those days were *The Singer Not the Song; West Side Story; Lilies of the Field; The Mark; The Guns of Navarone; Splendor in the Grass; Judgment at Nuremberg; El Cid; Psycho; Spartacus; Pollyanna;* and *Exodus*. There were just a handful of cinema houses in Dar es Salaam: Odeon, Avalon, Chox, Empire. We would buy the cheapest tickets but there was no money for snacks or soda. Before independence in 1961, the show would start with the British national anthem and a few adverts, including, for some reason, adverts for the new British aircraft the BAC One-Eleven and expensive watches like Rolex and Tissot. I couldn't understand who in the audience would want to buy an aircraft!

At school Ajmal and I had the delightful habit of putting salty peanuts into a full bottle of Coca-Cola or Portello (a drink made of grapes, raspberries, and black currants, known as Vimto in the United Kingdom) and drinking the mixture directly from the bottle. What a snack, what a treat! Late in 2017 in Toronto when Ajmal and I went to see a play at the Tarragon Theatre, I surprised him by making this snack (I had hidden the nuts and the Coke bottles in my jacket pockets) before going into the show. We had not had it since childhood and people were staring at us giggling away like kids!

Ajmal and I had met at the Aga Khan Primary School in Kisutu, Dar es Salaam, where we were in the same class level. We soon moved together to the well-established Aga Khan Boys Secondary School. It was considered the best boys' school at the time. Some students were given scholarships but most paid the reasonable tuition fees, as I did. There was at that time a separate girls' school but many years later the co-ed Aga Khan Mzizima Secondary School was created (Mzizima is the old name of Dar es Salaam). My brother Said was also at the same school but he was not in my class and was not very focused on studies—he had his sights elsewhere.

School was mostly fun. Ajmal was more interested in subjects like physics and math. Although I was good at arithmetic, I was never very good at math as a whole; I was much stronger in biology and the humanities; and I loved literature.

We had many friends. We were happy and gregarious and enjoyed each other's company. I was not much interested in sports. The surroundings were quite pretty with big mango trees in the school compound. Photographs of us show we were all skinny. We must have exercised more and eaten many fewer calories and healthier foods at home than most kids eat nowadays. We loved school plays. We acted together in several plays and Ajmal actually directed one. Our parents came to see the plays. The classes were not difficult, and I did well although I was often tired, having woken up at three to go to the abattoir. Ajmal and I remained at that school until I had to leave Dar es Salaam to go to high school in Iringa, in the southern highlands of Tanzania, while he stayed on in Dar es Salaam to complete his high school education.

Ajmal comes from the Shia Imami Ismaili community, whose spiritual leader is the Aga Khan. One way or another I have had much to do with Ismailis. My wife, Shahina, also comes from that community although she hasn't been a practising Ismaili since before I met her. As we grew up, Ajmal and I became closer and closer and spent most of our leisure time together. He became closer to me than my brother.

Ajmal shared my love of politics. We talked politics all the time. Tanganyika had gained its independence from the United Kingdom on December 9, 1961. I was thirteen at the time, and Ajmal and I went to the parade ground where the Union Jack was lowered and Tanganyika's flag was raised at midnight. It was exhilarating. I felt so proud. Suddenly all my friends and I were buoyed by a powerful new confidence. We had big smiles on our faces. *Our* country! (I would think of this shared moment of national pride many times in my life—especially when I became a front-row witness to events in Uganda when Idi Amin took power and the invigorating sense of "ours" became an ugly weapon in racist retribution.)

Three years later Tanganyika and Zanzibar formed a union called the United Republic of Tanganyika and Zanzibar (later renamed United Republic of Tanzania). So there was no shortage of political subjects to discuss. I think in our youthful idealism we learned to respect human rights and to sympathize with those being suppressed and oppressed, as was happening in South Africa.

As I said, my father really loved Ajmal and I still have no idea why. Ajmal named my father Blue Master because he had a blue car, an old German Opel Kapitan, which we could hear from afar. We would be at home, playing and talking loudly, and we would hear the engine of the car entering Aggrey Street. "Ah, Blue Master has arrived!" We knew it was time to tone it down and behave well.

Ajmal had a more forceful external personality than I. He always wanted to get his way. He had to have the last word in an argument or discussion! I suppose in many ways I would describe Ajmal as charmingly precocious; he was a dreamer and there was a bit of a rebel in him, which I liked very much. He could be very mischievous but not in a malicious or hurtful way. Early on in our friendship his mother approached me and said, "I want you to look after my son. He tends to be a little unfocused and naughty." I am not sure what she expected I could do. Ajmal always did exactly what he wanted!

Ajmal had a car when he was fifteen and he loved to drive around the neighbourhood and try to pick up girls. He loved to drive very fast and show off by skidding the car around tight corners or in circles while his sisters and friends would scream in the rear of the car. Girls loved him because of his wildness.

He was a natural leader; everyone loved him. He was a good-looking boy, smart and clever. I was more on the quiet side, and I think we got on so well because of the contrast in our personalities, and we respected each other very much. We developed a very strong and close bond. I was always calm and even-keeled, which I must have inherited from my mother. So calm that when people wanted to play practical jokes, I was always the butt of the jokes. They knew I would never get angry or react badly. One time a prankster at school poured a whole jug of water on me, knowing I would just smile it off. Ajmal was the opposite; no one dared play tricks on him. He had to be top dog in every situation. In some ways, he was very much like my brother Said.

Although Ajmal was an Ismaili, in most respects he was as irreligious as I. The Ismailis are a branch of Shia Islam, holding that their imams are direct descendants of the Prophet Muhammad through Ali, his cousin, who was married to the

Prophet's daughter, Fatima. The spiritual leader of the Ismailis is the Aga Khan, and it was the current Aga Khan's grandfather's focus on education that set them up for long-term success in Africa and beyond. He had built schools wherever there were Ismailis, and after independence these schools admitted not just Ismailis and other Asians but also Africans. I was one of the many beneficiaries of this school system.

Most of the prominent Ismailis in the West have come from East Africa, and most of those had come from India. They are highly respected, they do not proselytize, and they keep their religiosity to themselves. In some people who don't know them well, these attributes have tended to breed resentment and suspicion, compounded, for instance, by the fact that non-Ismailis are not allowed to enter their Jamatkhanas (a combination of an Ismaili mosque and community centre). Their business success and prosperity have made them targets of envy. They also don't talk much about their history, especially of their time in India, where they were converted from Hinduism. As a result, their beliefs and culture have incorporated a fair amount of Hinduism. We sometimes hear that Ismailis have more recently been moving a bit closer to mainline Islam, but I am not sure what that really means.

In Dar es Salaam we had many Ismaili friends and neighbours. Their Jamatkhana was just a few blocks from our house. It was very common to see Ismailis marching past our house in the dark just before dawn to attend prayers and meditation services.

Ajmal and I were inseparable as boys, and our close friendship continued even after I went away to high school. We communicated often. For instance, long-distance telephone calls were very expensive back then and had to be booked in advance with the postal telecoms service, so instead we would frequently write letters to each other, using blue-tinted aerograms (early versions of email!). At mid- or end-of-term, Ajmal would drive on the poor roads all the way to the highlands in Iringa to pick me up and take me home to Dar es Salaam. As my father became more ill, Ajmal would again come to pick me up from Iringa to bring me home to deal with some emergency or another. On a good day that trip was at least a ten-hour drive one way!

On several occasions my father needed me to take a train from Dar es Salaam to the cattle markets in Dodoma to load a shipment of cattle for the butchery business. Sometimes Ajmal would come with me. I remember one time in particular. We were riding back to Dar es Salaam on the train—in third class, as usual, because we had very little money—and we were desperately hungry. It had been a long journey, and all we could afford were a few boiled eggs that we bought from hawkers who mobbed the train wherever it stopped—and it stopped at every station on the way! After we left the station and the train was speeding to the next stop, we took our boiled eggs, opened the door of the moving train, closed it behind us, and sat on the metal stairs facing out. It was lovely and warm as the sun sank and the western sky was suffused with the beautiful combination of oranges and reds and violets, so close but so evanescent as the sun dropped rapidly below the horizon.

It was an ideal, peaceful moment, and the kind of time when we did not need to speak to each other and just being alone with your best friend seemed perfection. I was also incredibly happy because I had recently fallen deeply in love with an Ismaili girl, Farzana. Ajmal knew her well. For weeks I had been having a serious debate in my mind about when—and how—I was going to tell Ajmal. Would there come just the right moment to tell him of the happy news? How would he take it? I knew he respected me and I was his best friend, but did he have any faint prejudice where it concerned my love and potential marriage to a girl from his community? Even if he personally did not have these feelings, would he worry about members of his community having such biases, which I knew some had?

As I sat next to him nibbling at my boiled eggs, bits of coal aloft in the breeze were hitting my face and hands like sand—the lovely fragrance of coal—and me thinking, *I need to tell Ajmal about this wonderful, powerful, first love.* But the moment was too beautiful. I didn't want to spoil it. I kept silent.

Many years later I met up with Farzana again when I was a medical school student in London. This was before the time Shahina and I discovered our feelings for one another; it was obvious to me that I had some feelings still for Farzana and I was curious if she felt the same. We agreed to meet at the Serpentine Lake gardens in Hyde Park. It was an amazing afternoon. I felt anxious and nervous like a teenager all over again. At one point I asked her if she had given any thought to a future life together. She burst out crying and just wouldn't stop. I changed the subject and we agreed to meet outside an embassy in Kensington the next day. When the time came, I waited for her for more than an hour and, thinking that she had changed her mind, I left.

What I did not know and would discover only much later was that she had been unavoidably delayed—a problem with the subway—and had turned up to meet me only a few minutes after I left. I do not know what would have happened between us had she not been delayed. In a way it was another milestone—a turning point in my life. In retrospect I can see that my relationship with Farzana would not have worked. She was religious, devout, and attached to her family and community. She would not have disobeyed her parents, and marrying outside her Ismaili community at that time would have been very difficult for her.

Ajmal and I eventually did talk about Farzana and—of course—he was not at all perturbed by the news. Still, I find myself wondering about what would have happened. In my life I have come across taboos of one kind or another more times than I can count, which is one reason why I am so amazed by the wonderfully startling pace of social change we are experiencing today. It reminds me that change always has to start somewhere with someone—appeal to the heart and the brain will follow. What difference does it make where a person comes from or to whom they are attracted or what colour they are? It shouldn't be a question of *who* you love but *how* you love. When I have discussed these issues with my own children they smile indulgently. *Gee, no kidding, Dad*. Like it's the most obvious thing in the world. Only it hasn't been, not always. I know! And there are many places where it isn't still. One of the reasons I value my friendship with Ajmal as much as I do is that we have been friends for so long that we can remember going through all these changes together. What a long way we have come!

It was around the time I was in high school that Tanzania introduced National Service for boys and girls and most went to do this for six months after finishing high school. It involved being trained to be a soldier and doing community work. Because my father was ill, I was excused. Ajmal went and he and the people he met there, including many girls, had a great time. They were away from home, mucking about, working in the fields together, and I suspect the boys got to know the girls very well—and vice versa!

While in National Service, Ajmal became close friends with two Tanzanian boys of Indian origin who came from Tanga, the town where my father was to die in 1969. One day after graduating from high school, I was sitting in the butchery in Dar es Salaam and Ajmal came in with these two guys, Yusuf and Sultan. They had just finished National Service and I think were still wearing their uniforms. "These are two great guys. You should get to know them." By then I had already been selected to go to medical school and as it happens so had they. What a coincidence! Eventually Yusuf, Sultan, and later Ashni and I became very close friends at medical school in Uganda.

After high school in Dar es Salaam, Ajmal wasn't really sure at first what he wanted to do. He was accepted to veterinary school at the University of Nairobi and was also interested in going to a university in Beirut, but in the end he decided he was going to be a businessman. He started a business in Dar es Salaam at the age of about eighteen, rearing and selling poultry chicks. After a time he moved to Mauritius, where he started a dry cleaning business. He was slowly accumulating capital and later on immigrated to Canada. He has been in Canada much longer than I. Thirty years maybe. After trying his hand at one or two other businesses, he now has a well-established and thriving sportswear company called Jerico.

Except for about three years while I was at Oxford, Ajmal and I have kept in touch. I remember a very emotional moment for me: in May 1993 I organized and became president of a major conference in Singapore. The subject and the title of the conference was Transplantation in Developing Countries. It was hugely successful. Some of the best and most prestigious speakers and professionals came and spoke: ethicists, surgeons, physicians, and professors from Oxford and Cambridge and Harvard and from all over the world, including Peter Morris, my Oxford mentor, and Thomas Starzl, the famous American surgeon who, with Roy Calne of Cambridge University, had pioneered liver transplantation. It was at that conference that Starzl first announced his work on microchimerism—the observation that cells from a liver graft migrated out into the host's tissues and that this helped the host to accept the graft. This was a major scientific breakthrough that turned out to be a huge conceptual leap—and it was later found to be a common phenomenon.

It was a historic conference. I was so proud and elated to have conceptualized it and brought it to reality; at the time it represented probably the highlight of my career. It was also exhausting. The last night of the conference, I went to my hotel room and was lying down and thinking, just staring at the ceiling. I thought about the people I loved and the people who helped me to get where I was and the ones that I owed so much to: my wife, my family, my mother for her steadiness and encouragement—and Ajmal. Tears brimmed in my eyes.

I picked up the phone without thinking. I had Ajmal's Toronto number. He picked up the phone. I said, "Thank you for being."

He was taken aback. "Being what? Abdallah, what has happened?"

"No, I just want to thank you for being. For being you . . . for being such a great friend all my life. For always being there."

And then I just put the receiver down.

There are brothers we are born with and then there are the strangers we find who become brothers.

Chapter 8

Iringa: Life of the Mind v1.0

But perhaps you hate a thing and it is good for you.

— QUR'AN 2:216

Rejection is never easy, but some rejections are harder to accept than others.

For me, one such moment was failing my secondary school mock exams. I felt totally miserable when I failed and so was not accepted to go to high school. It was the end of any dream I had of obtaining higher education or going to university. I imagined I would end up a butcher's son and later a butcher. Or working for someone as a poorly paid employee. I felt ashamed that I was not good enough to pass a simple secondary school exam. The dream of becoming a doctor that had been nurtured for me mostly by my mother was extinguished. I would most likely lose all my friends as we went on to lead separate lives.

But this was in fact to be a lucky break. I have had a few lucky breaks in my life, perhaps the luckiest being this episode about how I was rejected and then got into high school. My maths results in the selection exam in the final year of secondary school, when I was about fifteen, were inexplicably poor and as a result I was rejected for high school. What a blow! I was despondent.

One day a group of us students were waiting in the office of the assistant headmaster, Mr. Banerjee. He taught English literature (which always included a Shakespeare play—in my year it was *Macbeth*). While we waited for him to arrive, I noticed the exam papers in a bundle on the floor by the door.

At this point I realized I had nothing to lose even if I were caught snooping—I would not be attending high school, so what could they do?—so I rummaged through the pile of exam papers until I found mine. I had to know how and why I had done so poorly. I was stunned. A full sheet of math problems had not been marked! Mr. Kabir, the examiner, must have missed the page entirely. No wonder my tally had been so low! Had the problems been tallied properly, I would have sailed to the top of the class and entered high school easily.

Mr. Banerjee walked into the office, saw me with my exam papers—and erupted in fury. When I explained the situation, however, he calmed down.

"Let me see this," he said, and held out his hand. I handed him my exam papers. He paged through them and sighed. He became sympathetic. "Follow me." He led me to the office of the headmaster, Mr. Greenshaw. He explained what had happened to the headmaster, who called in Mr. Kabir. The maths teacher reacted with outrage that a mere student dared question his competence; he even threatened to quit. The headmaster calmed him down; any suggestion of resignation was absolutely unnecessary; it had been a simple mistake. "The boy should not have reviewed the exam papers without permission," he agreed. "But considering the circumstances, I think his actions are understandable. Let's hear no more about this." Mr. Kabir seemed mostly mollified and after a few minutes—his dignity restored—he marched away.

"I will get you into high school if it is the last thing I do," the headmaster promised me. "Now run along. You are late for class."

It is impossible to convey my sudden sense of relief. I had not failed! In fact, I had scored near the top of my class. That was the good news. The bad news was that by now all placements at high schools in the country had been filled. The headmaster contacted the Ministry of Education and explained the problem. He told them about me, and about what an injustice it would be—not just for me but *for the country*—if this "promising student" were not allowed to go to high school. His shameless full-court-press pleading must have worked, because a place was found for me shortly thereafter. I was ecstatic, of course, until I found out that the school was not in Dar es Salaam. In fact, it was located far away in Iringa in the southern highlands of Tanzania.

Even today, it is rare that more than a few days go by when I don't find myself wondering what would have happened to me had I not lucked upon that pile of exam papers that day. And that was what it was: *pure luck*. Equally important, I owe so much to people like Mr. Banerjee and Mr. Greenshaw who interceded on my behalf to alter the course of my destiny. These are the true heroes. Imagine: a simple error—a single missed page in a single secondary school exam—and my future could have been derailed. I think of this often in my work today. I see so many young people in disadvantaged countries who are endowed with remarkable intelligence and creativity but who have not had the opportunity to shine. *Why me?* I wonder. I have another question—and a better question that has become a goal in my life: *Why not them too?*

Mkwawa High School in Iringa (from *lilinga* meaning "fort" in the local Hehe language) turned out to be the best and most prestigious school in East Africa. At the time only boys were enrolled, but the school was open to children of all races. I absolutely loved Mkwawa. The curriculum was demanding but I was in my element. I adapted to the challenge like a duck to water. I made many friends there, too, including Asians like Somji, Aziz Datoo, and Abji; and Africans like Jahazi and Ituga, who was the house prefect. I missed home, of course, and my large family, and I missed Ajmal.

I was away from home for the first time in my life—and away from the day-to-day obligations of working for my father. I have to admit it was a relief. On the other hand, I felt terribly guilty and ended up returning to Dar es Salaam as often as I could to help out and visit with my family.

At Mkwawa the majority of teachers, including the very senior staff, like the headmaster, Mr. Hobbs, were white, usually British. This was because of the history of the school. It had been established for the children of the British colonial rulers and its original name was St. Michael's and St. George's School. After independence it was renamed Mkwawa High School, in honour of a local chief who had defeated the Germans in 1891. It was established in the southern highlands of Tanganyika because of the cool weather and absence of malaria-carrying mosquitoes.

In those two high school years at Mkwawa, a transformation of sorts was happening to me. It was related to time. I had time to myself for the first time in my life. It was the first time I was away from my family and the first time I could think of, and for, myself. I had time to think beyond the daily concerns of the family. And I found a new set of friends of all shades and colours. In Dar es Salaam I had had many African friends but I did not spend much leisure time with them. I met them mostly in the context of the butchery business and they were older than me. At Aga Khan Boys Secondary School, there were only a handful of African students. But here at Mkwawa the majority of the four hundred or so students were black Africans, and they were all very smart and had excelled to get to this prestigious high school. We seemed to be the best and the brightest. It was an exhilarating feeling. It was also the first time in my life that I experienced the joy of a momentous academic move based purely on merit, and it had a profound effect upon me. I would never forget it.

The school grounds and buildings were beautiful. The soil was very fertile and so the campus had a lot of green areas, and flowers of all kinds grew profusely. The weather was cool and there were no mosquitoes. It had the feel of a small European university, and parts of it resembled the University of Oxford that I would discover a few years later. There was a big central hall, a dining room, and a library. The students lived in different halls of residence. Mine was called Magembe House, where we slept in one large dormitory each with our own single bed. The faculty had their own bungalows. There were several sports grounds; although I was not a keen sportsman, I see from my diary at that time that I played some badminton and went to watch some rugby matches.

I excelled at Mkwawa. We had wonderful teachers like Mr. Ashforth for physics, Mrs. Clayton and Mr. Desai for biology, Mrs. Rainbow who taught me what little French I know, Mr. Plant for chemistry, Mr. Fletcher for mathematics, and Mr. D'Arcy for English literature. Our education was rigorous, rounded, and comprehensive. In biochemistry I learned in detail about the electron transport chain in glycolysis, which had been described by Sir Hans Krebs and was named after him as the Krebs acid cycle. Later I was to meet Krebs in Oxford, where his office was just down the corridor from that of Peter Morris, my greatest academic mentor; I met Krebs again in Lindau, Germany, where as a Medical Research Council of Great Britain Training Fellow, I spent a week with many Nobel Prize winners, including Krebs.

Writing essays was a huge part of the curriculum at Mkwawa, and I enjoyed it immensely. It turned out I was very good at it and that fact really boosted my confidence. At my previous school in Dar es Salaam, I had participated in a number of activities that helped to shape me. I took part in debates, won an award for acting in plays, received a cup in an elocution contest, and founded and edited a primitive geography magazine—but my heart was not totally in those activities because of my father's need for me in his work.

At Mkwawa things were very different. Clearly my voracious reading had put me into an early and intimate relationship with words in general, and I took to the joys of mental creation with great avidity. It was not that I was not confident; until then my confidence was unfocused. Very quickly I found deep confidence in my academic abilities. Suddenly the life of the mind—the autonomous and intoxicating life of the mind—opened up to me like a borderless horizon of undreamed-of possibilities and opportunities. Up to that point, I was like the desert dweller who had never seen even a lake or pond and is told to picture the sea. Here I was embarking like an explorer upon completely uncharted and endless seas!

One day I walked into a meeting where students were talking about establishing a debating society, and at the end of the meeting they elected me to be its president. I was humbled by the trust put in me; the idea that I could spontaneously lead a group of intelligent people like that was very empowering. A few days later I had finished writing its statutes. One of the topics suggested early on for debate by the society was "The best place for a woman is the home." The debates were very spirited, well researched, and delivered as if we were at the Oxford Union. The fact that I could argue "for the other side" was very exciting and formative, and I was glad when that proposition was soundly defeated! Of course, not all my experiences were marked by triumph.

Biology class required us to find our own frogs to dissect, and for me the hunt was a miserable experience. I was quite lazy in this regard and often tried to save time by making use of frogs that had done me the courtesy of dying on the side of a pond or on the side of the road. It was like trying to dissect an old piece of rubber.

I remember having my specimens rejected for other reasons, too.

"No good, Daar."

"What's wrong with it?" I asked, staring at my frog.

"Well, for one thing that's not a frog."

"What do you mean?"

"It's a toad."

"What's the difference?"

I am absolutely convinced that were you to ask my biology teacher, Mrs. Clayton, back then whether she reckoned her student Abdallah Daar might one day become a respected transplant surgeon and global health professor who also worked with the UN and other prestigious organizations, she would have collapsed in hysterics!

One day when I was roaming the grounds outside the school searching for frogs, I walked into a swarm of stinging bees that attacked me viciously. I thought I was going to die. In a mad panic, I rushed into the closest house I could find. "A shower!" I screamed when I barged into the kitchen. "Shower! Shower! Shower!" I jumped into the shower and turned the water on to blasting. The bottom of the shower became a thick carpet of drowned bees. My face and hands were swollen like a rotten pumpkin but I survived. I went to the school dispensary where the nurse gave me some cream and aspirin. Even today I jump if a bee buzzes near me!

At Mkwawa I developed an obsession for chess. We had a small group of enthusiasts at Magembe House and we played every chance we had. I was not much of a sportsman so for me chess was a major substitute. I was absolutely fascinated by the game. We all slept in the dormitory and after lights out at 10 P.M. a few of us would sneak out and find a quiet place to play chess for an hour or two. If we'd been caught, we would have been punished.

I met at that time a fellow student called Peter Msolla, who in future years became the minister of communications and science and technology of Tanzania. It turned out to be an interesting connection because some of my future research work from the University of Toronto involved studying the innovation systems of different countries, one of which happened to be Tanzania. Every time that my Toronto colleague Peter Singer and I, with our graduate students, went to do this research, we would pay a visit to Minister Msolla. He and I became fond of talking about our old times at Mkwawa High School.

In the library at Mkwawa I discovered the venerable *London Times* newspaper. This was long before it was bought out by Rupert Murdoch and lost its credibility as a formidable newspaper of record. I loved reading all the sections, and especially its sister newspaper the *Sunday Times*, which featured long essays and was printed on lovely soft white paper. I recall reading the diaries of Harold Nicolson, a homosexual British diplomat who was the husband of Vita Sackville-West, a lover of Virginia Woolf of the famous Bloomsbury Set that included the colourfully exotic critic Lytton Strachey, artists Augustus John and Clive Bell, and others. It was a fascinating eye-opener to how the elite lived and thought in Britain. It could have seemed like an alien world to me, but in the excitement of the "life of the mind," I responded to the Bloomsbury stories less as a foreign cultural phenomenon than simply as a lens into a specific kind of life at a certain time: it seemed alive to me in a way that was deeply attractive. By the way, for his services to diplomacy at the 1919 Paris Peace Conference, Harold Nicolson was appointed a Companion of the Order of St. Michael and St. George (the original name of Mkwawa!).

Because of my enthusiasm for the Harold Nicolson diaries, I decided to keep a diary myself. It was mostly callow, sometimes pretentiously sophisticated schoolboy silliness, but I remember that exploring my thoughts was something I liked very much. A summary for a day in February 1966, for instance, deals with the importance of developing one's own life principles and the need to consciously strive to adhere to them. I had an internal monologue about human identity and on the subject of euthanasia (presaging my later work in transplantation and with brain death and where personhood resided). In yet another I wonder if plants can feel pain and how we should relate to them. Others are routine. I detail how poorly I was sleeping (a lifelong problem inherited by my son) while another entry records my enlightening encounter with the Indian barber and his gold cufflinks. Many are prosaic and gossipy: one entry describes our terrible driver in Dar es Salaam named Musa and the news that he had stolen our car. And many entries betrayed a common schoolboy issue: hunger. I write constantly about going to Iringa town to have a decent meal over the weekend!

The library was excellent for a high school but it didn't have that many advanced books. I did find biographies that gave me insight into political power and philosophy. I recall reading biographies of Gandhi, Mohammed Ali Jinnah (the "father" of Pakistan), Atatürk (the father of modern Turkey), and Aga Khan III, who was the grandfather and immediate predecessor of the current Aga Khan IV, Karim. Karim has made diversity and pluralism the cornerstone of his work. At a recent visit to the magnificent Aga Khan Museum in Toronto, I came across a quote from a lecture he gave in Toronto in October 2010: "When we talk about diversity, we often use the metaphor of achieving social harmony. But we might talk not just about the idea of 'harmony'—the sounding of a single chord—but about 'counterpoint' [in which] each voice follows a separate musical line, but always as part of a single work of art, with a sense both of independence and belonging."

One author who influenced me more than any other at that time was Ali Mazrui, a brilliant political scientist and writer who had been recruited to be professor of political science at Makerere University even before finishing his PhD at Oxford! When I met him in 1968 at Makerere I was awed by his erudition and I am comfortable saying that after all these years I have never come across anyone who can lecture like the late Ali Mazrui. He went on to become head of the Department of Political Science and later dean of social sciences. He was born in Mombasa, Kenya, of Omani and African ancestry and, therefore, was very much part of the Swahili culture that nourished and nurtured me. From him I learned about the richness of African history. His inaugural address at Makerere was entitled "Ancient Greece in African Political Thought." (Coincidentally, Mazrui, too, became a displaced person of Swahili heritage. Like me, he had to leave Uganda in 1972 because of Idi Amin.)

From reading Nyerere, I learned about what we would today call servant leadership. The works of Gandhi—his life—taught me that the impossible is always possible as long as you have the will and the commitment. Also, that heroes aren't born heroic; heroes rise to the historical occasion. To this day I believe each one of us has the resources to be heroic.

Mkwawa's British headmaster was Mr. Hobbs. I remember having long discussions with him. He was Christian. I think that in his own modestly proselytizing way, he was attempting to lure me into the fold—Muslims of my sort must have been tempting targets—but he was never aggressive about it and we generally ended up lost in discussions like two contented walkers on a path leading nowhere. I remember a time when we were cutting the grass on a long slope of the school campus. Everyone had finished and left, and I was still there, picking up leaves and stuff and the headmaster said, "Everyone is gone. It's getting dark. Why are you still here?" We started a long conversation about the life of plants. Are we hurting them when we cut them? Do they feel pain? And so on. It was classic schoolboy philosophy, and I can only imagine how many boys had subjected Mr. Hobbs to similar show-offy performances, but what I remember so vividly even today was just how wonderful it felt to have one's ideas and thoughts taken seriously. That kind of consciousness was beginning to mature in me.

Each school term was about three months long. I would go home to Dar es Salaam whenever I could because I missed my family a lot—and I missed the excellent food, of course. It was painful seeing my father so ill and getting worse. His cardiologist at Muhimbili Hospital, Dr. Nhonoli, looked after him very well but my father essentially had end-stage heart failure, a medical condition that is still a major worldwide problem today. Father knew there was no cure, just relief of his symptoms, which included weakness, shortness of breath, and swelling of the legs. My mother gave him tremendous support as his health deteriorated. When I was home, we would talk about his condition, and I would of course take him to the hospital when he needed to go. When we talked about the future, which didn't happen often, it was mostly about the family and what would happen to my mother and sisters. I would say to him, "Please don't worry, I am around, and I am sure Said would come back and together we will ensure all is well." But it was always in the context of staying on in Tanzania.

Mkwawa was stricter and more demanding than most other high schools in Tanzania, and because it was considered the top school in the country, a student developed a sense that you had to make it to university and that this was your best opportunity!

Chapter 9

Kampala, Uganda: Initiation into Medicine

We have not lost faith, but we have transferred it
from God to the medical profession.
— George Bernard Shaw

All day long my heart trembles like a leaf.
All alone at midnight, where did that beloved go?
— Jalal al-Din Rumi

Our home in Dar es Salaam was a modestly spacious, two-storey house that had previously belonged to my father and Uncle Ali but had been transferred to my father as part of the settlement after he recovered from his depression. On the ground-floor level of the house we had two tenants. One operated a tailor shop, but he was struggling to make a living. The other was a general practitioner, a very dashing Indian called Dr. Vellani, one of a handful of GPs in Dar es Salaam who catered to the needs of those who could afford their services—mainly the Asians. He would arrive in a white Peugeot sedan, his assistant would open the car door and take his doctor's bag from him, and he would walk the few feet from where he had parked on the street into his clinic. My mother admired him enormously, and he was really good-looking and seemed so smart in white shirt and trousers and a tie. I think it was from him that my mother, and later my father, first got the idea that I should become a doctor. I went to see him as a patient a few times; he seemed a competent doctor but I wasn't knowledgeable enough to judge if he was a good doctor. I never asked him about what it would take to become a doctor; such an ambition seemed so outlandish at the time, for there was only one medical school for the whole of East Africa (Tanzania, Kenya, and Uganda, with a combined population at that time of about thirty million or more), and what were the chances of me getting in?

My mother would watch him from our sitting room upstairs as he arrived at work. I think she had a mild crush on him. Almost every time he appeared on the street, she would catch my eye and nod approvingly. "You know, he's a doctor." And each time I would answer, "Yes, I know." Of course, she was trying to put into my mind the idea that I should go into medicine. *Look how well he is doing. He owns a car. He is always dressed in beautiful clothes.* That is when the thought of maybe one day becoming a doctor first entered my mind. In that period, if you wanted to break out of one level of life and do something at university that would take you to the next level, there was medicine, engineering, and law and very little else. Today our kids don't understand how limited our choices were. But at least we—I mean people like me who were from families who were relatively well off—*had* choices.

At the time, of course, I was not aware of the huge possibilities the future held for me. There was just one university in Tanzania during my teen years. And so when I talked about "the future" with friends and family—things like college or university or what I would do to make my way—it wasn't so simple. Of course I *thought* about a career in medicine. In fact, I remember even thinking that it couldn't hurt that as a butcher's son I would be way ahead of any classmates when it came to dealing with any queasy reactions to blood or body parts! Plus, for me, working in an abattoir in clothes covered in blood, becoming a doctor seemed a luxurious alternative.

For most people in the Tanzania I grew up in, treatment for illnesses was not first sought from Western-trained doctors. These were extremely rare, perhaps one for thirty thousand or more people, and they focused on treating the elite, who could pay. So when a person from the majority of poor Tanzanians fell ill, she or he first resorted to traditional healers—especially in the rural areas. Their remedies varied a lot: plant-based products like herbs, bark, roots, and leaves made into concoctions; prayers and incantations to intercede with supernatural forces and to banish evil spirits; and psychological interventions of various kinds. If the case were serious enough, the traditional healer himself would first have to become possessed by an ancestor using various means, including chanting into calabashes.

I recall one of our colleagues, Omari, who was working with us at Aswan Butchery. A handsome African man of about twenty-seven, his body began to swell and he continued to weaken week after week. I hadn't yet studied medicine and did not know what ailed him. He said he had been to see a local traditional healer who gave him some herbs and told him he had been bewitched. Neither the herb concoctions nor the fumigations and other measures that were meant to counter the bad spirit that was in his body made any difference. Towards the end he would come to the shop but was unable to work. He used to cycle in to work but had become too weak even to do that and now had to walk to work. I was quite close to him. We joked a lot while working at the butchery and we would have tea and mandazi together.

One day we took him to a Western-trained doctor, who said he probably had a bad kidney disease. In retrospect, as a physician I can see that he likely had nephrotic syndrome, a chronic kidney condition in which large quantities of protein are lost through the kidney into the urine. This results in very low levels of protein in the blood, too little to make up the osmotic component that keeps water in the bloodstream, and as a result fluid seeps into the tissues to give you swollen feet, arms, and abdomen. It is similar to those malnourished kids with kwashiorkor I saw later while at medical schools: they had swollen bellies not because their kidneys lost protein, but because their diets had not contained protein.

In any case, he was told nothing could be done. A few days later, he died.

The severe shortage of Western-trained doctors in Tanzania at the time was just another symptom of poverty and inequity. The vast majority of Tanzanians simply could not afford their services anyway. The few health clinics (dispensaries) that existed were staffed at best by nurses, they had few diagnostic facilities, and one had to wait for hours to be seen. As in many African countries at that time, there was one huge public hospital in the capital city that provided secondary and tertiary care, but getting to be seen there was a nightmare, and the conditions were also poor. It was in Tanzania's central hospital, Muhimbili, that my uncle Ali would die after a simple hernia operation. (So many of my memories are haunted by the senseless and unnecessary deaths of loved ones. I wasn't aware of those feelings at the time, but I can see now that my path into medicine had a lot to do with frustration and a feeling of helpless impotence.)

For a Tanzanian student who wanted to enter medical school in East Africa in 1967, the only one available was at Makerere University in Kampala, Uganda. Kenya, Uganda, and Tanzania were part of the East African Union and Makerere was the only medical school for all three countries. It accepted only about one hundred sponsored students annually, based on academic achievement alone. I was very grateful to my government for the scholarship. The need for doctors was huge (as it still is), and in the following years both Kenya and Tanzania went on to start their own medical schools. All three countries now have several new universities and medical schools, many of which are in the private sector.

I had spent a day in Entebbe and Kampala when I was travelling around East Africa a few years before coming back now as a medical student. It was such a lovely feeling being back. Besides how green the countryside was, I remembered mostly the rich redness of the soil, the colourful dresses of the women, and the gentleness of the people. I also loved the smell of the smoke from burning charcoal and firewood.

Kampala (the hill of the impala) is a beautiful place. Its population then, at 350,000, was bigger than Dar es Salaam's. The weather was very pleasant, allowing us to walk in the mornings the half hour or so from the university campus to Mulago Hill, where the Makerere University Medical School and the enormous Mulago teaching hospital were located. Makerere University had its origins in 1922 as the Uganda Technical College, the first institution of higher learning in the whole of East Africa. It rapidly grew into a full-fledged university and, with its world-class medical school, had a reputation as one of the two top universities in sub-Saharan Africa (excluding South Africa): the other was the University of Ibadan in Nigeria. Both had developed as extensions of the University of London, whose degrees they initially offered.

Kampala is situated very close to Lake Victoria, and some of its suburbs, like Port Bell, are actually on the lake. Although it was the largest city in Uganda, the political capital was at Entebbe, about 40 kilometres (25 miles) away. Entebbe is also where the main airport is today. It was where the hijacked Air France flight from Tel Aviv was diverted to in 1976, followed by a daring rescue led by Yonatan Netanyahu, who was killed in the fighting. He was the older brother of the current Israeli prime minister.

I had done well in my exams at Mkwawa High School in Iringa. The high educational standards now served me well when I got to medical school. There was a very special, energizing atmosphere at Makerere: a combination of service to the community, dedication to learning and teaching, excellence in clinical care, engagement in world-class research, and a sense that we were the best at the best university in Africa. My three close friends Ashni, a Punjabi from Kenya, and Yusuf and Sultan, both Tanzanian Asians from the Bohra community, were very smart. Almost every week when exam results were put up, two or three of us would be among the top ten, a list that also almost always included some of my closest African friends, like Zeph Gaya, Naphtali Agata, Jessica Semwogerere, and others. Unlike at primary and secondary school in Dar es Salaam, here the majority of students, all of whom came from the three East African countries, were African. But there were many Asian students. I still marvel at the generosity of the governments of those three countries for giving scholarships to us all. Particularly in the case of Asian students, the governments were investing in people whose contributions and whose futures, in the majority of cases, were to be away from Africa, mostly in the United Kingdom, Canada, or the United States. Do those governments now regret their decision to be generous and trusting? Are those Asians who left to prosper abroad grateful? Or do they believe they had a right to those opportunities and owe nothing in return? How many would later come back to serve their original communities? Some stayed behind, or came back, to serve and I know a few who stayed on in Tanzania who have dedicated their lives to serve their communities.

I had many African friends. The ones I remember most were all my classmates: Zeph Gaya and Naphtali Agata were both from Kenya and were very smart; they did very well as medical students and went on to have great careers. Agata was a very religious person, and over long walks and many discussions, I learned a lot about Christianity from him. Gaya, although a Christian, was not very religious. What I remember most about him was that he was going out with one of my other African friends, Jessica Semwogerere, a very pretty and very smart young woman that many of us quietly had a crush on. She was often at or near the top of the class. Her equally beautiful and smart friend, Praxides (Praxy), was also a close friend of mine—I often sat behind her in class—and I still remember the smell of her shampoo! The handsome Gaya would sometimes go out with my three Asian friends and me for a meal in town, sometimes followed by a movie.

Many years later, when I went back to Uganda to do some research, I tried to look up those wonderful friends of mine. It was difficult tracking them down, but I did manage to meet Praxy for lunch. And when I went to Kenya many years later, I drove to a suburb of Nairobi to find Dr. Agata. He was as warm and ebullient as ever. I was unable to get in touch with Gaya as he was in the west, in Eldoret, where he was an eminent surgeon.

The campus was divided into different halls of residence. Most students at the university lived in residence all the time we were at Makerere. My first hall of residence was Mitchell Hall, where I had to share a room with a sex addict. Most of us were really interested in women; we certainly talked about them a lot. For many of us it was the first time in our lives that we had an opportunity to mix freely with young women. But my roommate really had it bad. He was a Ugandan of Goan Indian origin and could speak the local language, Luganda, proficiently. He neglected his classes and brought a woman to the room almost every day. It was miserable for me because I had to vacate the room a lot. That situation didn't last long, however. At one point I moved into a new hall of residence, Lumumba Hall, where each student had his own room.

I loved hanging out with girls and had many friends, including Jennifer Bennett, whose father was professor of preventive medicine at the university. She had a car of her own and we used to go out driving often. We also had a number of visiting medical students from Europe, but I never met any from other African countries. One of those visiting medical students was Anna Lawson, a remarkable person who was to play a major role in my life. She was British and half-Jewish. I had never until then knowingly met a Jew. I liked her immediately. She was a medical student in London and had come to do an elective at our medical school. She was a real character. She was very pretty, laughed loudly, and smoked cigarillos. She was competitive, independent, and very curious and could ruffle feathers when she wanted to. I remember how smart she was.

The very first time I met her in the medical ward, she talked confidently about Wolff-Parkinson-White syndrome, a relatively uncommon problem caused by abnormal electrical circuitry in the heart. She seemed interested in so many things. I have always been attracted to intelligent women, and Anna was catnip to a tom! We became instant friends. We went out in the evenings to explore Kampala's suburbs and restaurants. We attended classes together, during which she loved to show how smart she was. We developed a loving and respectful relationship.

I first saw Shahina, my future wife, in the main hall of the university. She was also a medical student, two years my junior. She was playing table tennis and I recall very clearly that the first thing I saw of her were her beautiful legs clad in leather straps that wound all the way up to her knees and I thought, *Anyone who wears such beautiful boots must be interesting.* The rest of her was beautiful, too, and I would love to have gone out with her if she hadn't had so many admirers and boyfriends! However, we did become friends and only fell truly in love with each other when we were in the UK a few years later. Shahina became the most influential person in my adult life.

I was a good medical student, but I also liked to have fun. At least, I thought I did. I remember drinking for the first time in my second or third year. Actually, the recollection is very embarrassing! I had been invited to a wedding, and I had decided—something not uncommon among non-drinkers—that I wanted to satisfy my sweet tooth for wine and spirits by trying "a little bit of everything." Well, a lot of everything, as it turned out. Huge mistake. The funny part was, I had actually asked my three close friends to keep an eye on me, which they promised to do. But I was completely naïve to the effects of alcohol and to the law of inverse proportion: the more I drank, the weaker my resistance.

At first I assumed I was fine. Before too long I had essentially lost any taste for what I was drinking. "This isn't so bad!" Of course, what my friends around me were hearing sounded more like "Siz izznt zo—zo bad." I was leg-buckling, word-slurring, body-weaving drunk. At one point I demanded my friends take me to the women's hall of residence, and being friends, that is exactly what they did. Actually, I think they were amused by my situation and could not resist the temptation. I think they wanted to know what their crazy drunk friend Abdallah would get himself into!

The women's residence was most improbably named Mary Stuart Hall. Imagine being in the middle of Africa, attending a very African university in the twentieth century, and living in a residence named after a sixteenth-century doomed French-Scottish Catholic queen! Truth is, I was headed to a bit of an emotional beheading myself. Somehow I managed to hoist myself over the wall, stumbled into the residence, and slurrily asked in a very loud voice for Parvaneh Kara's room. Parvaneh happened to be a beautiful classmate I had a crush on but had not the courage to approach. So what better opportunity to properly make an introduction than when soused to the gills?

I burst into her room. "Pavane, schmiz me, adblah!" I shouted. *Parvaneh, it's me. Abdallah*! Needless to say, the object of my bewitched adoration appeared less than impressed. In fact, Parvaneh was staring at me like a stunned rabbit frozen in the headlights of an oncoming sixteen-wheeler on a highway at night. I was looming in front of her, bobbing and weaving, a huge stupid smile contorting my face.

As they say, it seemed like a great idea at the time.

Parvaneh screamed and dived under her bed and out the other side, rushing out into the corridor, me stumbling after her and confessing my undying love. She rushed into Shahina's room. "Help me!" Parvaneh pleaded. "Help! Help!" She must have known that I was a friend of Shahina's. Sadly, Parvaneh's rejection seemed only to make me desire her more (I had not yet encountered Freud, though I am not sure he would have been any help). I kept reaching for her, attempting to apologize but slurring my words, which made her even more anxious.

Seeing me, Shahina just shook her head. She calmed Parvaneh down. All I recall is Shahina scolding me for "making an idiot" of myself and that "the best idea was to leave before making it worse." At this point, I decided that as I had struck out with Parvaneh I may as well shift my attention to yet another young woman I was lusting after, Pricilla, who had a room not far away. Pricilla asked me to sit down next to her, held my hand, and asked me what I was trying to do.

I had no idea, really. I explained how the evening had evolved and how my terrible friends had let me get drunk and then abandoned me at the women's hall of residence. We talked for a while, and then she gently escorted me outside and I stumbled home to my residence hall. The rest of the night I spent bent over a toilet, vomiting.

* * *

Coming from a British system of education, we went straight from high school to university medical school, but spent six years there (including a year of internship) instead of the four that is the norm in the United States and Canada, where entrants would already have completed a bachelor's degree. For me, university life was first and foremost about freedom. It was the first time I was away from home for months at a time. Medical school itself was not as tough as I had expected. The first year was predominantly spent dissecting human cadavers but for me the major problem was being in the presence of formaldehyde: the smell was overpowering and I hated it. It made me wheezy. However, I was pretty good at dissection and I did very well in anatomy, as I did in physiology and pathology, the other two major subjects in the early period of medical school. I recall very early on getting hold of the huge *Dorland's Illustrated Medical Dictionary*—it was not required reading and I didn't know anyone else who had a copy. I must have read through most of it in the first year of medical school: I kept it beside my bed all the time. I was particularly interested in the etymology of medical terms and would spend endless hours browsing through it. I became fascinated by the vastness of the field of medicine. I couldn't imagine how anyone would be satisfied specializing in just one branch of it.

This awareness contributed greatly to why later at grad school in Oxford I studied not just surgery but also internal medicine, immunology, and genetics, and why later in my career I took up bioethics and finally global health: I found a unity in all these that was satisfying and appealing and useful. And all because of the influence of a rarely read book at medical school!

The first two preclinical years at Makerere were more stressful than the later clinical years. There was a huge amount of material to learn and memorize, often without understanding the context or need. We had theoretical classes in the mornings and afternoons, and in between we had practical sessions and laboratory work. In the evenings we had a lot of studying to do on our own. We were not exposed to patients in the first year, but towards the end of the second year we began to learn how to take a history and examine patients, and then from the beginning of the third year we started clinical rotations through the medical specialties of internal medicine, surgery, paediatrics, and obstetrics/gynaecology. By then, we were really launched into our careers, for it was unusual to fail in the clinical years. I don't recall struggling with any subject at medical school. Our education at Makerere was really excellent, and as I later discovered, it was better than at medical school in London, where I went after the mad rule of Idi Amin caused me to become a displaced person.

We had some wonderful professors. To me the most memorable included Professor Richard Wheeler Haines, who made the otherwise "dead" subject of anatomy come to life: his handbook of embryology was the first book I came across written by our faculty. His most famous quote was "I went to South Africa once. Nothing much happened. But I brought back a wife!" Among his assistants was Dr. Kulwant Bhangoo, who was learning anatomy for the tough FRCS exams: he went on to become a famous plastic surgeon in Buffalo, New York. Professor Enyinnaya Nnochiri was a very serious, unapproachable microbiologist originally from Nigeria but British trained; almost all the parasite life cycles I know I learned from his superb lectures. These would become very useful to me in later years when I was writing chapters on tropical diseases like schistosomiasis, round worm infestation, and liver flukes in the *Oxford Textbook of Surgery*. But the greatest professors we had in the first two years, and later in the clinical years, were in the department of pathology: Michael S.R. Hutt, Raphael Owor, and Dr. Walker. I learned more medicine more quickly and comprehensively at the pathology department's midday post-mortem teaching sessions than I ever did anywhere else in my career. There were also a number of remarkable Ugandan rising stars, including professor of anatomy Sebuwuffu, Dr. Olweny, and Dr. D'Arbella. Professor Hutt had come to Makerere from the University of London and was instrumental later in getting us refugee students to transfer to British medical schools.

In the clinical years, some of the outstanding professors were Ian McAdam, a large ebullient man who was reputed to have wooed (and won) the British ambassador's wife; he was an amazing surgeon who took a personal interest in me. I later became very fond (unrequited!) of his beautiful daughter Elspeth, who had previously gone to the very British and prestigious Kenya High School in Nairobi that Shahina also went to. I don't think any professor at Makerere had a greater influence on me than Ian McAdam. He was not only large but larger than life, in attitude and physically. His surgical skills were legendary. If not yet committed to becoming a surgeon, I was now committed to giving surgery a real shot. He had a wicked sense of humour, but like most leaders, he was serious and tough when he had to be. Here was an example of leadership that I found attractive. Peter Morris, my great surgeon-scientist mentor I was to meet later in Oxford, was cut of the same cloth in many ways.

In internal medicine, the American head of department, Professor Russell, was less inspiring but he was methodical and I learned from him how to take a careful medical history from patients. In preventive medicine we had Professor Bennett, Jennifer's father. He was renowned as a hands-on practitioner of his discipline and was very close to the African students and faculty. From him I first learned about pit latrines and how important sanitation was to health. It was great preparation for my career later in life as professor of public health sciences/ global health in Toronto. I admired greatly his close friendship and respect for African students and colleagues. There wasn't a prejudicial bone in his body.

My memories of Makerere are some of the happiest of my life. But there is one memory that is extremely painful for me to remember. My sister Alwiya had a beautiful daughter named Fatma. I visited the family not long before I left for medical school and Alwiya mentioned that Fatma seemed unwell. I asked if she had seen a doctor. My sister shrugged. She had, but no one seemed that concerned about it and that was about it. A couple of years later I received a call from my sister; Fatma, who was about twelve, was desperately ill. "Her heart is pounding as if it wants to burst from her chest. Is there something you can do?"

I arranged for Alwiya and Fatma to come to Kampala to see our cardiology professor, Dr. Sommers. He diagnosed rheumatic disease that had destroyed Fatma's heart valves. Rheumatic fever is rare nowadays in rich countries but was, and is still, relatively common in poor ones because in conditions of poverty, streptococcus throat infections, of which this is a complication, are not treated adequately or treated at all. Better living conditions, less congestion in housing, the ability to diagnose strep infections, and not sharing cooking utensils or cleaning tissues would help reduce the transmission of the bacteria. Unfortunately, by the time of the consultation with Dr. Sommers, the heart valves were so damaged that even surgical treatment could not be carried out.

Fatma and my sister returned to Tanzania. A short time later Fatma died. It just breaks my heart every time I think of that beautiful child and the grief her parents went through. Can there ever be consolation for a lost child? Alwiya herself died a few years later from complications of an easily treated illness.

It was about the time I started medical school that a historic medical advance occurred that had a profound impact on me and in ways that I could never have imagined at the time. On December 3, 1967, Dr. Christiaan Barnard performed the first human heart transplant—in Cape Town, South Africa, no less! Unimaginably, almost no one I knew was discussing this medical breakthrough. Of course I had no idea at that time that I too would enter the medical field of organ transplantation, nor could I have any inkling that a subsequent heart transplant by Dr. Barnard—on January 2, 1968—would, as we shall see, have very real implications for me and for my career.

It was on that day that Dr. Barnard did the unthinkable: he transplanted the heart of a Cape Town coloured man into the chest of a white man. Twenty-four-year-old Clive Haupt was a lower-middle-class machinist when he was brought to Groote Schuur Hospital in Cape Town after suffering a stroke (a subarachnoid haemorrhage). On admission he was considered a potential heart donor for a patient named Philip Blaiberg, a white dentist who was dying of heart failure at the age of fifty-two in the same hospital. Mr. Haupt's family consented to the heart donation, knowing full well it was going to be transplanted into a white man.

Of course it was a sensationally controversial decision not only in South Africa but also around the world. The United States had passed the Civil Rights Act only a few years earlier and in 1968 race riots erupted in major cities all over the country. It was the tumultuous year that witnessed the assassinations of Senator Robert Kennedy and Martin Luther King Jr.

The American magazine *Ebony* beautifully captured the exquisite irony of racist outrage: "Clive Haupt's heart will ride in the uncrowded train coaches marked 'For Whites Only' instead of the crowded ones reserved for blacks." Jokes were shared about Haupt's posthumous violation of the Group Areas Act, which prevented blacks from entering white neighbourhoods. Foreign headlines read "Brothers Under the Skin" and "The Heart That Knows No Color Bar."

As a transplant surgeon I would come to know first-hand the empirical truth of our fundamental sameness. Not once in my career did I find myself staring at the kidney of a white man, or that of a black man, an Arab, or any other racial identifier. Healthy or unhealthy, that was all that mattered. And when I think about it in those terms today, it all sounds so simple.

Maybe because it is.

Chapter 10

A Career Aborted? Idi Amin and the Evil of Racism

Although some people felt Adolf Hitler was bad, he was a great man and a real conqueror whose name would never be forgotten.

— Idi Amin

Evil, when we are in its power, is not felt as evil but as necessity, even a duty.

— Simone Weil

[E]very man may know, and most of us do know, what is a just and an unjust act.

— John Ruskin

Uganda had been under British rule as a protectorate from 1894 to 1905 and then as a colony to 1962 when it gained independence. During this period the British brought in Indians and instituted policies that, as in Tanzania, specifically favoured Asian Indians in education, commerce, administrative jobs, tariffs, and so forth, seeing them as a buffer between themselves and the local Africans. Indians had also come to Uganda in the 1890s as indentured labourers to build the Uganda Railway—some of these went back to India while others stayed behind.

The first prime minister of Uganda was Milton Obote. To face down political opponents and build up his power base, he suspended the country's constitution in 1964. He then oversaw major changes to the constitution, including creation of a presidency with immense powers. Obote then took over as president. His rule came to an end when Idi Amin, a former cook with a fourth-grade education (his claim to have trained at Sandhurst was refuted by that military academy), overthrew the government of Milton Obote in 1971, giving himself the title of Field Marshal.

There is little doubt that the Asians, about eighty thousand of them out of a population of about eight million in 1971, controlled much of the commerce and owned most of the over five thousand firms in Uganda. Thus 1 percent of the population earned 5 percent of the national income, but in many ways it was their overt and subtle control of commerce that was resented more. Many owned shops and worked in banks. In my time as a medical student I met hundreds, perhaps thousands, of poor, ill, malnourished children and their sad parents at the teaching hospital, in Kampala itself, and in small towns and villages. I never met one Asian who fit this description. During Obote's time, a policy of Africanization had been instituted but not implemented properly. Idi Amin seemingly wanted to accelerate this process dramatically with his announcement in August 1972 ordering all Asians to leave Uganda within ninety days. The Asians were accused of many things, including commercial domination, cheating Ugandans, lack of integration into the broader Ugandan society, racial segregation, a sense of superiority, and not appreciating the talents of local Africans. As happens in such complex situations, there was some truth to all these accusations.

Amin's exact motivation for expelling Asians, however, has never been clear. Apart from commercial domination by the Asians, other reasons were also possible, including a desire to hit at the British for their refusal to arm him so he could invade Tanzania. Like most dictators, Amin was a strange hybrid: on one hand he was a narcissist bewitched by his own power, charisma, and invincibility, and on the other a deeply suspicious personality bordering on paranoid schizophrenia. It was not long after his takeover, of course, that the economy began to slow down and stumble; having absolutely no experience as an economist, Amin decided on the next best thing: find a scapegoat. For Hitler in Germany it was the Jews; for Stalin in Russia it was the peasants. And on and on it goes.

In Uganda the finger was pointed at the Asians, and one day Amin announced that he had had a dream the night before. It was in this dream, he claimed, that he had had a vision from god and that god had instructed him to get rid of all the Asians. By decree, all Asians in Uganda had ninety days to leave. Imagine! People who were born in Uganda or who had come to work, study, or live and had raised families and built businesses were suddenly told, *No, we don't want you. You are not one of us. Go.* And where would all these people go? To whom could they appeal?

It was a terrible time. It was the first time in my life when my identity was being questioned at its most existential level. Of course, I was not a black African; I knew that. I don't look like a black African. But I had been born in Tanzania. I was at least a third-generation Tanzanian. I was without doubt a true African! But here is Idi Amin telling me that god has told him that I am not who I know I am. It made me incredibly angry but what could I do? How do we prove we are what someone says we are not? In any case, the reality was that none of us had a choice. If I stayed, I would be imprisoned or killed in the chaos that ensued.

I had a double burden. First, I looked to be Asian. Second, I carried a Tanzanian passport, and Idi Amin had compelling reasons to hate Tanzanians: Milton Obote—the man he overthrew in the coup—had been granted asylum in Tanzania (which was also supporting Ugandan exiles who had fled Amin's regime). Idi Amin had requested military hardware from the British for the purpose of invading Tanzania to rid Uganda of this rebel "cancer," but the Brits refused. Tanzania, meanwhile, was arming itself for eventual war against Amin.

One afternoon I was in my room studying when I was interrupted by a knock on the door. I didn't recognize my visitor at first. "Oh. It's you," I said, brightening at the recollection. "How are you? What are you doing here?"

"I want to stay with you." He was an engineering student I had met at an elective summer semester in Syria. We had roomed together in Damascus, where he was a student. He was very nice and very generous. This fellow, whom I will call M, was part of the Zanzibari diaspora of the thousands of people of Arab background who had been displaced after the 1964 Zanzibar Revolution.

"Of course!" I said. "Come in." I noticed he had no luggage, just a small duffel bag. He also seemed rather dour and tight-lipped, not at all like the open and gregarious friend I remembered from Damascus. Every morning he would get up early and disappear. I would not see him until late in the evening. I would ask him where he had been or how his day was, and he would mumble and utter something evasive and change the subject. One time, he said he had been to "the ministry"; another time he said he had met "a person." He wouldn't say which ministry or what person specifically. It was very odd. This went on for about a week. Then one day he was gone. Disappeared without a word. Now I became worried. Had he left the country? Had he been arrested? Or had he been killed? The next day there was another knock on my door. I assumed it was M.

"For heaven's sake," I mumbled, "what now?"

Three men were standing at my door. They were all wearing suits and reflective aviator sunglasses. "Yes?"

"We think you are a spy."

A spy? It was ludicrous! I wanted to laugh, but their manner dissuaded me. "No," I assured them. "No. I am a student. I have been here three and a half years. I haven't been in politics. Why do you say this?"

"You had someone staying with you."

Yes, I admitted, he was an old acquaintance. "Who are you?" I asked.

"Where is he from?" they demanded.

"He was born in Zanzibar," I said, "but as far as I know he is an engineering student in Syria. Why?"

"He is a spy. He went to see the chief of our army, General Hassan, but when he didn't find him, he went to see the foreign minister and gave him a letter from a politician abroad. Why?"

"I have no idea."

M apparently had been seen making several visits to different government ministries and had been seen meeting with people the government suspected of being part of a secret political movement. It transpired later that the foreign minister, Michael Ondoga, was indeed secretly plotting with the Tanzanians to overthrow Idi Amin. Amin would soon murder him.

M had been under surveillance, I suddenly realized. These men must be Amin's secret police. And they assumed that I was working with M and whatever he was involved in. I had been confused up to that point, but suddenly I was very afraid. How does one prove one is not a spy, or that I had not been sheltering a spy? *What did they know?*

"I know nothing of his activities," I said. I explained that I had not seen him since Damascus.

"What is he doing here?"

"I have no idea," I said.

I could not tell if they believed me or not. *What the heck was going on?*

"Do you know John Okello?"

"No, but I have heard of him. I am from Dar es Salaam, not Zanzibar."

John Okello was a Ugandan who had left home to work in various menial jobs in Kenya (where he was imprisoned for rape) and then headed to Zanzibar, where he worked as a house painter. Importantly, he ended up playing a short-lived but crucial role in the January 1964 revolution that overthrew the Omani Arab dynasty of al Busaidis. (It was in the al Busaidi royal court in Zanzibar that my Circassian great-grandmother had grown up.) Apparently, Okello had a talent as an organizer and a revolutionary. In 1964 he led a small group of about twenty rebels in an attack on a police station in sleepy Zanzibar. The police fled in shocked panic and Okello—surging with adrenaline—redirected his rebels in an assault against the palace. The frightened Seyyid Jamshid, the last Sultan of Zanzibar, and his court escaped in boats and later settled in Portsmouth (which is where I went to do my internship after medical school in London). In his brief, mysterious moment of glory, Okello named himself Field Marshal and notoriously gave orders to his rebels to murder all Arabs aged eighteen to twenty-five, but to spare pregnant and elderly women and refrain from raping virgins! Up to twenty thousand Arabs who had been in Zanzibar for generations, some of whom had intermarried with the majority Africans, were massacred. Many women were raped or forcibly married to the revolutionaries. Okello was mentally unstable and a Christian fomenting revolution as a front man for other, hidden, forces in a Zanzibar that was almost wholly Muslim.

He spoke broken English with an Acholi Ugandan accent and was generally totally out of place in Zanzibar. The government was taken over by Abeid Karume of the Afro-Shirazi Party. Okello, not surprisingly, was not allowed to come back to Zanzibar after a short visit he made to mainland Tanganyika. After a while he went back to Uganda, where he was last seen in 1971 with Idi Amin.

After Amin promoted himself, Okello quipped, "Uganda now has two Field Marshals!" It is suspected that Idi Amin put him to death at some point. He was too much of a potential enemy to keep alive. Perhaps it explains why the police were suspicious of M, for he too came from Zanzibar and was acting suspiciously in Kampala. In any case, the three men at my door warned me about what might happen if I was lying.

"We are going to keep an eye on you. Don't disappear."

Don't disappear? Here I am . . . visibly Asian, a Tanzanian. Idi Amin has just decreed that all Asians must leave. But now I am apparently a suspected spy or sympathetic to someone who is and I've been ordered not to leave? It was very confusing. I was also scared to death.

(Years later, M confirmed most of the above but said he had nothing to do with Okello. He had met with General Hassan and the foreign minister, but says he didn't know the contents of the letter. He told me about how he escaped from Uganda. He was being followed by the secret police. In cloak-and-dagger style, he entered a mall, went into and out of several shops, and exited by the back door, losing his pursuers. A travel agent advised him against buying a ticket to the Middle East and instead to buy one to a neighbouring African country. He took a taxi to the airport where he found a two-mile-long line of Asians waiting to escape. He stood in the line, but it didn't seem to be moving at all. He caught the eye of a soldier carrying a rifle and somehow, perhaps through a twisted explanation but almost certainly with some bribery, he was ushered through another door and later caught a flight out of Entebbe.)

The following three months were the most stressful of my life. Amin's army, police, and military police were everywhere. Tanks were in the streets of Kampala and on campus. You had to do whatever they said or they would shoot you on the spot. If a girl was kidnapped on campus and taken off and raped, there was nothing you could do. We sometimes heard screams coming from the women's residences, where soldiers would shoot at the girls and take them away in cars. On one or two occasions, I heard the screams of female students as, in desperation, they jumped off balconies to their death to avoid being attacked by Amin's thugs in the night. It was a terrible time.

Many people were robbed by soldiers or forced to pay bribes, or were beaten up for no reason. On campus during the day, it was relatively safe, but there were tanks and police everywhere. After the first few days of chaos, classes were suspended so we did nothing all day but talk and play cards and keep from being noticed. After about a week the local shops in Kampala—almost all of them operated by Asians—began running out of food. Who was there to keep them going and supplied? Everything stopped. There was no trade. And people who had been bringing food or supplies into the city soon stopped doing so since there was so much graft and corruption and violence. The situation was completely disorganized and chaotic. No one bothered studying anymore. What was the point? Ironically, it was the only time in my life I was able to put on weight. There was very little food available and all we could find were industrial-sized tubs of peanut butter. Peanut butter: morning, noon, and night. Week after week after week. Even today I can't look at a jar of peanut butter without groaning.

At the time of the expulsion, about thirty thousand Asians had Ugandan citizenship or were in the process of having it granted. About fifty thousand Asians were citizens of the United Kingdom and its colonies, but their passports did not grant rights of residency there. Obviously the key question was where eighty thousand deported Ugandan Asians were supposed to go. Britain at first refused to take them until international condemnation forced a reversal of that decision. Kenya and Tanzania closed their borders to the Asians, and some countries—India, for instance—created strict quotas. Since many of the Asians were Ismailis, the Aga Khan contacted Canadian prime minister Pierre Trudeau, and Canada agreed to take in many of the Asians, both Ismailis and non-Ismailis. At one point, when the situation became desperate, Canada actually arranged an airlift. It turned out I was very lucky. I was among a group that qualified for Canadian residency, but I opted instead to go to the UK to continue my medical studies. My future wife, Shahina, was already at the University of Bristol for an elective period and she stayed on to complete medical school. My three Asian friends and classmates, Ashni, a Kenyan, and Yusuf, a Tanzanian, also decided to go to the University of Bristol, while Sultan, a Tanzanian, decided to join me at the University of London.

The largest percentage—about twenty-seven thousand Asian Ugandans—opted to go to the United Kingdom; six thousand went to Canada, and about a thousand ended up in the United States. Only about four thousand remained in Uganda, and of those, many later left.

Another question during those ninety days was what would happen to all the properties left behind by deported Asians. Amin had banned any transactions to transfer the properties. As it happened, most of the firms and shops were "re-allocated" to individual Ugandans favoured by Amin and his cronies; the rest went to government or para-statal organizations.

I was obviously at great risk during those ninety days and needed to flee as soon as possible. Our group of four students had decided we were going to go to Kenya for a time, then we would leave for London. We had been lucky to get transcripts of our record as medical students at Makerere: we would need these when applying for future medical schools and jobs. So the day came before the end of the ninety-day deadline when we headed to the airport. Along the route to Entebbe airport there were many police checkpoints. They stopped everyone, and all the police did was steal from people who had money or valuables hidden away that they wanted to smuggle out. Long lines of taxis would be stopped and the occupants dragged out. Suitcases were forced open and whatever was of interest was stolen. Anyone who resisted or put up a struggle was roughed up, severely beaten, and even shot. I think much of the time the soldiers or police simply enjoyed showing off their power. They understood that they could do mostly what they pleased and get away with it. The four of us got into a taxi and put whatever money we had into our socks (I had about thirty dollars). We had few other possessions. When they stopped us we didn't look wealthy. We had no family or kids, or big bags. The soldiers took a few little things.

We arrived at the airport. It was totally chaotic. The lines were miles long. Everyone was shouting and pushing to get to the front of the line. Finally, after hours of waiting, we managed to get a flight to Nairobi. The nightmare was at last behind us. Those of us who managed to escape Idi Amin were the lucky ones. Others were not so lucky. More than three hundred thousand African Ugandans, including chief justice Benedicto Kiwanuka in 1972, foreign minister Michael Ondoga in 1974, and archbishop Janani Luwum in 1977, were murdered during Amin's reign of terror from 1971 to 1979, when he was overthrown by the invading Tanzanian army. He fled to Libya and later was given asylum in Saudi Arabia, where he lived in Jeddah.

An incredible conjunction between his life and mine occurred at his death. On August 16, 2003, Idi Amin—his health having rapidly deteriorated—was admitted to King Faisal Hospital in Jeddah, Saudi Arabia, for treatment.

Amin died shortly thereafter of kidney failure. He had not been allowed home to Uganda to die. To do so, the then Ugandan president said, would result in Amin having to "answer for his sins." Instead, he would be buried without fanfare at a modest grave in Jeddah—himself an involuntarily displaced person sentenced to exile for eternity.

The physician who declared Idi Amin dead was Dr. Anna Lawson, chairperson of the Department of Family and Emergency Medicine at the King Faisal Hospital. Being both white and female—not to mention being half-Jewish—her appointment had been a rare and distinct honour. It was also yet another example of the odd intersection of trajectories I have experienced in my life. Anna, you see, was not only a colleague and a friend but also my girlfriend, and the big reason I went to London from Uganda.

Chapter 11

Medical School, Racism, and the Streets of London

As I look ahead, I am filled with foreboding; like the Roman, I seem to see the River Tiber foaming with much blood.

— ENOCH POWELL, *a British parliamentarian in a speech some time before thousands of immigrants from Uganda arrived in the United Kingdom*

Even long after I relocated to the United Kingdom, Uganda and its traumas never receded too far into my memory. Amin's brutal assault on my identity seemed—seems—real to me even now.

On the flight from Nairobi to Heathrow Airport in London, I was thinking about why I was heading to London and not, for example, to Canada, where I had residency papers, which had been issued to those escaping Idi Amin. There were other reasons for choosing London, but the main one was Anna.

I was also thinking that I had little idea what was coming next. What would medical school be like? How would I cope? What would people think of me, and me of them? I was worried but I was also very excited about the prospects of meeting many new people, of making new friends, and of living in one of the largest cities in the world. A door had closed in Uganda and I was pushed over the threshold, but I could not yet see clearly what was on the other side. I would soon be joining one of the world's best universities and health care systems, institutions where I would have to prove myself. I asked myself: Will I also rise to the top? In retrospect, the years 1972 to 1975 were some of the most densely packed, exciting, and formative years of my professional and personal life. So much was yet to come, including developments in my relationship with the two women in my life. I had no difficulty getting through British immigration because as a Commonwealth citizen I didn't need a visa. Anna was there as I walked out of Heathrow Airport at about four in the afternoon. She had a big smile on her face.

"Daar!" she called out.

"Juanita!" I called back. We hugged.

(In January 2018 I found among my papers a greeting card she had sent me while we were still in Uganda in 1972. It was signed "from Juanita." Here is how that name came about: One day soon after her arrival in Uganda, Anna had dropped in to the medical school canteen in Kampala.

("Hi!" she announced to a group of us—some had not yet met her. "I'm Anna." There was stunned silence, then my friends burst out laughing. They apologized immediately, of course.

("Anna happens to be the name of a very well-known prostitute!"

("Ah," she said. "No doubt you are aware that I am *the other Anna*? The famous medical student?"

("No doubt," one said, and we started laughing again. From then on, Anna became "Juanita" to her close friends.)

She took me to her car and we drove off from Heathrow towards London. The traffic was very heavy but Anna deftly changed lanes and overtook. It was a cloudy day and a bit foggy. Instead of heading straight to London, Anna took a detour to Windsor and stopped at a tea room not far from the famous

Windsor Castle. I had not yet realized how the Brits love their tea! The tea room was beautiful, with large glass windows looking out on a garden full of flowers, lending it the feel of a well-lit greenhouse. As we walked in, I immediately noticed two things about the people there. They were immaculately dressed, as if they were going to a party. And they were obviously curious about this young white woman with a brown man, but they did not stare—my first encounter with British stiffness and reticence!

We found a table and an Italian waitress came to take our order. "We will have the afternoon tea service," Anna said. *Tea service, not just tea? What was that?* Soon we were served a large pot of fragrant tea that smelled of bergamot. I found out it was called Earl Grey tea. It was served with plates of sandwiches and scones and cream. I fell in love immediately with English scones and Cornish clotted cream, which became a minor obsession with me for the rest of my life: today I will go a long way to find that combination. (It is sometimes served on British Airways flights, where they use a brand of clotted cream called Rodda's.)

By the time we finished our tea an hour later, I was full and ready to go home. As it happened Ashni, one of the group of four of us who escaped from Uganda together, had arranged that we would stay with his aunt in Hounslow, not too far from Heathrow. But Ashni, Sultan, and Yusuf had not yet arrived, so I went to stay for a few days with Anna at her apartment in Streatham, a short driving distance from Anna's college, St. Thomas's Hospital Medical School in London. One of the oldest and most prestigious medical schools in the country, it was established as a hospital in 1173, became a medical school in 1550, and joined the University of London in 1900. That evening we went shopping for breakfast items and again I encountered that instant flash of curiosity about Anna and me, but again, no comments or stares. "That will be a pound sixty," the cashier said. Now I was really worried. I heard "pound" and "sixty," put two and two together, and said to myself, "Oh my god. We have to pay £60 just for bread, butter, and jam?" I laughed out loud when Anna explained it was only one pound and sixty pence!

After a few days of staying with Anna, I moved to Hounslow to stay with Mrs. Soni, Ashni's aunt. Sultan and Ashni himself soon moved in, while Yusuf went to stay with his relatives elsewhere in London. The house had four bedrooms, and I shared one with Sultan. TV news was dominated by the Watergate scandal, which I found riveting. I wondered about the recklessness and stupidity of it all, but I also learned a great deal about US politics, and the country's leadership, constitution, and governance. I was particularly impressed with its system of checks and balances (which today seems to be failing!).

I was waiting for letters of acceptance from medical schools but had little else to do except enjoy Mrs. Soni's superb Punjabi food and watch TV. None of us had computers and there was no email but the UK postal service was incredibly efficient. The arrival of the mail every morning was the exciting highlight of the day. As it turned out, I was accepted to three different medical schools in the United Kingdom. The choice, however, was easy: St. Thomas's. Anna and I would be classmates. Sultan also decided to go to St. Thomas's.

The day came when Sultan and I had to move to St. Thomas's to start medical school. We didn't have much luggage so we went by subway, which Londoners called the "Tube" or the "Underground." We decided to head for Waterloo station instead of Westminster station, which was closer to St. Thomas's, because we wanted to experience changing subway platforms. In the subway compartment I noticed that no one, absolutely no one, spoke to their neighbours. Everyone was reading his or her newspaper or book, avoiding eye contact at all costs. Now, I just love talking to people and tried several times to start a conversation with my fellow passengers. No one responded.

"You better stop," Sultan said to me.

"But what's the harm?"

"Don't you see they are not interested? They might think you are a homosexual, trying to proposition them."

"Oh that's funny, Sultan. No, I won't stop until someone responds!"

And I developed a habit of doing just that whenever I got into one of the compartments. It took months before someone actually responded, and I felt I had achieved a huge success. When I later told Anna about this, she laughed her head off. "What an idiot!"

We arrived at Waterloo station, the busiest in London. In front of it was Waterloo Bridge, which is where a few years later a dissident Bulgarian writer, Georgi Markov, was assassinated using an umbrella tip laced with ricin. We walked the short distance to St. Thomas's, where I had a small room to myself at St. Thomas's House, the student accommodation next to the medical school and the hospital, where I would spend most of the days, doing ward rounds and attending classes. St. Thomas's is situated right across the Thames River from the Houses of Parliament, and close to Lambeth Palace, the London home of the Archbishop of Canterbury. The students were organized into separate groups and neither Anna nor Sultan was in my group, but I sometimes met one or both in the dining room for lunch. I could see Big Ben from my room.

The first day at St. Thomas's, I hurried through the paperwork, obtaining lockers, getting a stethoscope and the short white jackets that medical students wore, opening an account at Barclays Bank, and then I headed to my first class, which became a watershed moment. It was an obstetrics class taught by the dean, Professor Philip Rhodes. I found a seat in the middle of the small classroom and thought to myself, *You will be okay*, even though I was definitely feeling unsure of myself. I was thinking, *What if I am asked a question and I don't know the answer? It will be embarrassing and they will all think I came from a poor medical school and I know nothing*. After all, this was considered one of the best medical schools in the country and the standards must be very high. Professor Rhodes started with an anecdote about how his own wife had been able to hold off delivering her baby for a few days until he himself returned from a conference overseas. Then he quizzed us on the hormonal changes that initiate labour. He asked a question and no one responded. My fellow students stared back with blank faces. I knew the answer and raised my hand and he liked my answer. This was repeated several times during that first class, and I realized then just how good my medical education had been in Uganda.

Professor Rhodes was impressed with me and at the end of the class asked me to stay behind, and we had a chat about Uganda and how I was settling down at St. Thomas's. In the coming months, he wrote me a great reference letter and he also gave me a testimonial, signed in his beautiful handwriting. I have treasured that testimonial and have kept it with me since.

Looking back, that particular obstetrics class may well have initiated me into the system that culminated later in my acceptance at the University of Oxford, which in turn would launch me into an academic career spanning surgery, internal medicine, organ transplantation, bioethics, and global health.

I realized I was going to shine in London. I became more and more confident of my abilities. It will sound like bragging but in Uganda we were trained to a much higher level than what I found in London. The students in London had not trained nearly as hard and, in my opinion, were woefully unprepared compared to us foreign students. In fact, St. Thomas's, I am afraid to say, at that time had a reputation as a party school. Far more time was spent on sports, drinking, and carousing in what was still "Swinging London" with its sexual liberation, Carnaby Street culture, and miniskirts than on serious study. St. Thomas's (Tommy's) turned out to be, in large part, the kind of place that was congenial to the children of the privileged and entitled. The charming and carefree indolence of many of my new colleagues—their casual and bemused appreciation for their status as permanent fixtures at the top of the social order—reminded me in many ways of the Sebastian Flyte character in Evelyn Waugh's acerbic comic novel *Brideshead Revisited*.

As we got nearer to the final exams the following year, some of the students began approaching me to give them private tutorials for which they were willing to pay what were for me princely sums of money. We held these tutorials in our rooms at St. Thomas's House, constantly bombarded by loud music. One of the rooms belonged to a pale, thin, shy, bespectacled Thai medical student; he might have been from the Thai royal family. He rarely came out of his room and while in there he played Neil Diamond songs, very loudly, almost all the time. This interfered not only with the tutorials I was giving but also with my own studies. In this the Thai student reminded me of my sex-addicted Goan roommate at Makerere! But here at Tommy's it was noise that was the biggest bane of my life, and the main culprit at night was Big Ben. I am a light sleeper and the bells of Big Ben kept waking me up. I was annoyed with it but almost every time it rang it would remind me of the immortal lines about death from John Donne's "Meditation XVII":

> Any man's death diminishes me,
> because I am involved in mankind,
> and therefore never send to know
> for whom the bell tolls;
> it tolls for thee.

In those early days at medical school I moved in with Anna for a while. In the evenings we would sometimes go to restaurants for dinner. In the beginning I was not earning and had a tiny stipend from a London charity that helped refugee students, so most of the time Anna paid the restaurant bills. Anna was big-hearted. She didn't mind paying, and I said to myself, one day I should try to repay her. But it isn't like Anna to accept payment. However, with my new earnings giving tutorials, I was able to send a little money home and pay for meals with Anna and for the movies we went to with Sultan.

Life in London was an education, often a humorous one. I learned that were I out and about and felt the call of nature, the best option was to go down to the subway station—ideally the loo at busy Piccadilly Circus. There were lots of urinals with no partitions between them, and when urinating the guy next door would often look at you and then look down at your member and back again at you. I found it very peculiar. A typical conversation would have gone this way: "Why are you looking at me?" I would say. A blank and sad stare would result. "Ah, I'm sorry . . . I thought you . . ." and he would mumble the rest.

I later learned that this was a favourite way for homosexuals to meet. I would get very annoyed in the early days but later would just laugh and say something like "Good luck with the next guy!"

One Friday morning soon after I arrived in London, Anna suggested we go to Paris for the weekend. "How are we going to do that? It will be expensive." Don't worry, she said. We will take a very cheap flight and stay in an inexpensive hotel. I really couldn't resist so I hastily packed the few things I needed and threw my passport in the bag. We arrived that same evening on a charter flight at the small Paris Orly Airport just as it was about to close at around six in the evening. The immigration officer allowed Anna into France but would not allow me in because I had no visa in my Tanzanian passport. Anna refused to go in without me. We argued back and forth until the immigration officer closed his kiosk and left. We were stranded in no-man's land, looking really sad. After about ten minutes, a West African lady pushing a cleaning cart saw us looking miserable and walked over to ask what the matter was. We explained. She asked us to wait and went inside behind the kiosks. We waited for about fifteen minutes and she returned and asked us to follow her. The senior immigration officer in his back office was just packing up to leave for the night. We told him we were young lovers, medical students, who just came to Paris for the weekend. He took pity on us and allowed us into France with a warning and a wink!

Paris was enchanting. We checked into a two-star hotel, showered, and went out walking to explore the sights of the City of Lights and its many delights, including for the first time for me eating oysters, frog legs, and snails smothered in garlic. Back in London I asked Anna about the apparent prejudice around us and she said this was something so prevalent that I would soon get used to it and I should just ignore it. When I asked again later, she explained that these were tense time in the UK About twenty-seven thousand Asian refugees from Uganda, including me, had suddenly descended on the country and there was a lot of resentment. Politicians were making moves to limit immigration. Prejudices that had been just under the surface were now rising to the surface. Riots broke out, especially in areas where there were already large numbers of visible minorities. Among these the most prominent were black people (some people still called them Negroes in the UK at that time) from the Caribbean (also known as West Indians, go figure!) and Asians from various parts of the Commonwealth. Most of these folks had entered and settled in the UK as full citizens and so had rights to health care and other services, and they were therefore seen as competing with the whites. Asians were congregating in London and in cities in central England and the Midlands like Birmingham, Leicester, and Wolverhampton. In London, West Indians tended to settle in Notting Hill. Partly in reaction to the prejudice around them, they started what became the biggest street carnival in Europe, usually held in August every year.

Just a few years before I arrived in London, a senior Member of Parliament, Enoch Powell, had delivered his famous "Rivers of Blood" speech. He was talking about the dangers of letting in large numbers of foreigners, claiming that in time this would lead to violence in the streets. His exact words were "As I look ahead, I am filled with foreboding; like the Roman, I seem to see the River Tiber foaming with much blood." Powell actually made an appearance at a notorious hangout for mostly rich but all-white right-wingers—the Monday Club—to denounce what he perceived to be the Heath government's lax policy of taking in Ugandan refugees. Many of the Monday Club members at St.

Thomas's had surnames I recognized as sons of Tory leaders; they were evidently Tories themselves.

I remember thinking, *What is this all about?* I started investigating the history of the Monday Club and discovered that its members were right-wing fascists who supported the regime in Rhodesia. They lionized Ian Smith and supported his Unilateral Declaration of Independence in 1965. Their greatest hero was Cecil Rhodes, who had started his ignominious career in Rhodesia (named after him!). He became insanely wealthy in South Africa and was a colonialist to his core. He brutally and oppressively expanded the British Empire in Africa. He and his white cronies accumulated all the benefits and privileges, while the blacks in his path were mostly suppressed and kept in a menial state. The only time I myself felt excluded at St. Thomas's was by these Monday Club types. Their conversation was often about beer, rugby, and the themes of the larger conservative Monday Club: monarchy, strong defence, an elite form of Christianity, and a sense of superiority. They were anti-immigration and were considered racists. In today's world they would be natural leaders of the Brexit movement, and with their hard exclusivist views would have supported Donald Trump.

We sometimes forget that South African apartheid did not start with the Boers (known by various other names, essentially we are talking about the South African whites of Dutch and Huguenot, and some German, descent). The Boers put into practice an official and brutal form of apartheid when they came into power. But the British before them had brought in many of the policies that segregated communities and restricted the movement of black South Africans. And of course slavery had existed in South Africa well before the Boers and their National Party took over power in 1948.

I obviously had no sympathy with these racists. I thought it very odd that here we were in the 1970s and these supposedly well-educated and intelligent people should have such repulsively outdated ideas. People like that tended always to congregate on their own and were often superficially accommodating. The estrangement was passive. They smiled as if they actually saw you but you had this feeling that all they saw was "another brown immigrant" who could be ignored. In those early days at Tommy's it made me feel alienated and out of the loop.

Racism is racism, however; it hardly matters whether it is passive or overt.

For instance, during the expulsion crisis, advertisements had been placed by the city council of Leicester in many Ugandan newspapers aimed at dissuading expelled Ugandan Asians from setting down roots in the city. "In your own interests and that of your family," it warned, "you should accept the advice of the Uganda Resettlement Board and not come to Leicester." In fact, the Asians came anyway and in one of the lovely ironies in the war between races, the Asian community from Uganda that settled in Leicester became among the most affluent and productive in the UK—I dare say model Englishmen!

Enoch Powell spoke to this deeply held prejudice and fear among many white Britons. I hadn't heard of the River of Blood speech until I arrived in London. It chilled my blood. Apart from the special case of Ugandan Asians, many of whom had British passports, the Conservative Party's policy generally was to stop immigration and encourage re-emigration. Yet at the same time, these very same minorities did menial jobs that the whites did not want to do. Interestingly, immigrants from the Commonwealth staffed much of the National Health Service (NHS) as doctors and nurses, and soon I would be joining their ranks.

In the United Kingdom in the 1970s, race was a common, visible, and very controversial issue, although it was often clothed in typical British understatement when people wrote or spoke about it in public. It was everywhere. Not just in some areas—but everywhere. The assumption for many was that blacks and browns had come to England—or were in England—for only one reason: to work as servants for the rich or in undesirable low-wage labour that no self-respecting Brit would take on. That is the way it had been for a long time. Had I not become so busy soon after starting medical school in London, these racist prejudices would have affected me deeply. I tended to ignore them at that time, but they must have taken a toll on me subconsciously. I am pretty sure this is also how my Asian fellow medical students from Uganda reacted.

Much of the racism touched us only passively. For instance, I might see an African or Asian sitting in a crowded subway, and a white person coming onto the train would avoid the empty seat next to her. A clerk at a shop might put change on the counter instead of in an African's hand. A few times while shopping, I would notice that a white customer would be assisted ahead of a visible minority. There were protest marches and disturbances by skinheads. Some of my Asian medical friends ended up with internship jobs in remote places because the choicest spots were given to white graduates. And to keep Asians and Africans from getting the good jobs, advertisements in the *British Medical Journal* specified that applicants must be British-born but when this didn't keep brown and black people from applying, since many were British-born, the ads asked for photographs of applicants to be submitted with the applications. These were things that would make me angry but being angry is not what I wanted to do. It was not who I wanted to be. I did not want to become a bitter person. I did not want to hate. I would deal with inequities later in my life. At that point in my life, my focus was on my studies and building the foundations for my future career, which I was beginning to suspect would at some point lead me to global health, with that discipline's focus on reducing global health inequities. Furthermore, Britain was not all black and white. There were many vocal white Britons who spoke out against racism.

For the most part St. Thomas's was upper echelon, rich, and white. But before I arrived I had no idea what it was like. If I had known, I might have considered it a major challenge. Tommy's was bound in tradition: until very recently there were lines drawn along the hospital corridors: on one side walked the doctors and on the other side walked everyone else; and you were not permitted to talk to people on the other side of the line. Junior nurses could talk to doctors only through the ward sister. One of my memories is of crates of Veuve Clicquot champagne bottles outside the consultants' dining room. They met there every day for long lunches, the equivalent of the US's three-martini lunches of the time. In nearby London suburbs poor people were living lives not too dissimilar from those of many African suburbs—totally unseen by these privileged consultants at Tommy's.

The nurses were called Nightingales, for good reason. The nursing school at St. Thomas's had been established by Florence Nightingale, The Lady with the Lamp, who had revolutionized war nursing during the Crimean War (1853–1856) and reduced fatality rates among injured British soldiers from 40 percent to 2 percent. She single-handedly created the modern nursing school and the nursing profession. One of our hospital wards, Scutari, was named after the place in Turkey where she had worked. Our Nightingales at St. Thomas's wore elegant, distinctive blue uniforms and white hats, and were incredibly beautiful. It wasn't at all difficult to fall in love with them. In fact, my friend Sultan fell head over heels in love with one of them, a gorgeous young lady called Jane. They got married a few years later.

In 1973 Sultan and I bought a very old green Morris Minor car for £30 from a Mother Teresa–type of nurse who was a friend of Yusuf and Ashni in Cornwall, where they were doing their internships. We had so little money that we paid for the car by instalments! We used it until 1975 after I had settled in Oxford. It was a beautiful little car, one of the original ones that had a split-screen windshield and red turn indicators that stuck out of the door frame. Sultan courted Jane in it (and Samantha before her!) and I often took Shahina for rides in it. By 1975 it was starting to require a lot of repairs that we could not afford. However, we loved it so much that when it was time to let go of it, we just parked it on a quiet street in Vauxhall in London, left the key in the ignition, kissed it goodbye, and hoped someone with deeper pockets would take care of it after us.

For weeks before medical school started, I lived in Hounslow, and even after starting school I would go whenever I could to eat Mrs. Soni's lovely food. I loved Punjabi food. When we had escaped from Uganda, we stayed for a short while with Ashni's family in Nairobi. That is when I learned how delicious Punjabi food was. Hounslow, which is near Heathrow, was home to a lot of people who had emigrated from India and Pakistan—especially from the Punjab regions. Many of them worked at the airport in mostly menial jobs; some had started small shops or sold fruits and vegetables in small stalls on the street or in small markets. You would often hear white thugs yelling insults at "Pakis" or complaining about them stealing their jobs. "Skinheads" of various types marched in the streets, shouting slogans against immigrants and threatening violence. During those years, proper skinheads would wear tight ankle-length jeans, Doc Martens boots, leather jackets, and swastika-emblazoned T-shirts. These Nazi emblems indicated that these thugs were not just against recent immigrants: they bore ancient prejudices.

Of course, no jobs were being taken by the immigrants. None were stolen. All the jobs were ones that Brits didn't want or wouldn't take or stay with. It is always that way. Bars and restaurants would often give "Pakis" the cold shoulder. The skinheads were increasingly active then. I tried to keep to myself and ignore them but it was happening all around us. Brown and black people were being targeted and sometimes beaten up; shops were attacked and windows smashed. Now, it might have been that I felt a bit removed from the day-to-day reality of racism because I was a medical student and in our university life such matters were not dealt with in a confrontational way. It could be odd or awkward but it was rarely confrontational. I have no doubt that many people in areas like Hounslow had become politically engaged as a result of their experiences. But it did not touch me in that way, although I did feel humiliated at times. And in time it started to make me angry. But I forced myself to take the long perspective.

They will learn in time that we are no different from them, I kept repeating to myself like a mantra. After all, we are of one species and actually all of us ultimately came from Africa! It helped, but it helped because I also believed it to be true. I still do. I've always had the view that I might have an opportunity one day to make a difference. That feeling sprang from the knowledge and experience of the poverty and deprivation all around me when I was a teenager in Tanzania, and it kept on growing in me. It came down to this: it does not so much matter what the problem is;

what matters is the solution. Once you have a comprehensive, lasting solution, the problem disappears. Those were the kinds of internal dialogues that were going on in my mind.

I don't doubt that another person in my shoes with a different attitude—I think of my brave older brother Said, for instance—would have reacted differently. I have no doubt that Said would have cheerfully walked up to one of these bullies yelling insults and offered to fight him. And he would have won. But that was not who I was. My feeling is that most fights you win with your fists end up not being won. The fight is merely postponed.

Anna might have been the first Jew I ever met. She was absolutely non-religious: she never attended synagogue or practised any common Jewish rituals and I cannot recall her ever even mentioning being Jewish other than as a fact. I visited with Anna's family a few times. Her Jewish father was a successful GP, and when we met he was very polite and welcoming and if there was any surprise on his part about my "foreignness" he never showed it. On the other hand, I am not sure that either he or Anna's Christian mother had any idea that Anna and I were linked romantically. I had the sense her parents figured I was merely a friend from her "Uganda phase." Anna was a free spirit, however, and the kind of woman who seemed to enjoy speaking her mind so it could be too that her parents practised an early version of "don't ask, don't tell" with their daughter.

Both were unfailingly polite in that uniquely British aristocratic way. They were wealthy and didn't talk politics but I suspect were good Tories. According to Anna, her father never went to synagogue either. They lived in Sloane Square, an exclusive section of London. It's possible, of course, that the family's Jewish secularism was strategic. Anti-Semitism was part of Britain's rich history, too; I knew that key members of the British royal family as well as many powerful aristocrats had been sympathetic to Hitler. Downplaying one's Jewishness might have been considered a necessary move to fit in British society. All I can say is, I never felt any discomfort in their presence. They struck me as genuinely decent people. Now, might the atmosphere have been a bit frostier had they known I was romantically attached to Anna?

Immediately upon completing our final qualifying exams in 1973, Anna and I went on a long camping trip in Devon and Cornwall. It was on this trip that I first heard Ralph McTell's song "Streets of London": it became a favourite of mine.

Anna had given me a book that has influenced me a lot and I have treasured it all my life: *The Little Prince* by Antoine de Saint-Exupéry. From that book I learned how to think with the heart, and to be forever childlike but not childish, to continue for life to have a sense of wonder, enchantment, and magic. And to treasure the people who have brought joy to our lives; for as the Fox says in the book: "You become responsible forever for what you have tamed. You are responsible for your rose."

On the way back from our camping trip, Anna and I were driving near Southampton and we were talking about what the future had in store for us. We seemed to be in love and had just spent a week together in a tent! She said, "What do you think we should do? Should we get married?"

"Yes," I said. "It's a lovely afternoon. Why not just drive to the registrar's office and get married?" We turned around in a big circle and headed to town and looked for the registrar's office. Our body language started changing the closer we came to town.

Let's slow down. Let's not rush. I think we instinctively felt at that moment that we were not made for each other over the long run.

Not long after this Anna went to a party—it might have been one of our graduating parties—where consultants and professors were mingling with students. One of those consultants walked into the room and his eyes fell immediately on Anna: "That is the woman I want to marry." He was a radiologist, and soon after, they were married. And that was that. It hurt like hell, of course, but there was a part of me that realized Anna and I had such different life priorities that a marriage between us would not have worked out.

It was a brief love affair that was doomed; another love affair, however, a love affair of a very different kind, flourished.

Looking back at my life at St. Thomas's and London after all these years, one particular experience stands out above all others. One of the many admirable things about Tanzania in the 1960s and 1970s was that it had faith that the Asian students it gave scholarships to would serve the country. My departure from medical school in Kampala in 1972 had been so abrupt, however, that it wasn't until I was settled in London that I realized how much I had been given by Tanzania. It had provided me a scholarship to study medicine in Uganda; had that scholarship not appeared, I never could have afforded medical school. After settling in, I recall feeling depressed that I had "abandoned" my country. I sat down and composed a letter to the ministry of education explaining what had happened and reassuring them how grateful I was—for all that Tanzania had done for me. I had been forced to flee from Uganda, I said, and intended to finish my medical training in London but I had every intention some day to repay my debt to Tanzania, the country of my birth. It seems a rather emotional and naïve thing to have done—probably no less naïve than expecting a reply.

About a month or two later, I received an official letter from the Tanzanian ministry of education. "We understand the situation," the letter read, "and we thank you for considering the needs of the poor in Tanzania." I was encouraged by the government official to continue my studies in London. "We know you will do the right thing," he concluded, "and when the time comes we have faith you will perform excellent service for Tanzania." The official who replied was Mr. D.M.S Mdachi, the student registrar.

This was one of the most cherished love letters I have ever received, and one of the most important influences on my life and career. To this day it remains one of my most treasured mementos. I keep it with other mementos in a beautiful black leather bag that I call my James Bond bag. Every now and again when I am feeling blue or depressed about not making as much progress as I would like, I take it out and read it. That faith expressed in me has been a powerful influence. One of these days I will go to Tanzania and look for Mr. Mdachi, or his family if he is no longer with us, to offer my thanks for that letter and for what it meant for me.

In fact, that letter is a big reason why I devoted much of my work later in life, particularly after I moved to Canada in 2000, to serving the health needs of Africa. I know I am not alone. We never are. We just have to know where to look.

Chapter 12

Tough Exams and Injecting Heroin in London

Insist upon their quiet and rest, for their limbs are weak;
Try to lift their spirit through welcome words and pleasant company;
Give them sweet-scented perfumes and flowers;
Obtain happiness and music for them;
Spare them somber thoughts and fatigue

— Avicenna (ibn Sina)

The past is never dead; it's not even past.

— William Faulkner

Before my internship, my first paid job after medical school was as a locum (a temp) where I soon learned a very important lesson. The locum placement was at a nearby small branch of St. Thomas's at the northern side of Westminster Bridge. (This is very near the site where a terrorist mowed down innocent people in 2017, using his van as a killing machine.) I recall clearly the very first patient I helped operate on with the surgical registrar (roughly equivalent to a second-year resident in the United States and Canada). The patient was a young woman with excessive sweating in her armpits, a condition technically known as hyperhidrosis. The registrar removed part of the skin of the right armpit, stitched the wound, and discharged her home the same day.

I was on duty, staying in the hospital building, and four nights later I was called to see her in the middle of the night. She had returned to hospital because the stitches were too tight and painful. Being very new, I thought that four days was probably enough for the wound to have healed and I removed the stitches. The next morning she returned with a gaping hole in her armpit, and I had to apologize, own up to my error, and stitch it all up again. The lesson: if not sure, ask!

The next locum job before my proper internship began was in Colchester in Essex, reputed to be the oldest town in England and to have been the capital of Roman Britain. The hospital was quite small, and as I recall, most of my time there I was doing two things: either performing sigmoidoscopies (an examination of the lower colon) or standing by in my role as the duty doctor when patients were given electroconvulsive therapy (ECT).

Soon after that, I started my one-year internship at the Queen Alexandra Hospital in Cosham, Portsmouth, about an hour's drive south of London. This was part of the St. Thomas's orbit; serving an internship was necessary before one could be licensed to practise. After that I went back for about a year to St. Thomas's, so in reality I was attached to St. Thomas's Hospital Medical School one way or another for about three years.

Internship consisted of two six-month stints: one in surgery and the other in internal medicine. It was hard work. You could be on duty for forty-eight hours at a stretch. The day would begin with a pre-ward round on your own at about seven, followed by a ward round with the registrar at seven-thirty and twice a week with the consultant (the attending, in US and Canadian parlance). Three times a week this was followed by outpatient clinics, where you might see up to forty patients. You had to take a history, examine the patients, make a working diagnosis, order investigations, prescribe treatment, and so on. If the patient was coming for follow-up, you would still have to go through the whole medical record to be sure all was well, read the results of the prior investigations, examine the patient, and change medication if necessary. If the patient had had surgery, you ensured that the wound was not infected and that healing was good. Then in the late afternoon or evening, you had to write to the general practitioner looking after the patient in the community. And then you did a last ward round in the evening or night. If there were very ill patients in the ward, you would probably do another ward round at night before going to bed—and you were often woken up in the night by the nurses who wanted advice or asked you to come in to see a sick patient.

This went on and on, every week. You learned a lot—that was the idea. You learned from the patients, registrars, and consultants, but you learned more of the practical details from the nurses, with whom you spent a lot of time in the wards and outpatient clinics. You became exhausted, but you got used to that, and you just carried on. You don't imagine that you will show weakness, and you don't complain, because that's the way everyone worked. There is one big disadvantage: people made mistakes, and these sometimes harmed patients. I recall being woken up one night at about 2 A.M. An elderly patient that the Australian registrar and I had operated on that afternoon for a bleeding peptic ulcer was not doing well, the nurse said. Her pulse rate was high and her blood pressure was on the low side. I went to see the patient; I should have diagnosed internal bleeding but I had seen what a great piece of surgery the registrar had performed and couldn't imagine that the patient could be bleeding, so I diagnosed heart failure instead and prescribed medication for that. I went back to my room, the nurses didn't call me back, and I went to sleep at about 4 A.M.

At our ward rounds that morning, the registrar was furious with me for not waking him up.

"I didn't want to disturb you. I know how tired you are. I saw what a great operation you performed and I didn't think you could do much at three in the morning," I said.

"You are wrong. You are totally wrong. Things can go wrong in surgery and the patient comes first. This lady has been bleeding."

This was my second major lesson: the patient always comes first. Don't spare the registrar at the patient's expense. I never made that mistake again. However, such mistakes were common, and a few years later the practice of making junior doctors work such long hours was stopped. Working hours were cut back further when Britain joined the European Union and was forced to comply with Europe's more humane working conditions.

The monthly pay for internship came to less than £100, of which I sent £60 to support my family, who had moved from Tanzania to Aden by then (Said remained in Dar es Salaam). We supplemented our meagre income with what we called "ash cash." If a patient died in hospital and the family wanted to cremate them, by law, the body had to be examined by a doctor, who was paid for this extra duty. Ash cash could add up to £20 or more a month, which for me was a godsend. We had to be in the good books of the morgue attendant, because he was the person who chose which intern to ask to undertake this lucrative work! At first I thought how morbid this was, but like much of what we were experiencing that year, I just got used to it.

At the end of the internship year, I moved back to St. Thomas's to work in accidents and emergency and take up a job as a "demonstrator"—the lowest rung in the academic hierarchy—to teach anatomy in the medical school. And I would be preparing for some serious exams.

* * *

The past and present are close in my mind. Many memories just keep coming back to haunt me, painful memories that also instruct.

The first encounters I had with large numbers of poor people in poor health, suffering silently, was in Uganda when I was a medical student. I saw patients at small hospitals and at the teaching hospital. I can still see the faces of malnourished children with swollen bellies and stick-like limbs, with that characteristic apathy and slowness of movement—the kind of faces you see today on TV in ads asking you to donate the equivalent of a cappuccino a week to save their lives. I can still see the faces of countless mothers waiting in the outpatient clinic all day, only to be seen for five minutes by an exhausted doctor who would prescribe something banal like an aspirin or an antibiotic without having the time to examine her properly; the mother would still have to walk several hours to get to her village. I can still smell the pus on the leg dressings of the patients being discharged from the ward because many others were awaiting admission. And when they came back, those limbs were gangrenous and had to be amputated and the poverty was suddenly made massively worse. I see the mother crying for her stillborn baby in a small white bundle. I see the patient running on his own into the emergency department with burns on 80 percent of his body, and I knew he would die no matter how good the treatment he received. I still see the hundreds of blind people, only a few of whom would be lucky enough to have their sight restored.

When I moved to London in 1972 to finish medical school, things were very different. But even at St. Thomas's, later on in the accidents and emergency department I would see the homeless and the lonely and the defeated and the mentally ill, like the eighteen-year-old boy who jumped off Westminster Bridge and landed on a barge passing underneath and broke his legs: it was the first serious manifestation of schizophrenia, which often starts around that age; the girl admitted after the police found her wandering the streets of London in a mental state of "fugue"; the hundreds of patients admitted for overdosing on alcohol, narcotics, or just paracetamol (acetaminophen) for which we would do gastric washes to save their lives. In winter, the department was like a warm home for the multitude of London homeless, many with mental health issues. Our nurses were the most compassionate imaginable, real Nightingales, who would sister and mother and talk to and entertain and feed and care for the many, many patients who walked in twenty-four hours every day.

And oddest of oddities for me: when on duty I had to inject heroin intravenously for usually homeless addicts. In a way Britain was pretty advanced in dealing with drug addiction, for the model of legally sanctioned, medically supervised injection centres is now common in the Western world. I remember one man, a rather elderly unshaven white man who I saw regularly for his injections. He had large ulcers on his leg. We would change the dressings for him as part of the service. On one occasion, he came in with a high fever and his dressings were bloody and pus-stained.

"Mr. Ross, how are you feeling?"

"I am very well, Doc. No problem."

"But you have a high fever and you need to be admitted so we can give you IV antibiotics and take you to theatre to really deal with those leg ulcers."

"No need, Doc. I will be okay. I don't want to come in. Just give me my heroin injection and I will be okay."

I did. He went away, and I never saw him again.

My working hours when I went back to St. Thomas's after the internship in Portsmouth remained very long. I had to study very seriously. I developed a great capacity to place social life, work, and study in different silos. To get on in the world of surgery, I needed to pass the primary FRCS (Fellowship of the Royal College of Surgeons) exam, which was devilishly difficult. Anatomy was the most difficult part, but advanced pathology and physiology, with all their subsidiary subjects like immunology, were not that easy either. The reason I chose to teach anatomy back at St. Thomas's was so that I could really learn the subject well enough to pass the forthcoming primary FRCS exam, but halfway through the course, I had the opportunity to go to Houston and so only taught for three months, during which I also started a research project—my very first one—studying muscle proteins of small birds. I would work during the day and study during most of the night. *Gray's Anatomy* and *Last's Anatomy* were the two textbooks I had to read from cover to cover. In addition, of course, there were tomes in the other subjects, but those were easier to read, and I began at that time to develop an interest in immunology, which was later to be the main part of my PhD research in Oxford. I was overworking and was chronically exhausted but I had to learn to focus. Simone Weil comes to mind now: "Attention, taken to its highest degree, is the same thing as prayer." How true. But as for prayer, I don't remember that it was part of my life and it was also not part of anyone's life around me. Not that we were atheists or anything like that. There was just no space in our lives for religion, and certainly no one I knew went to mosque, church, temple, or synagogue. In fact the whole of the UK was kind of post-religious. Sunday church attendance was dropping, and many churches were becoming increasingly liberal; even the evangelical movement was becoming more "charismatic." There were no TV or radio programs that I encountered that were pushing religion. A few years later, however, there was a reaction of sorts, with the rise even in the UK of many new churches. In Oxford two years later, some of my closest friends were joining such churches.

* * *

Over the years I have gone through several evolutionary stages of "religious" reflection. The trigger for my days of serious reflection was the publication of *Knowledge and the Sacred*, based on the 1981 Gifford Lectures by Seyyed Hossein Nasr at the University of Edinburgh. He was the first Muslim in the history of the Gifford series to be invited. Nasr argues that in all cultures throughout history the quest for knowledge has been a sacred activity as we seek, knowingly or unknowingly, to discover the Divine. It was a monumental piece of scholarship, drawing from Judaism, Christianity, Islam, Buddhism, Hinduism, Zoroastrianism, Confucianism, and other traditions, and from modern philosophical thought. Nasr had gone from being a scientist at MIT and Harvard to one of the leading scholars of Islamic thought and became a distinguished university professor of Islamic studies at George Washington University. From his work, I was led to the work of Frithjof Schuon, whose book *Understanding Islam* is a gem and a classic that influenced me profoundly, and of course to the works of mystics like Meister Eckhart and others among the Perennialists, including Aldous Huxley. It was from Nasr's great book, which I have re-read recently, that I came across this gem: "One wonders who knows more about the coyote, the zoologist who is able to study its external habit and dissect its cadaver or the Indian medicine man who identifies himself with the 'spirit' of the coyote?"

A later evolutionary step for me occurred when I discovered the work of the enlightened Moghul prince, Dara Shikoh, especially his short but profound masterwork, *Majma-ul-Bahrain* (Mingling of the Two Oceans). That book is very difficult to get hold of as it is out of print. After seeing a copy with Shahina in a museum in Kolkota, I spent months trying to get the book, but the search was successful and worth it. It opened my eyes to the commonality between Islam and Hinduism, and therefore to Buddhism. Shikoh also reinforced my interest in Sufism and its incredible emphasis on the concept of *fanaa* (annihilation of the self). It is Rumi who captures this best for me:

I died a mineral, and became a plant.
I died a plant and rose an animal.
I died an animal and I was man.
Why should I fear? When was I less by dying?
Yet once more I shall die as man, to soar
With the blessed angels; but even from angelhood
I must pass on. All except God perishes.
When I have sacrificed my angel soul,
I shall become that which no mind ever conceived.
O, let me not exist! for Non-Existence proclaims,
"To Him we shall return."

As an adult I did start to pray, but the meaning of praying changed for me: it went from being a habit to being a deep meditation. I do believe in the existence of a higher power in a Sufi, mystical way, approached from a Muslim cultural perspective. I have no scientific explanation for this, and I keep asking and trying to understand more. My position is, I think, akin to that of Einstein, who is quoted as saying: "I'm not an atheist, and I don't think I can call myself a pantheist. We are in the position of a little child entering a huge library filled with books in many languages. The child knows someone must have written those books. It does not know how. It does not understand the languages in which they are written. The child dimly suspects a mysterious order in the arrangements of the books, but doesn't know what it is. That, it seems to me, is the attitude of even the most intelligent human being toward God."

To me this debate about the existence of God is both important and unimportant—immeasurably so—and I think that the way Islam defines God is spot-on: God is ineffable, unknowable, neither begets nor is born, and there is nothing in the cosmos, in the whole of what exists, that is comparable to God. In other words you cannot fathom God, and what you imagine as God is not God.

It serves no useful purpose to create God in one's own image. Since we belong to one human species, if we believe in the ultimate oneness of the God who created all, then we logically all believe in the same God.

What about the relationship between different "religions"? Here, I am with the Perennialists as I have come to understand them: every major religious tradition has arisen from and shares the same metaphysical truth. Every major religious tradition has its own culture, its own history and evolution and emphases—in other words, its own genius—and they are all worthy of respect. And if we believe this, then there is every reason to live together in harmony; conflict arises out of greed and the politicization of religion.

In this context one does not need to abandon one's religious identity. Simply recognize that others have taken a different historical, cultural, and evolutionary path to where they are today with their religion. There is of course more to it than that, and

I continue to explore and learn. Perhaps at its most profound level this ecumenical perspective was summarized by the great Islamic philosopher Mohyiddin Ibn Arabi, who was born in 1165 A.D. in Spain during the heady days of Arab-Spanish culture:

> O Marvel! a garden amidst the flames
> My heart has become capable of every form:
> it is a pasture for gazelles and a convent for Christian monks,
> and a temple for idols and the pilgrim's Kaa'ba,
> and the tablets of the Torah and the book of the Quran.
> I follow the religion of Love: whatever way Love's camels take,
> that is my religion and my faith.

And I believe that it is not possible to have faith without having doubt.

Confused? Mystified? I hope so, for to me one of our greatest of human problems is *certainty*. For those who hold on to certainty as an antidote to fear, Rumi has an answer: Fear "is the non-acceptance of uncertainty. If we accept that uncertainty it becomes adventure!" or, as he says elsewhere, "Sell your cleverness and buy bewilderment; cleverness is mere opinion, bewilderment is intuition." Truth is, there are as many different definitions of what God is as there are individuals who think about it. There are "as many religions," Gandhi wrote, "as there are individuals." And when he was asked if he was a Hindu, Gandhi replied: "Yes, I am. I am also a Christian, a Muslim, a Buddhist and a Jew." (In the movie version of his life he adds, "And so are you.")

Well, then, the next question might be, if that is so, does it really even matter? I mean, does it matter how we define God, who is indefinable and unknowable, or is the much more important question to ask, What does it mean for us to love, or relate to, God? Here we may resort to Hafiz, who lived in the fourteenth century and remains one of the greatest of Persian poets. In "A Divine Invitation" he writes:

> You have been invited to meet
> The Friend.
> No one can resist a Divine Invitation.
> That narrows down all our choices
> to just two:
> we can come to God
> dressed for Dancing
> or
> be carried on a stretcher
> to God's Ward.

Discussions about religion can seem endless and confusing. At some point most of us become tongue-tied, so to speak. That is why we need poets like Hafiz:

> I wish I could speak like music.
> I wish I could put the swaying splendour
> Of the fields into words
> So that you could hold Truth
> Against your body
> And dance.
> I am trying the best I can
> With this crude brush, the tongue,
> To cover you with light.

* * *

I remember the day the results of the primary FRCS exam were announced. We gathered in the drab examination hall in Russell Square, London. My memory is of a big room with grey concrete walls that looked like a basement room. It was not rare for candidates to fail this exam as many as ten times and so we were all tense and nervous as the exam numbers of the passing candidates were called out. Shahina was with me. Then my number was called out. It is difficult to imagine the joy and relief that I felt at that moment. The memory is so very vivid in my mind. For the many others, both British and "foreigners" whose numbers were not called, there was dejection, disappointment, and anger, and they started walking out even before all the numbers were called out. I thought at the time that this was the most crucial day of my life, a watershed moment. In fact this was only one of many like it with regard to their effect on my life and career. But I was so excited that on the way back, crossing Westminster Bridge with Shahina in the passenger seat of the Morris Minor, I was stopped for speeding.

"Sir, are you in a hurry?"

"I'm sorry, Officer, I was just too excited. I have just passed the most important medical exam of my life. I'm sorry." (I had learned quite a bit since my last encounter with police officers many years ago in Tanzania!)

"Are you a doctor?"

"Yes. I work at St. Thomas's across the bridge over there."

"Oh, that's our hospital. What do you do there?"

"I work in the hospital accidents and emergency department and I teach in the medical school." He smiled and said something like "I could be a patient of yours one day. You better be careful." And he let me go. I had had no idea that St. Thomas's was the official hospital for the police in London!

At this time I was also preparing for another exam, the first part of the MRCP (Membership of the Royal Colleges of Physicians) exam, which was equally tough. I didn't have to do the

MRCP, because that was for people aiming to become internal medicine experts; I was aiming to become a surgeon. It was unknown for anyone to take both exams, but I just couldn't understand why I should not follow my curiosity and learn everything I could, even if that killed me. Luckily I passed that exam too. The fact that I had passed both exams was a crucial factor in getting a place in Oxford the following year, 1975.

* * *

Shahina and I were spending more and more time together. I remember kissing her for the first time on Bristol's Clifton Suspension Bridge (described in W.H. Auden's beautiful poem "As I Walked Out One Evening"); at one point it became very obvious that I was deeply in love with her and that she was definitely the woman I wanted to spend the rest of my life with. She obviously felt the same way and we began talking about marriage. My sisters say I never formally proposed marriage to Shahina and that may actually be true! It just seemed the most natural of things to do. In December 1975 we got married in Aden in Yemen where my mother and sisters were. Then we went back to Oxford.

Our original plan had been to wed in Nairobi, where her father, Fatehali, lived. Unfortunately, he absolutely refused to countenance the marriage: he objected to the fact that I was "an Arab." He was a man with a very high regard of himself. He worked as a chief accountant for a law firm called Kaplan and Stratton in Nairobi and spent a lot of time socializing with white Kenyan Brits. You can tell much about his priorities from the fact that he made it to being the Grand Master of the Masonic Lodge in Nairobi. When Shahina wrote to him in 1975 to say we were planning to come to Nairobi to get married, he said, "Don't come. I won't be here. I don't approve."

I was very disappointed. And Shahina was surprised as well because although after her mother had died when Shahina was only ten and her relationship with her father became strained, she didn't expect him to be so bigoted.

Two years later, when our son Marwan was born and we took him to meet his grandfather in Nairobi, there was a 180-degree change in Fatehali. He became totally besotted with Marwan, and from that day he and I had the best of relationships!

A few months before we got married in 1975 and before I went to Oxford, I had an unusual opportunity to travel to the United States. I jumped at it because I thought it would be great to have a change of scenery for a while. And I found it.

Boy, did I ever find it!

Chapter 13

Houston? I'm Having a Problem …

But race is the child of racism, not the father.

— TA-NEHISI COATES, *Between the World and Me*

We haven't lost everything,
We just have it all to gain. Again.

— DEBORAH MOUTON, *Houston Poet Laureate*

While I was teaching anatomy in 1975 at St. Thomas's Hospital Medical School, I was offered a position at the University of Texas in Houston and teach anatomy. And so, in 1975 I found myself on the way to the United States aboard a cheap Laker Airways charter flight that cost me less than forty pounds sterling for the flight to New York. (Laker Airways, by the way, was the prototype "no frills" budget airline launched by flamboyant entrepreneur Freddie Laker in the late 1960s. In a way, Freddie represented the entrepreneurial Mount Everest of British "cool" at the time: loud, colourful, a bit obnoxious, and sensationally original. After a spectacular run, the airline was forced into bankruptcy in 1982).

I found my seat and sat down.

"Hi," announced the fellow to my right, "the name's Ken. I'm heading to San Francisco after New York. What about you?"

I nodded and smiled. "Yes. What a surprise. I mean, me too. I'm headed to San Francisco as well." Ken turned out to be an American who had been on a short trip to London and was headed back home. He was about my age with shaggy hair and a slightly hippie appearance.

"Where you staying?" he asked.

"Do you mean in San Francisco?"

"Yes."

"I don't know. Maybe at a cheap hotel somewhere near the bus station."

"How come? You can't see much of San Francisco from a bus station hotel."

I shrugged. "I have to be in Houston two days later." He seemed interested and we talked a while about my background and what I was going to do in Houston. He told me he worked at an art gallery in SF and had been to London to look at some paintings the gallery was thinking of acquiring. Then we talked about San Francisco and its recent hippie history and how he had been a hippie himself. It was a long flight and there were no in-flight movies or iPods for distraction and after a while we both fell asleep until we got to New York, where we had a two-hour stopover. We had to go through customs and immigration in New York and then transfer to the flight to SF. We boarded together and sat next to each other again.

"Look," Ken said at one point, "I have a car parked at the airport. I can give you a lift into town."

"That would be great. Thank you."

"In fact, why don't you stay at my place? I have a couch that extends into a bed."

We got to the airport at around noon and got into his beat-up Saab and drove into town, talking animatedly, mostly about life in San Francisco. He had planned a party at his place that evening; it sounded great but I was exhausted.

I explained that I might want to turn in early.

"It'll be fun. You'll love it. Trust me."

I was not what we euphemistically call a "party animal," and I hated loud music. Yes, I loved socializing and I relished the thought of meeting new people in a new city. San Francisco struck me as one of the more beautiful cities in the world. We got to his small apartment in the Castro District and took our bags in. The apartment was quite large and was decorated with many posters depicting hippie values, the counter-culture, and the Summer of Love. One was called "The End of Western Civilization," and another showed a street sign of the intersection of Haight and Ashbury streets. I was exhausted and soon dropped onto a couch in his sitting room and took a nap for about forty-five minutes. At about 6 P.M. his guests started to arrive. There were about fifteen of them, all dressed very casually; like him, they were all white with an air about them of being former hippies. Drinks were poured, but recalling my injudicious experience with alcohol at medical school in Uganda, I wasn't going to drink much.

I noticed that someone smoking a cigarette took a long drag and then passed it to her neighbour. Well, I thought, that seems odd. The cigarette made its way around a small circle of guests until the person next to me took a drag and passed it to me.

"Hey, man. Wanna hit?"

It was my first encounter with marijuana. Immediately I had images of Hollywood-movie federal agents kicking down the door in a drug raid and hauling me off to prison. I was not a smoker, even of ordinary cigarettes, and knowing how inept I had been with alcohol I wondered if I should heed the angel on my shoulder who was warning in my ear, "Better not!"

Unfortunately, my natural curiosity got the better of me.

I nodded. "Absolutely . . . man. Yeah. Far out. Love it."

I took the joint between my fingers and inhaled deeply. I held in the smoke and waited for the moment of velvety ecstasy and blissful transcendence I had heard so much about. *This is it,* I thought. *I am a brilliant, hip, and charming doctor from London in San Francisco in the great U S of A at a cool party with sophisticated jet setters who are smoking drugs and living life to its fullest.* I smiled at my friends and nodded sagely. "Excellent grass," I had meant to say.

Instead, the bomb went off.

The smoke that I thought I had comfortably ingested and settled like a soft cloud decided it needed to get out and didn't mind turning my lungs literally inside out to get there. It felt like someone was taking a cheese grater to the soft tissue in a runaway elevator from the ground floor up. My coughing was so intense it sounded like someone had loosed a mad barking dog into the room. And the dog wouldn't stop barking. Of course, I was also lunging for air and gasping and my eyes were watering so much my reality was a complete sopping blur but somehow I managed to pass the joint on and wheeze an almost inaudible "Sorry."

It was too late. I had lost my cool.

The party, however, was not a complete loss. After a while my humiliation was forgotten and the party dissolved into a haze of loud talking, thumping music, and drunken passes. I noticed couples here and there making out with surprising vigour. I was so tired, however, I could barely stand up straight.

Eventually the party wound down. Ken insisted again that I stay the night. I was too tired to argue but wondered if he might be gay. I had met two gay guys in Dar es Salaam and knew they could be subtle in their approach. This was 1975, and homosexuality was still a topic that polite society was happy not to talk about or acknowledge. In African societies, in fact, homosexuality was taboo, and later especially with the influence of evangelical churches, several countries, including Uganda, tried to make it a capital crime. And it is hard to imagine now, but the horror of AIDS was still seven years away.

But nothing happened. We were both exhausted after our long flights and we soon fell asleep. The next morning I awoke with a mouth so dry it would cure tuberculosis. I thanked Ken for his generosity and made my way to the Greyhound terminal to board a bus that would take me south across Arizona and New Mexico to Houston.

It was the longest two days of my life. Along the way, there were vast open spaces, interspersed with small towns that looked Spanish or Mexican and indeed much of the population looked Mexican and spoke Spanish. I loved the red colour of the soil and the occasional views of forests and the flat-topped low mountains that they called mesas (Spanish for table) along the way. We stopped in small towns to change buses, go to the toilet, stretch our legs, and eat in small restaurants. I slept on the bus at night or whenever I was tired. To keep boredom away, I was reading *Tinker, Taylor, Soldier, Spy* by John le Carré. And then I arrived in Houston.

* * *

Five of us from the UK were hired as visiting professors to teach anatomy in Houston. The UK was renowned for its anatomy teaching. Budding young surgeons like me taught it for a while to learn it deeply enough to be able to pass the primary FRCS exam. The University of Texas had advertised for anatomists to come teach in Houston, and the five of us applied independently and were accepted. Only two of us, Alan Wolfenden and I, were medical graduates and we were both heading for a career in surgery. None of our group had met previously and we did not know each other at all, but we quickly became very close and spent much of our leisure time together. We rented cars and had to find our own digs. I rented a two-bedroom apartment, which I shared with another anatomy teacher called Patricia (Pat), who later became a good friend of my wife, Shahina, in Oxford. Alan was married and had arrived with his wife. They were from Liverpool, a mostly industrial working-class town in northwest England known for being the birthplace of the most famous rock and roll band in the world, the Beatles. Alan's wife, Sue, was a police officer back in Liverpool.

One day we all decided to take a sightseeing trip to Dallas, about 370 kilometres (230 miles) north. All I knew of Dallas at the time was that it was where President John F. Kennedy had been shot and that its football team supposedly had the most gorgeous cheerleaders in America. I had never seen an American football game and had no idea that it and the European game had nothing in common. Not that it mattered. To be honest, I hated sports but loved the idea of gorgeous women! Plus, I was interested in seeing as much of America as I could. I had not realized it at the time but Texas is an absolutely enormous state. People in London can basically travel the length and breadth of the entire country in a day. Driving across Texas could take three days. And as I was to discover, a huge percentage of it was flat and monotonous.

We took two cars. I rode with Sue and Alan in one car, while Pat and the other anatomists were in the other. We had not driven too far outside the Houston city limits when we heard a blaring siren roaring up behind us. Sue shot a look at the speedometer and laughed. "Not used to the speed limits here," she joked. "I'll take care of this." She got out. This worried me because I had heard that when stopped you were not supposed to get out of the car. I could see from the backseat that the patrol car's door had swung open and the officer had stepped out.

I couldn't believe it. He looked exactly like a Hollywood cutout of the no-nonsense Southern sheriff. He was about medium height but incredibly fit with anvil-like forearms. He was wearing mirrored aviator sunglasses and a cowboy hat with a brim whose edge was as sharp as a razor; his uniform was immaculate and crisp. He tipped his hat to Sue and looked into the car. I noticed the enormous gun holstered high on his hip.

Immediately I was reminded of the scrubby soldiers and police who showed up on the streets in Kampala after Idi Amin's order of expulsion. This American policeman, of course, looked nothing like Amin's thugs. Most of them were criminals in the employ of a dictator who robbed and stole and brutalized for profit. Also, they were all black. This man was white. Very white.

When he walked I could hear the thud of his boot heels on the gravel pavement. I noticed too that he tended to carry one hand up and slightly at his hip, and it reminded me of a Western movie when the two gunfighters turn and face each other for the final showdown. The minutes passed and we waited.

"What the heck are they talking about?" I asked Alan.

"Hell if I know," Alan answered. "But they seem to be having a few laughs." It's true; the two of them seemed to be getting on very well, more like old friends. Finally Sue fished some identification from her wallet and handed it to the officer and he took it in two hands and examined it in minute detail.

He seemed satisfied and handed it back and smiled. Sue smiled back. And then he tipped his hat again and walked back to his patrol car and roared off. Sue jumped into the car with a big smile on her face.

"We got away without a fine!" she said, turning to me in the back seat with a thumbs-up.

"How'd you manage that?" I asked.

She flashed us a coquettish smile. "Charm, of course."

I frowned in mock doubt. "No, seriously. What did you do?"

She flipped me the bird. "Fine. If you must know, I told him I was on the job too. That I was a copper back home. Cops stick together."

Alan looked serious for a minute. "Do you think it was because you were white?"

We drove away. For quite some time, I kept thinking about being pulled over and what might have happened had I been the driver and not Sue. What if the policemen had seen me—a dark-skinned man—exiting the car and not a very pretty white female? I kept thinking about Amin's thugs too.

What if this police officer decided he didn't like my looks? What could I have done? It reminded me of so many times during those horrific ninety days in Uganda when the law was whatever the person with the gun or the uniform said it was. When I was growing up, policemen essentially did what they wanted to do: they were paid poorly and had little training. I also recalled the terrifying night in Dar es Salaam when I was tossed into jail when I was only thirteen. Thirteen!

There were no Muslims in Houston, at least not any that I had met. I had seen plenty of churches, but never a mosque. I wondered who the white officer who pulled us over would have seen had I stepped out of the car. Had he ever met a Muslim? Had he ever met an African? Would he know where Tanzania was on a map? Not for the first time in my life I found myself puzzling over the irony of identity.

When I arrived in Houston, it was one of the fastest-growing cities in the United States. The oil business was booming and the local economy was on a skyward trajectory. It also had one of the country's largest populations of African Americans, more than 420,000 in 1975. At the same time, virtually the entire African-American population lived in all-black communities. If any blacks had a share of the booming economy I did not see it. There were no black doctors at the university where I taught and I didn't see any in the nearby hospital. There were no black students in the classes I taught. I can't recall ever seeing a black man in a nice suit going into or coming out of any of the luxurious glass and steel office buildings downtown.

When I saw blacks they were always at the low end of the wage scale: janitors, custodians, working in fish-fry joints, manning shoe-shine stands, and working as bathroom attendants at fancy hotels and restaurants.

I do recall drives down to Galveston and other places when we would detour down long hot dusty roads where clusters of shacks and lean-tos sagged with age and neglect, pretty much like the people who lived in them. It reminded me of a "land-time-forgot" scenario: old black couples sitting on front porches in rockers and sometimes little children and dogs running around in the dirt.

At times the scenes reminded me of growing up in Tanzania. I have seen many instances of poverty in my life. Too many, to be honest. But this was different. This was the United States. The land of unlimited opportunities. The American Dream!

Is that what it was? A dream? Soon after the episode with the policeman in the car, another, ominous episode occurred when we were back in Houston. The scene is truly etched in my memory and every encounter with a policeman, or even the sight of one, in the United States brings it back to me very sharply and I get a mixture of feelings: outrage, fear, disgust, anger. A few of us from the university went to an outdoor concert at a nearby grassy knoll. It was late afternoon in early summer, warm and humid, but there was a soft cooling breeze blowing. Birds were singing in the trees and there was a bouquet of lovely smells from the myrtles, oleanders, and gardenias growing nearby. We were sitting on the grass, listening to the music, and every now and then one of us made a comment relatively loudly, but it didn't seem to matter because of the outdoor setting and the loud music.

A young black man next to us also made a comment. His voice was not much louder than ours. Suddenly a big white police officer nearby whipped out his gun, came across, and pointing his gun to the young man's head, said, "If you don't shut it, I'm going to blow your brains out."

The young man was terrified. We didn't know what was going on. It was all so sudden. He meekly raised his hands in the air and faintly said, "I am sorry, officer."

Ignoring that the concert was still going on, the police officer replied angrily and very loudly, "You better be, motherfucker, or I am going to toss your ass outta here." Others around us, all white, didn't show fear, or even surprise. It was as if this was a common thing. After a short while the young black man got up and left. When the police officer had gone away Sue said, "Oh my God, that would never happen back home. For one thing, we don't carry guns."

"It was so unnecessary and so pointless to humiliate him like that," I replied.

"Maybe that was the point," added someone in our group. I don't think I really understood then what she meant. But now I think I do.

In Houston, many men walked around wearing ten-gallon (from the Spanish *tan galán* meaning "very gallant") hats and leather boots and talked loudly. Real cowboy country. So was it a cultural shock for me? The terrible racism I saw around me, the poverty of the black population, upset me a great deal, even though I was learning a lot, observing new things, and attempting to fit in quickly, which I managed to do.

After arriving in Houston, there was some paperwork to be done to become an employee in the United States. I was given a social security number. And my papers and identity card identified me formally, and for the first time in my life, as a professor. I didn't realize this at the time, but this was also the actual launch of my lifelong academic career.

At the university the workload was not demanding. We wore informal clothes. For men in my group, it was Bermuda shorts and T-shirts. On weekdays we went to teach at about 10 A.M. and finished by about 3 P.M. We did some dissection of cadavers with the students and the nasty smell of formaldehyde came back strongly; and I hated that as much as I had at my first medical school in Uganda and later in London. The students were mostly white, with a few Latinos, but there were no black students. No one showed any overt prejudice to any of us. I think the students had a little difficulty understanding our British accents, especially in my case, tinged with my East African Swahili accent. After a while the students relaxed enough to talk to us informally. I really enjoyed discussing with them what the cadavers we were dissecting had died of. In some cases there were obvious tumours and I would tell them about the cancer and how it progressed and how it would have killed the patient. For those who died of infections, there would be pockets of pus or signs of inflammation somewhere in the body. And some cadavers showed signs of the violence that had caused their deaths—a bullet hole or a knife cut. We also became friends with the students and occasionally we would go out to a café or a restaurant with them. In our spare time we would catch crabs or crayfish in creeks, rivers, and bayous around Houston (it was called Bayou City) or drive down the coast to Galveston and have a barbecue.

One evening I decided I was going to go with the group to a bar in downtown Houston. The group was joined by a few of our students and friends, one of whom was a beautiful Latina. We really hit it off. I had never before had a drink called the White Russian, so I ordered one and enjoyed it very much. It didn't taste much of alcohol and I assumed it had a low alcohol content, so I ordered another and another.

At the end of the evening, I was truly drunk and my friends agreed that it was time to leave. On the way out, however, I saw a man who looked exactly like Sheikh Yamani, the famous Saudi minister of petroleum at the time. This being Houston, I assumed Yamani was here on business. I broke away from my friends and walked unsteadily up to him.

"Hello, Sheikh Yamani! How are you?"

He looked at me, very puzzled. "What are you talking about? Who the hell are you?"

"Don't worry," I assured him. I was weaving a bit. I set my feet apart for stability, which made the weaving worse. "I know," I gabbled, "you are a Saudi and are not supposed to drink. I won't tell anyone I saw you in a bar in Houston." I was so drunk, however, that he could not understand a word I was saying.

"Look, buddy, I don't know who you are talking about. But I'm the goddamn manager of this bar. Do you have a problem with that?"

I stared at him, smiling knowingly. I winked. *Your secret is safe with me,* I meant to say. He thought I was flirting. *Houston? I'm having a problem.*

Perhaps the wink was not a smart move. The manager suddenly squared his shoulders angrily; his chest puffed out like he was about to explode in rage. Luckily, my friends rushed over to drag me away and hustled me into the car.

We ended up at my Latina friend's apartment. It turned out she helped me up the stairs, having for some crazy reason taken pity on me. Perhaps she was worried about abandoning me to the care of my male colleagues. For the second time in my life, I spent an entire night hunched over a toilet. The next day, dragging myself off her couch, absurdly thankful simply to be alive, I made a promise never to become inebriated again. I have stuck to that promise.

* * *

The University of Texas Health Science Center was the largest such medical centre in the world at that time. Its staff included two world-renowned heart surgeons, Michael DeBakey of Baylor College of Medicine and Denton Cooley. I was really interested in DeBakey because of his great contributions to heart surgery and his Lebanese origins.

All my life I have been fascinated by origin stories and their link to identities. One reason I think I was drawn—and continue to be drawn—to the world of the mind is that excellence is what matters. To achieve excellence in mathematics, for instance, or to compose a beautiful symphony or write a classic novel or play is completely unrelated to one's background or ethnicity, religion, or anything else.

DeBakey inspired me, despite his well-earned reputation as an incredibly tough supervisor for his trainee surgeons. I remember thinking, *His ethnic background has not mattered. This is a country that recognizes merit.* He was a remarkable surgeon, researcher, and educator, and he became something of an important role model for me.

One thing I have realized over time, too, is that we often don't seek out the role models that end up making the most difference in our lives; they seek us out. We have to be open to them, however. The effect of a role model can be subtle, too; the power of a mentor's or a role model's influence can be indirect—even subconscious. And you may not realize the existence or value of that influence until much later in your life.

Denton Cooley was the founder of the Texas Heart Institute and had pioneered transplantation of artificial hearts. He and DeBakey are often talked about together because of their long-running feud, which started when Cooley had apparently taken away an artificial heart from DeBakey's laboratory. I had read books about—and by—them before going to Houston and was fortunate during my stay to attend and observe several open-heart operations performed by Cooley. It was like surgery in a moving assembly line: incredibly efficient. His assistants would open the patient's chest; Cooley would come and do his magic; Cooley would leave the assistants to close the chest while he went to the next table to operate on another patient. There were at least six surgical tables, and when one patient was wheeled out, another was brought it.

But my mind kept going back to that episode at the outdoor concert, and its implications. I began to reflect: here I am, a brown

African from London (whose future father-in-law didn't want me to marry his daughter because I was "different"). I am on the teaching staff of a prestigious university in the fastest-growing city in the United States that has a huge population of black Americans. But at the university I only see whites. I see no black or Hispanic professors. I see one or two Hispanic students but no black ones. Where do black Americans get their higher education? Do they get any? Where do they go to receive medical care? I don't see any black or Hispanic doctors at the hospitals around me in Houston. Are there any at all?

It looked and felt to me that Houston could justifiably be described as an apartheid city. I hadn't yet started working with Bill Hoffenberg, my future friend and colleague, but I knew of his story of opposing the apartheid regime in South Africa and the terrible price he had to pay for his courage. The organ transplant he was involved with in 1968 in Cape Town had some of its scientific precedents right here in Houston but I am sure neither of the two giants of heart surgery here, Michael DeBakey and Denton Cooley, would condone the exclusion of blacks in the life of their famous city. Neither would they have condoned the behaviour of the South African apartheid regime that allowed the heart of a coloured man to be transplanted into a white man when all coloured persons were forbidden by law to even visit a park where there were signs saying "For Whites Only."

Like in Houston, quality medical care in the South Africa of the 1960s was not available for non-whites. In fact, even today I am still shocked by seeing what a privileged life the whites lead in South Africa, particularly in the Western Cape region, where I go to work in Stellenbosch once or twice every year. There the majority coloured and black people are still poor. There is a township nearby called Khayelitsha, which I see stretching for several miles whenever I drive to Cape Town. Here the level of poverty and the quality of life are appalling. A large portion of the population of Khayelitsha still lives in cardboard shacks.

But for me, after witnessing the episode of the gun pointed needlessly at the young black man at the outdoor concert, it seemed that Houston police *wanted* to keep black Houstonians out of places frequented by whites. But more than that, they wanted to humiliate them, just as the whites in South Africa wanted to humiliate blacks at every opportunity during the apartheid era. Here in Houston they had their own system of apartheid.

These observations were building in me a resolve to make a difference. *Someday.*

I recall a party at the house of the head of department. Unfortunately, he was a heavy, nonstop drinker and about halfway through the party he had become totally drunk. There were more than a few times I remember him being on duty with bloodshot eyes and reeking still of booze. "How is it possible to run a major department of a major university while being so incapacitated?" I used to wonder. "This is a very tolerant society!"

I found nothing in Houston that spoke to an Islamic presence. I do not recall meeting another Muslim. Based on my experience with how blacks and Mexican Americans were treated, I have doubts that Muslims would have been welcomed. I don't know. It could be very different today. So much is.

Progress is always possible. And maybe it is precisely when we surrender to doubt—the moment of personal or collective fatigue when we think, *It's bad and it won't change*—that is *exactly* the moment when we are most receptive to change: the moment when change is really possible. It is hard for me to see what is going on today in North America and around the world and not think of my experiences in Houston. I think of the civil rights movement and leaders like Martin Luther King Jr. "Darkness cannot drive out darkness," he said, "only light can do that. Hate cannot drive out hate; only love can do that."

One moment I will never forget: I am at a small, dusty, run-down ranch outside Houston. I am sitting on an old rocking chair on the porch. There is no one around me. The sky is blue and there are a few mosquitoes around but they are not bothering me. It is not dissimilar to the experience of floating I had as a child. Suddenly I am lost in a kind of formless—disembodied—but intense reverie. *What is life all about? What will it all add up to? Will I have peace?* I remember thinking, *At the end of my life, were I to find myself on a porch on a rocking chair like this, that would be more than enough for me.*

How else do you measure happiness, if it is at all achievable? It's a remarkable moment. And just as suddenly as it appeared, it disappeared. On the flight back to London, I looked out the window just before landing at Heathrow. I saw a very crowded, grey city and I suddenly felt terribly glum and dejected. I went to Houston needing a fresh perspective and instead I came back to England with the same old recycled misgivings. I knew my beloved Shahina was waiting for me, but I had no idea where I was heading with my career. Over the weekend I found myself browsing through the *British Medical Journal* when I came upon an advertisement that caught my eye.

Chapter 14

Working the Dreaming Spires: Life of the Mind v2.0

And that sweet city with her dreaming spires,
She needs not June for beauty's heightening,
Lovely all times she lies, lovely to-night!
— Matthew Arnold

Back in England, I went to stay for a few days with Shahina in Brighton. I had by then fallen deeply in love with her, and it was then that I saw an advertisement in the *British Medical Journal* for a senior house officer job (equivalent to between a first- and second-year resident) in the department of surgery in Oxford. I had already passed the first parts of both the surgical exam, FRCS, and the internal medicine exam, MRCP. The job sounded like just my cup of tea because I figured it would combine my interests in surgery and internal medicine, and I would learn a lot about immunology. But I wasn't sure, so I called the professor of surgery, Peter Morris, and, being a bit cocky, asked him if I could meet him to discuss the job to see if I would like it. Most English professors would say, "Go take a jump; I do the interviewing, not you!" However, Peter Morris was different. He said to come over that same day at six. I couldn't place his accent but it reminded me of the

Australian surgical registrar in Portsmouth where I had done my internship. That already told me a bit about him.

Now I had to get to Oxford from Brighton, where Shahina was doing her surgical internship at the Royal Sussex County Hospital. Luckily, my friend Sultan and I still had the beautiful green Morris Minor car (the second important Morris) we had bought together. Shahina was able to take the half-day off and we thought it would take us only about two hours since Oxford was just 128 kilometres (80 miles) away, so we decided to take scenic country routes. Big mistake! Before we got to the country roads, the traffic was terrible, and when we got to the countryside, some of the roads were single lane and muddy. The Morris Minor was beautiful but underpowered if you were in a hurry and hopeless if the road was muddy. We found ourselves often blocked by tractors and sheep, and we got lost several times (no GPS at that time). We thought we might stop for scones and cream, but we had to abandon that idea. We were in a good mood but as my appointment time approached, I was getting really nervous: the great professor would be waiting and in a bad mood, or would have left. Either outcome would be disastrous. As it turned out, he was still in his office at the old John Radcliffe Hospital in the centre of the city when we arrived a half hour late.

Peter Morris was emphatically Australian. He had been to medical school in Melbourne and early on decided to train overseas, as did many Australians at that time. After a brief spell in England, he went to Harvard to train with some of the leading researchers and practitioners of the young field of organ transplantation and its related immunology. On returning to the University of Melbourne, he set up service and research laboratories and a clinical transplant program. In Melbourne he trained John Fabre (who was to become my PhD (DPhil) supervisor in Oxford) and Alan Ting (with whom I was to co-author my very first scientific paper) and a string of other young Australians who followed him to Oxford after he moved there in 1974.

Over the decade I worked with Peter Morris, he loved telling the story of how he was recruited by the great (so many greats in Oxford!) Sir Richard Doll, who had discovered the link between smoking and lung cancer. Doll was the Regius Professor of Medicine (called Physic until the twentieth century) at Oxford. Regius Chairs had been founded by Henry VIII in the mid-sixteenth century and continue to this day; they are royal chairs and the reigning monarch appoints the holders. The most interesting parts of the story of his recruitment were about the negotiations between a brash young surgeon from down under and a true stiff-upper-lip Oxford professor who was determined to bring him to Oxford no matter what. The outcomes of those tough negotiations with regard to such things as facilities, staff, and laboratories set the scene for the pioneering transplantation work Morris did in Oxford.

So here I was sitting across from him in his quite modest office, and down the corridor was the small office where the Nobel Prize winner Sir Hans Krebs worked (more about him later). After listening to Peter Morris, I was sure that this was exactly the job for me. I told him about my background, my time in London and Houston, and Shahina, explaining that we were thinking of getting married soon. I could see he was impressed with me; he said he would let me know about the upcoming job interview after he talked to Desmond (Des) Oliver, the nephrologist with whom he was setting up a transplant program at the Churchill Hospital at Old Road, Headington (everything about Oxford is old!).

A week later, I was on the shortlist of two for the interview with Morris and Oliver. The other, older candidate went in first. He had already completed the second part of the MRCP and might well have got the job. My turn came next. I thought my interview went well; Morris and Oliver told me to wait outside while they talked to the first interviewee again. After about ten minutes, they came out beaming, told me I had gotten the job, and congratulated me. They explained that the first interviewee was overqualified for the job, which was a training one; they explained this to the other candidate and he graciously agreed to forgo the opportunity.

I came to realize that I have had similar make-or-break, fork-in-the-road moments in my life: in Dar es Salaam accidentally coming across my math marks, the math teacher threatening to resign, and the headmaster overruling him to get me a spot in high school, which turned out to be the best in East Africa; the escape from Uganda and getting into St. Thomas's; that first class with Professor Philip Rhodes at St. Thomas's; and others. And there were more to come. Oxford was to mean a lot of things for me: identity, crossing thresholds, transformations, meeting and learning from remarkable people, personal relations, and a look at history's own intriguing surprises and connections.

In October 1975, I started work at the relatively new transplant unit at the Churchill Hospital. I asked Peter Morris to recommend books about transplantation and he said there were very few, but recommended one by Jean Hamburger, a French transplant pioneering physician. I learned a lot of the early history of transplantation from it, but not how to take care of desperately sick patients, hour by hour, in the ward. Only a small handful of patients had been transplanted at the time. My predecessor, Chris Khoo, had worked there for a few months and left intimidatingly high standards for me to follow. He was originally from Singapore and went on to become a renowned plastic surgeon in England.

The transplant unit comprised just Peter Morris and me. I was the only doctor on permanent duty in the unit and reported directly to Morris at any time of day or night. On an average day I started working at about 7 A.M. and got home to our apartment on the hospital grounds at 10 P.M. at the earliest, and I was often woken up in the night to deal with emergencies. By this time working hours had been reduced in the UK, but this was not a typical NHS job.

Another huge life-changing event appeared on my horizon. By this time, Shahina had finished surgical internship and had moved with me to Oxford in October 1975. The following December we took off for a few days to Aden to get married. Later Peter Morris gave me a few days for a honeymoon that we took in Tangiers, Morocco. Soon after that, Shahina started working at the nearby Banbury Hospital, where she developed a lifelong interest in hematology. She went on to do research for a Master's degree at the famous Hammersmith Hospital in London, and then obtained an advanced research degree at her alma mater, the University of Bristol. It was not unusual in the British system of that time for young married couples pursuing medical careers to be separated on and off during their training period. Shahina later ended up as a professor of hematology at Sultan Qaboos University in Muscat, Oman.

I have many memories of the patients I looked after in the transplant unit. One of the earliest was a Glaswegian. People from Glasgow are wild compared to those from Edinburgh. Glasgow has the highest mortality rate in the UK and some of its denizens will tell you, "We die young here. But you just take the hand that life deals you and get on with it."

They also drank a lot and called each other Jimmy: "aye Jimmy" is the way they greet each other. This lovable Jimmy who became a fond patient of mine could not afford normal alcohol and started drinking methyl alcohol, one of whose metabolites is formaldehyde, which I hated in anatomy dissection rooms in Kampala, London, and Houston. One day Jimmy binged on methyl alcohol, probably by drinking windshield washer fluid, and it burned his optic nerve and made him blind. In addition, it gave him severe pancreatitis and destroyed his kidneys. He was lucky enough to be placed on temporary dialysis and sent to Oxford for a transplant. That went very well. He was a happy, gregarious patient; nothing seemed to bother him. When he went back to Glasgow we all missed him, hoping he had learned his lesson, would keep off methyl alcohol, and would stick to his immunosuppression therapy.

Another patient I recall from those early days was a high official of the Jockey Club. I think his name was Andrew but I cannot recall his surname. Whenever Andrew came into the ward for a few days, he was very stoic and not at all demanding. I would sit and talk to him, and one day he told me that what he missed more than anything else was a soft-boiled egg for breakfast—the eggs that came on the hospital meal trolley were always overdone. One morning I decide to surprise him. In the ward kitchen I make him two eggs just the way he loved them. You should have seen the disbelief and joy on his face when I took the eggs to him! He couldn't stop thanking me. It was as if he had just won a million-dollar lottery. He was a shy man but I think he actually got up and hugged me for the eggs. That simple gesture completely transformed his hospital experience.

One day Andrew came in to the hospital as a day-care patient to have tests done. He left about four; I said goodbye and accompanied him to the door. At about eight that evening a family member called to ask where Andrew was, because he had told them he would be home around five. I said he had left the ward and was going to drive straight home. I went out to the car park to see if he had left. His blue Volvo was still there. He was slumped over the steering wheel. I knocked on the window and he didn't respond. He must have had a massive heart attack and died a few minutes after we said goodbye.

Oh, how fragile life can be. And how rewarding also, as was the case of the beautiful, thin, young woman called Anne Cox. She had fair hair and pale skin made paler by anaemia. At that time most patients with kidney failure were very anaemic because the normal kidney produces erythropoietin, a hormone that stimulates production of red blood cells by the bone marrow, and without it you become anaemic. Years later, a biotech company learned how to make erythropoietin, and at least that one of the many problems of end-stage renal failure became manageable. Anne was about twenty and rather shy. She looked a bit vulnerable. We transplanted her with a cadaveric kidney (i.e., from a dead person). This worked slowly but about ten days later it stopped clearing toxins from her body; in other words, although her new kidney was producing a lot of urine, that urine was almost just water. So she had to be put back on dialysis and on the waiting list for another transplant, maybe years in the future. I saw her frequently as she came in for dialysis and blood transfusions. Everyone wanted to give up on her and stop immunosuppression but I asked Professor Morris if I could continue her on small doses and he agreed. I explained that I had a feeling her kidney would recover. We had taken a biopsy that showed cortical necrosis rather than severe rejection changes, and cortical necrosis, if not complete, can recover sometimes. Week after week she would come in carrying her two white plastic cans containing the urine she had passed over the previous twenty-four hours. We had our own labs nearby and I would test it for its concentration, pH, urea, electrolytes, protein, and so on. Very, very slowly the quality of the urine improved, and one day, after about four months, she was able to come off dialysis; she went on to lead a normal life with a working transplant.

Most of the transplants we performed in those early days were from cadaveric donors. But it was possible every now and then to use kidneys from living volunteers, usually family members. When we did this in Oxford, we worked with the Nuffield professor of medicine, David Weatherall, the greatest hematologist of his time. He would interview the patient and the donor and members of the family to ensure there was no coercion of the donor and that everyone understood the risks and benefits. He reviewed the test results to ensure the donor was perfectly healthy and willing to become a donor. I was so impressed with this important ethical step that I wanted to learn more about the ethics of living donor transplants. This is what started me off on a lifelong interest in bioethics. In later years, I did much work on this subject, published extensively, and became a World Health Organization expert. On reflection, I realize now how this one incredible but humble person, without even knowing that he was a mentor, came to be such a profound influence on my life and career.

A normal day for me in the two years when I worked with Peter Morris in the transplant unit started with walking to the ward at about 7 A.M., being briefed by the nurses (throughout my career I have learned a huge amount from nurses) before I did my own ward round and reviewed the test results for each patient, recorded those, and wrote up patient records and filled out a huge green chart pinned on the wall outside each transplanted patient's room. I would then go talk to the nephrologists, usually Des Oliver himself: he was always around tinkering with instruments, placing peritoneal dialysis catheters into patients' abdominal cavities, and so on. Des was a huge, gentle New Zealander who had come to England many years before. In Oxford he married a nurse who herself had kidney failure and was on dialysis, so Des understood such patients and their detailed needs and he was always there for them. He was a physician but also very good at making shunts and fistulae for hemodialysis; he was the one who taught me how to fashion them using his meticulous techniques.

After that I would go and perform kidney biopsies (also learned from Des)—there were always a few of those to be done—and then go to the lab to look at them with the pathologist. This way I was able to learn what a normal and a damaged or rejecting kidney looks like under the microscope when fresh (what is known as a frozen section) or after fixing and staining with special dyes. This was a period of intense learning for me, and I was rapidly being transformed by the people I was working with. Then I would go to the radiology department to look at X-rays and scans (and soon thereafter at MRI scans; some of the basic science research for MRI technology had been done in Oxford). By about midday and continuing into the afternoon and evening, I would greet new admissions, read their referral letters or previous medical records, take their history, examine them, make a working diagnosis, communicate with them, and order investigations, often taking blood samples myself.

Some days there would be seminars at lunchtime where, while eating sandwiches, we would review all patients and make unit-wide decisions. Here I would learn how important it is to listen carefully to everyone's opinions, and to make life-and-death decisions based on as much information as possible, knowing that it will almost always be incomplete and so you make decisions on probabilities based on past experience and knowledge. This was thrilling. When Peter Morris attended these sessions, there would be academic research presentations by junior doctors or scientists from the Nuffield Department of Surgery (NDS) or from the medical departments. Here I was being exposed to critical thinking and the process by which knowledge is being created; when that knowledge is published, as mine was just a few months into the job, it gets disseminated for use by others around the world.

After these lunchtime sessions, Peter Morris and I would see our patients and review those big green charts. We would talk about the results that were being produced from patient samples by the research labs at NDS. Alan Ting was running the tissue-typing labs there and one of the things we were studying were antibodies in patients with transplanted kidneys; soon we published a short paper in *The Lancet*, one of the most prestigious medical journals in the world.

That was my very first paper published in a scientific peer-reviewed journal. It is difficult for people not in academia or not involved in research to appreciate just how important a milestone it is for a young clinician-scientist to publish her or his first-ever paper. And in *The Lancet*! Another time after the afternoon sessions, Professor Morris and I were reviewing those green charts when I pointed out that patients having rejection episodes do not have a rise in their white cell counts, as would be expected in processes that involved inflammation. We collected more data, analyzed it, and wrote it up; it was published in the *British Medical Journal*. These early projects were significant because they were my introduction to scientific research and were the beginnings of my later life as a surgeon-scientist.

In the afternoons, much of what I did in the ward in the morning was repeated and I would record all observations and results. Going into the room of a patient who had just had a transplant required wearing sterile gowns and masks and paper overshoes, all adding to the time spent in the ward. By the time I returned home, late and exhausted, Shahina would be there, and after eating a quick dinner I would get into bed and fall asleep, hoping against hope I would not be woken up by the ward or a hospital saying they had a brain-dead patient on the ventilator and would we come "harvest" (I never liked that term) the kidneys. Those night-time calls came quite frequently, and if it couldn't wait till the morning that meant getting our team together and heading there; the whole process disturbed the routines of the hospitals we were going to, especially their operating theatre scheduling, so we preferred to go overnight. Jim Corbett was our transplant coordinator and thankfully he organized the communication, equipment, our operating instruments, transport, and so forth and we would be off, returning as the sun was rising. After a quick shower, I would be back in the ward, coffee cup and a half-eaten sandwich in hand. I would call Professor Morris to inform him of our nocturnal work, and we would work out from the ever-changing waiting list which patient would receive the kidneys. Jim would then call them to come in, and I would start preparing them for theatre. Jim would negotiate with theatre staff to make room for the transplants.

Once the transplants were done, usually by Peter Morris himself in those early days, I would stay with the patients and call him at home in the evenings to let him know how the patients were doing and we would discuss medication, fluids, any need for antibiotics, what to watch out for, and so on. If we had two patients transplanted on the same day, I would spend the whole night in the ward. God forbid if we had to go out again to get kidneys that night!

During those two years and later in the UK, I was always amazed at how much trust patients placed in doctors and their decisions about their health. I would do a PR (per rectum) finger examination, suspect a cancer in the low bowel, perform a sigmoidoscopy to confirm it, take a biopsy, and say to the patient: "Mrs. Hoskins, I think you have cancer. I have taken a biopsy and will know for sure in a few days."

"Thank you, Doctor. Will I need surgery?"

"Yes. Depending on what we find on the surgical table, we might have to removed the whole of your lower bowel and you might have to have a colostomy for life."

"What's a colostomy, Doctor?"

"It's a pouch we create on your abdomen so you can evacuate your bowels into it."

"Oh, okay. Whatever you say, Doctor. Just let me know when I should come in for the operation."

Scenarios unfolding in this way were very common. They cemented in me the conviction that good medicine is performed in an atmosphere of trust and honesty. When that trust is abused, patients suffer and careers can be destroyed.

My world for those first two years in Oxford was largely the world of transplantation. One of the things I dealt with all the time was death, and more specifically, brain death (see the short portrait about Bill Hoffenberg and about the youngest transplant in Oman). I was so absorbed with my work that I kept forgetting there was a much bigger and much different world out there. But unbelievably that bigger world was thriving in its own inscrutable, chaotic way.

Chapter 15

Abdus Salam: Persecuting a Nobel Prize Winner

> The heart of the issue is whether Pakistanis can be silenced by fear. Because if we can be silenced when it comes to Ahmadis, then we can be silenced when it comes to Shias, we can be silenced when it comes to women, we can be silenced when it comes to dress, we can be silenced when it comes to entertainment, and we can even be silenced when it comes to sitting by ourselves, alone in a room, afraid to think what we think. That is the point.
>
> — Mohsin Hamid, *Discontent and Its Civilizations: Dispatches from Lahore, New York, and London*

> If he were allowed contact with foreigners he would discover that they are creatures similar to himself. . . . The sealed world in which he lives would be broken, and the fear, hatred, and self-righteousness on which his morale depends might evaporate.
>
> — George Orwell, *1984*

> If you possess enough courage to speak out who you are, you will find you are not alone.
>
> — Richard Wright, *Black Boy*

My introduction to Abdus Salam at Oxford was not propitious. I had never met the man but had a superficial knowledge of him and of his incredible achievements in the world of mathematics and physics. To be honest, it was a point of pride with me that this world-famous scientist was a Muslim. When I met him at Wolfson College, Oxford, however, I was unaware of his commitment to his faith. At the time I believe I must have shared the fashionable distrust most scientists in general have for individuals of faith and religion. He had been invited to lecture at Wolfson and arrived well before the start time and I decided to introduce myself. I waited until he was momentarily alone and when the time was right, I swooped in.

"Professor Salam, I am a PhD student here!"

He looked surprised at my sudden appearance and a bit confused by my declaration. "I see," he said. The frozen smile on my face would not thaw; I was too scared to think of anything else to say. After a painful silence, Salam asked, "What is your research about?"

I breathed a huge sigh of relief. "Immunology and immunogenetics."

He brightened immediately—as if this odd little student had done something actually worthy of attention.

"Ahh! That sounds interesting. Maybe we can talk about that later." He smiled. I waited, too terrified still to think clearly. *Should I set a time for us to discuss my work?* I wondered. *What if he says no? What will I do then? Maybe I should wait? Or, better to strike while the iron is hot?*

He shifted a bit impatiently. "Do you have a question for me?" he prompted, too courteous to resume ignoring me.

"You are a Muslim," I blurted.

He chuckled. "I am, yes," he said. He sighed wistfully. "Although there are those who say I am not!"

I was puzzled by his response, but plunged ahead. "My question is this: How has your religion affected your work?"

He seemed genuinely curious at my question. He thought for a minute. "It hasn't at all," he answered. "It has made my work easier!"

I did not understand what he meant and was too much in awe of him to admit my incomprehension by following up with the obvious question, "How?" and by the time he was pulled away by the college president it was too late. *Damn*, I remember thinking.

Salam's lecture was fascinating although I cannot recall the details today. I just remember how proud I was that I had met him. Back home, I told Shahina I had met and talked with the great Abdus Salam. She asked me what we talked about.

"Nothing," I said. "I asked him if he was a Muslim."

"You didn't!" she said, laughing. "What did he say?"

And that started me thinking again. Back when I was a medical student in Kampala, I used to see a large mosque as we walked to the medical school in the morning. To be honest, at the time I thought nothing of it. As I have said, religion did not play a big role in my life. I do recall, however, remarking to a fellow student that it was an enormous mosque and that I had no idea there were so many Muslims to warrant a mosque that size.

The fellow student—a devout Muslim—reacted with a horrified shudder. "You should never go to that mosque!" he warned me. He seemed very upset.

Frankly, I was mostly amused by his reaction. "Why not?" I asked. "What could possibly be the problem?"

"It is an Ahmadi mosque!"

"So what?" I asked.

"Ahmadis are heretics," he pronounced decisively. "They are very bad people."

I wheeled and shot him an angry, withering look. "You must be joking. Do they not worship the same Allah as you?"

He shook his head. "You do not understand," he said, and walked away in a huff. *No,* I thought. *Most certainly, I do not understand.*

I remember this event whenever I think of Abdus Salam. You see, he was an Ahmadi. Even as a boy in Dar es Salaam, I was aware of mainstream Muslims looking down at Ahmadis and shunning them as vile heretics and apostates. The precise reasons for the schism are complicated; I will describe them briefly below. In Pakistan, the persecution of Ahmadis has included discrimination, isolation, arrest, violence, and even death. It is very difficult to put a figure on the number of Ahmadis killed in the violence—estimates range from hundreds to millions. When it comes to senseless barbarism, of course, numbers hardly seem to matter. What cannot be argued away is that Ahmadis historically have been subjected to organized violence and that violence has often been ignored or even abetted by the government.

In 1974, for instance, Pakistani prime minister Zulfikar Ali Bhutto, under pressure from religious extremists, passed an amendment to the constitution declaring Ahmadis as non-Muslim. Overnight they were barred from calling themselves Muslims in a bizarre Orwellian-like nightmare of identity theft. Their passports carried a stamp declaring them to be heretics. A decade later, a new law was passed that barred them from calling their places of worship "mosques" and forbade them completely from propagating their faith in Pakistan.

Of course, for people like Abdus Salam, religious faith and principles were a form of identification imprinted on something far more durable than an official identity card: the human heart.

* * *

Abdus Salam was born in 1926 in a small, poor farming village, Jhang, in Punjab in what was then India but is now Pakistan (India was partitioned in 1948). His father, a schoolteacher, predicted his son would go places and he was right, but his son would also go places by becoming a displaced person from his own country.

As a boy Salam did incredibly well at school, coming first in local and national exams, despite studying at home without the aid of electric lights (an interesting irony considering that his Nobel Prize–winning work would probe the depths of the material world to explain phenomena related to electricity). He won a scholarship first to the University of Lahore, where he obtained an MA in 1946 and another to the University of Cambridge in England, where, among other giants in the fields of mathematics and physics, he studied with Nobel Prize–winner Paul Dirac, one of the greatest physicist of the twentieth century—and the strangest: he has been described as "pathologically reticent, extraordinarily literal-minded and almost unable to empathize with most people, even his family."

As a graduate student, Salam shot to the top and won many prestigious awards and became something of a celebrity in his field. His PhD thesis, published in 1951, contained groundbreaking, fundamental insights into quantum electrodynamics that cemented his global scientific reputation. Feeling an obligation to give back to his country, he returned to Pakistan in 1951 to establish a research centre at Punjab University, where he was appointed head of the mathematics department. Unfortunately, his efforts failed to meet with success and reluctantly he returned to Cambridge in 1954 to become a lecturer and fellow of St. John's College.

Just three years later, Patrick Blackett, a professor involved in the establishment of the physics department at Imperial College

London, and himself a Nobel Prize winner, walked up to Salam and without any introductions asked: "Do you want a chair?"

Salam answered that he did.

"It is done."

Cambridge tried to dissuade Salam from moving to Imperial College by, among other things, offering him a bottomless supply of sherry, a doomed seduction given that Salam—an observant Muslim—was a teetotaller! In 1957 Salam became professor of applied mathematics at Imperial College, but switched to physics, where he believed his true vocation lay. He settled in Putney outside London but close to the Ahmadi mosque in Southfields, which dates back to 1924. It was here that the Ahmadiyya community established its first branch outside of Asia.

Between 1960 and 1974, Salam became a scientific advisor to the Pakistani prime minister, and he has been credited with establishing the foundations of the country's space and nuclear programs. Yet when this first Muslim to ever win a Nobel Prize in science returned home to Pakistan in 1980, he was threatened with physical violence for his Ahmadi identity: invited to a celebratory ceremony at the physics department of Quaid-i-Azam University (QAU), he could not enter because so many angry protestors—most of them students belonging to a powerful Islamic party!—barred his access to the building. A colleague who was present recalls how tense the situation was; he said he feared very much for Salam's physical well-being. The ceremony was cancelled.

Quaid-i-Azam of course refers to Jinnah, the Great Leader, and "father" of Pakistan. He was a fascinating person (too complex to capture here), inexorably and inevitably, it seemed to me, hurtling towards a solution—Pakistan—that in time became something very different from what he had envisioned. He envisioned Pakistan as a new country that respected and encompassed all religions, not just Islam or any branch of Islam. Had he not died so soon after Pakistan's creation, he would have been ashamed to witness the unseemly battles to pigeonhole him as Sunni or Shia. To me he was an example of a man who transcended petty religious differences. He would also have been ashamed of the persecution of the minority Ahmadi community. In a presidential address to the first Constituent Assembly of Pakistan, in Karachi, on August 11, 1947, he famously declared that everyone was "free to go to your temples, you are free to go to your mosques or to any other place of worship in this State of Pakistan. You may belong to any religion or caste or creed. That has nothing to do with the business of the State."

Salam never abandoned his contacts with the Pakistani scientific community, however, nor his advocacy and championing of science for the developing world. Nor did he abandon his faith or his faith in the people of Pakistan. "Scientific thought and its creation," he has written, "is the common and shared heritage of mankind." And it's possible progress is being made.

Perhaps his greatest legacy to colour-blind achievement in science excellence is his founding of the International Centre for Theoretical Physics (ICTP) in 1964 in Trieste, Italy, a sustaining monument to his genius and vision to bringing scientists from around the world (e.g., from Israel and Palestine, Pakistan and India) together to help solve the problems of humanity. Over the past decade, I have been lucky enough to visit Trieste many times in various capacities in my global health work. It is mainly a white city, and there is a funny saying that if you see a "dark" person on the streets, assume he or she is a great scientist! (Whenever I visit York University in Toronto, I am also reminded of the Ahmadiyya community, because it is there that I met their current spiritual leader, Mirza Masroor Ahmad, the Fifth Caliph of their community, in October 2016. He gave a lecture entitled "Justice in an Unjust World" at a gathering that was hosted by my poker-playing friend Greg Sorbara, the chancellor of York University. The Ahmadiyya community is said to number in the tens of millions in two hundred countries, with four or five million still in Pakistan, mainly in a city called Rabwah.)

Another legacy of Abdus Salam is The World Academy of Sciences (TWAS), which is housed in the same building in Trieste as ICTP. I am a proud Fellow of TWAS, and that is one reason I have been going to Trieste so often.

I have a vivid memory of an episode that occurred when I was head of surgery at Sultan Qaboos University in Muscat. I had seriously planned to invite Professor Salam to speak; it was my hope that our faculty and students would find him as fascinating and inspiring as I did. Of course, I was also wonderfully excited at the opportunity of reuniting with the Great Man after all these years. I had no illusions that he would remember our brief conversations back in Oxford, but for me it did not matter. Imagine my shock—my bewildered confusion—when the university authorities turned me down flat.

"Why ever not?" I demanded angrily. "There must be a mistake. The man won the Nobel Prize in Physics! He is a giant!" I was told the selection would be too controversial. "What on earth are you talking about? Controversial? How?" As long as I live, I will never forget their answer.

"He is an Ahmadi."

In fact, in 2017 Prime Minister Nawaz Sharif of Pakistan attempted to correct the wrong done to Salam by naming the same QUA's physics department the Professor Abdus Salam Centre for Physics. A local newspaper noted that it had taken four decades for Pakistan to honour a globally renowned

Pakistani scientist, which it described as "a sad reflection of the priorities that hold sway here . . . and his faith rather than his towering achievements was the yardstick by which he was judged." Sadly, small steps in the right direction have been met with giant steps backwards. Nawaz Sharif's belated attempts to posthumously honour Salam were met with a violent backlash. It is doubtful if the momentum and the meagre moves away from Ahmadi persecution will be sustained. I suspect, however, that were Abdus Salam alive he would tell me that obstacles will always exist in order to be overcome. That is what science is.

When I first met Abdus Salam, of course, I knew nothing of the persecution of the Ahmadis. It reminds me, however, how powerful the shadow cast by a great personality can be. In time I would come to learn and deeply respect Salam's passionate devotion to his Muslim faith. I would come to appreciate his stubborn goodness and generosity, his open-mindedness and commitment to humanity.

After his community was declared heretic by legislative fiat, Abdus Salam added Muhammad to his name to honour the Prophet and show his deep personal commitment to Islam. His religion did not occupy a separate compartment of his life; it was inseparable from his work and family life. "The Holy Quran enjoins us," he wrote, "to reflect on the verities of Allah's created laws of nature; however, that our generation has been privileged to glimpse a part of His design is a bounty and a grace for which I render thanks with a humble heart." In other words, for him research in advanced physics and mathematics was an attempt to understand God's design. I think that is largely what he meant when he told me in Oxford that his religion actually helped him as a scientist.

But what is the religious issue that has so angered the extremists and caused such sectarian violence? The Ahmadis, of course, consider themselves to be Muslims, but those against them consider them to be heretics because of the accusation that their late nineteenth-century founder, Mirza Ghulam Ahmad, declared himself a prophet of Islam, which goes against the strong Islamic tenet that the Prophet Muhammad was the final prophet and there could not be another after him. However, some sources say that Mirza's message was more nuanced in that he claimed to be like a "reflection" of the Prophet and did not claim to be a prophet per se. He did not bring forth a new law and was only a Mahdi, a divinely guided redeemer who had been prophesied in Muslim eschatology. There have been other Mahdis in recent times, including the famous Sudanese Muhammad Ahmad bin Abd Allah, an Islamic revivalist cleric who declared himself the Mahdi in 1881, seeing himself also as a divinely guided redeemer fighting the forces of injustice, tyranny, and evil, and the one who would prepare for the second coming of Jesus Christ, also prophesied in Sunni Islam.

His great-great grandson Sadiq al Mahdi, politician and Imam of Muhammad Ahmad's followers, became prime minister of independent Sudan from 1966 to 1967 and again from 1986 to 1989. And this brings us to another personal connection for me. Sadiq's cousin, Abda Yahia Abdelrahman El Mahdi, is the wife of a close friend of mine, Mohammed Hassan, who had been the executive director of ICTP and a close friend of Abdus Salam for a long time.

I still find it puzzling and painful that as kids growing up in Tanzania we were warned to "be careful" of members of the Ahmadiyya community. What were we all so afraid of? The situation for Ahmadis has changed for the better, but not enough. In 2016 I read a BBC report about a south London mosque where leaflets were found calling "for the killing" of Ahmadis unless they subjected themselves to immediate conversion.

In times past in England and Spain, it was the Muslims (Moors) and Jews. In Uganda in the seventies, it was Asians. In Rwanda genocide erupted over the difference between two tribes, Hutu and Tutsi. In the United States in 2017 it was the Muslims. In Muslim-majority Pakistan today it is *unacceptably Muslim* Muslims. And on and on. Times and names change but the message is the same: *We don't want you.*

I met Abdus Salam a few more times when he moved to Oxford towards the end of his life; he was not well by then and we never exchanged more than basic formalities. He would never know, of course, what an important role model he became for me: I admired him because he was a great scientist; he understood the social role that science can play; he created powerful, innovative research institutions to which he brought scientists from countries in conflict to work and live together on neutral ground in Trieste. He understood to the core the link between science and peace. In later life I benefited from those institutions, including The World Academy of Sciences. I could not do the same at his scale but he was always on my mind when I also tried to resolve conflicts by bringing people together.

I have another, more personal, reason for considering him such an important role model. I think I shared with Salam the sense of fraternity that comes with the shared experience of exile. Was he also a father substitute, filling a void left by my father's death so many years ago? I think many of the mentors and role models I had as a young man were idealized versions of my father. Abdus Salam believed that "scientific thought and its creation is the common and shared heritage of mankind." I share that view strongly, and through my membership on the council of the

Israeli-Palestinian Science Organization (IPSO), which at one time had six Nobel Prize winners, we have brought together and funded Palestinian and Israeli scientists to do research and build scientific capacity among themselves. I believe strongly also that our modern understanding of human rights, as codified in the magnificent non-religious UN Universal Declaration of Human Rights, brings humanity as close as it can to being wise about how to live together in peace. It is because of this that I devote time on the executive board of the International Human Rights Network of Academies and Scholarly Societies, where over the years we have successfully reduced or eliminated the persecution of many professionals and scientists in many parts of the world.

Like so many people who have inspired me over the years, it is doubtful Abdus Salam had any idea what a powerful influence he was on me and on those around him. Amazingly, Pakistan has a second Nobel Prize winner. Her name is Malala Yousafzai. She was awarded the Nobel Peace Prize in 2014 for her struggle to allow girls to be educated. It is a miracle she survived the bullet aimed at her brain by a Taliban gunman outraged that she was advocating for girls to be educated. Malala, who has become an inspiration to millions around the world, was a shy schoolgirl of fifteen when she took her courageous stand against the Taliban. I doubt even she had any idea how tall she would stand. Most heroes never do. She enrolled at the University of Oxford in 2017.

In November 1996 Abdus Salma died in Oxford. I was very sad when I read the news but heartened to learn that when his body was returned to Pakistan for burial, as many as thirty thousand attended his funeral prayers.

I still think of that mosque back in Kampala—I remember thinking how huge it was. And that makes me think of Abdus Salam. A true giant, not only of the mind but also of the spirit.

A man who was—is—a true inspiration for me. Not long ago I read that the epitaph on his tomb was to have honoured Abdus Salam as the first Muslim Nobel Laureate. Apparently this proved too controversial and the word "Muslim" was excised.

Chapter 16

Dancing to the Inner Music

I've become obsessed with the idea of reconciliation, particularly reconciliation with nature but with people too, of course. I think that travel has been a kind of search for that, a pursuit for unity and even an attempt to contribute to a sense of unity.

— Jan Morris

By 1977 I had successfully completed the final parts of both the FRCS and MRCP, and in 1979 I embarked on a PhD (DPhil), moving to Wolfson College. Something unusual happens in the UK when you become an FRCS. You stop being a doctor! You are now referred to as Mr. followed by your surname. It's an old tradition dating back to the time when surgery was performed by "barber surgeons" but in this context it marked the crossing of a major threshold and was quite an honour.

In Oxford almost no one called me by my full first name; it was always Abdul or Ab, a name Peter Morris gave me and by which he still calls me. At least these resemble my first name. In Dar es Salaam for several years I had been called "Said," which is the name of my grandfather—this came about because when I entered Aga Khan Boys Secondary School I had to register and some official (as they did at Ellis Island) decided to give me a name he liked and used my first name, my father's, and my grandfather's, and not my surname! But now at Oxford I had another appellation: I was called the "Whistling Surgeon," a name given to me by Peter

Morris's secretary Joan Cracknell, because she could tell from far away that I was approaching her office by the way I was whistling a tune "in two keys at the same time."

I loved walking past her office on the way to my lab because on the wall opposite there were these large black-and-white photographic portraits of the lecturers. I had been appointed to the faculty as a lecturer, so one of those photos was of me. Looking at those photos now I cannot believe just how thin I was (that tonsillectomy hadn't kicked in yet!). There were also photos of the whole Nuffield Department of Surgery staff and faculty taken annually: you could see not just how fast the department was growing but also how we were aging gracefully.

Both Oxford and Gloucester, 69 kilometres (43 miles) to the west, are embraced by the Cotswolds, a most beautiful part of England, renowned for its Cotswold stone, which has a particular golden colour from the geological characteristics of the area. In the 1970s a big regional hospital was built in Gloucester, rising ten storeys with two wards on each floor and a big accidents and emergency (A&E) department. The Cotswolds and this hospital with its facilities attracted some really good medical and surgical staff, including some who had trained at some point in Oxford. One of these was Michael Gear. He worked with Peter Morris to develop an extension of the Oxford surgical training program at the Gloucestershire Royal Hospital.

From 1975 to 1977, while I was in the Nuffield Department of Surgery in Oxford, most of my work was in transplantation. However, I also did a fair amount of general surgery, some of it at the Churchill and some at the old Radcliffe Infirmary. In 1978 Peter Morris asked me if I would like to spend some time in Gloucester, and I agreed because of the great reputation there and the fact that it would give me a lot of "cutting" experience.

And so at some point in 1978 Shahina and I packed our stuff in our battered old orange-coloured Datsun and moved to Gloucester. It was fortunate that in their emergency department I could get plaster of Paris to patch the rusting wings of the Datsun every few weeks! I worked with Michael Gear, from whom I learned a great deal about gastric and biliary surgery; Hamish Thompson, from whom I acquired a lot of innovative techniques in general surgery; and Denis Calvert, a urologist who taught me a lot on that subject and in addition taught me how to perform thyroid and parathyroid surgery safely. I performed a lot of surgical operations. Because of the crowded theatre schedules, I had to learn to operate very fast; I could perform appendectomies in nine minutes "skin to skin." At a younger age, surgeons are proud of such achievements but with age and wisdom we learn that good surgeons are really good physicians who are occasionally forced to operate. In fact in later life, I taught my students that a good surgeon is a good biologist who is occasionally forced to operate.

While in Gloucester, I also did a lot of research on gastric biopsies I obtained while performing many upper GI endoscopies. We were doing so many at that time because a lot of people had peptic ulcers and this was the better way (compared to barium meals) to make a diagnosis and exclude malignancy. In some ways this was primitive medicine, because in 1982 two Australian scientists, Barry Marshall and Robin Warren, discovered that peptic ulcers were caused by a bacterium called *Helicobacter pylori*, and the treatment changed completely from using ineffective antacids and surgery (unnecessary, in retrospect) to using antibiotics. (Half the people in the world harbour *H. pylori* and most are asymptomatic.) This discovery totally revolutionized treatment of peptic ulcers and the two Australians were awarded the Nobel Prize in 2005.

In Gloucester Shahina continued working part-time in hematology, and we became close friends with a surgical registrar called Nabil el Hoss and his wife, Sally. Nabil was a relative of then–Lebanese prime minister Salim el Hoss. In 1979 Peter Morris called me back to Oxford, where there was an opening as surgical tutor (at senior registrar level), and I was then soon appointed as a clinical lecturer in the NDS. The main duty of the surgical tutor was to organize the teaching of medical students, but it also included providing "moral guidance" to the students and advising them regarding any personal issues they might have.

On returning to Oxford for another five years or so, I would discover a higher level of the life of the mind and what was meant by "effortless excellence" in Oxford. I developed a kind of madness whose main features were hectic, unrelenting, unquenchable curiosity about everything, and almost superhuman capacity for work. This is not a good combination. Besides my own work in clinical surgery and immunological research, I had developed an abiding interest in bioethics and therefore in philosophy, and in how moral action is affected by religion. Therefore I had to explore how most religions approached issues at the beginning and end of life. From the work of Derek Parfit, a professor at Oxford who was considered one of the greatest moral philosophers of the past century, I was to learn more about personal identity. I later came to know him personally, for his partner, Janet Radcliffe-Richards, was a member of our International Forum for Transplant Ethics (IFTE) group. Oddly, what I remember most about Derek was his insistence on squeezing into the tiny boot (trunk) of Janet's packed car on our way to dinner one evening in Oxford. Derek's passion in life was photographing beautiful buildings in Venice and St. Petersburg.

In 1980 I was awarded a three-year Medical Research Council of Great Britain Training Fellowship to finance my DPhil studies. This was really helpful for me but the greatest thing about it was the opportunity it gave me to attend the Triennial Convocation of Nobel Prize winners in medicine/physiology in Lindau, Germany, in 1981. Of all the events in my life that I could say were most influential in opening my mind to wider horizons and that led me to approach life as an open research question, this was it. For a whole week we lived with, ate with, and talked with almost all the then-living Nobel Prize winners in medicine/physiology. Among the more memorable occasions was a walk around the beautiful gardens with Hans Krebs, the Oxford chemist who had described the Krebs Acid Cycle, so fundamental to cellular life, and the Australian neurophysiologist John Eccles, for his work on brain synapses.

But the most colourful and tragic of the thirty or forty great minds present that week was Carleton Gajdusek, the American who had won the Nobel Prize in 1976 for his discovery that the fatal disease kuru was transmitted among Papua New Guinea highlanders by eating the brains of recently deceased relatives as part of their funerary rituals. Gajdusek was accompanied in Lindau by a number of young black boys. It transpired in court later that Gajdusek was sexually molesting some of the fifty-six Papua New Guinea children he had brought to live with him in the United States. He had recorded these abuses in his diaries, pleaded guilty, and was imprisoned in 1997. Publicly admitting to molesting children, he also defended incest.

The most useful thing I learned that week in Lindau was to demystify these great scientists. You got to say to yourself, "They're great, but they are just like you and me; just human." But each encounter with them was influential and instructive in some way and added to my enlarging repository of confidence.

One of the most interesting experiences I had with anyone in my entire tenure in Oxford was extremely indirect but nevertheless powerful and influential in the way I thought of identity.

Around the time I arrived at Oxford in 1975, I came upon a book by the same name (published in 1965) by a brilliant travel writer and historian named James Morris (the third Morris of my Oxford Holy Trinity!). Morris of course would skyrocket to fame with the brilliant *Pax Britannica* series of books. What I did not know initially was that James Morris was actually Jan Morris. Not long after *Oxford* was published, Morris began gender-reassignment treatment.

Jan Morris was born James Morris in 1926, studied at Christ Church, Oxford, and married Elizabeth Tuckniss, with whom he had five children. James began gender transitioning in 1966 and went to Morocco in 1972 to undergo sex-reassignment surgery; British surgeons refused to perform the operation unless she divorced Elizabeth, which she refused to do. Although they eventually divorced, Jan and Elizabeth continued living together, and in 1982 they were again legally reunited in a civil partnership.

Most of my surgical life has been dedicated to organ allo-transplantation (i.e., between human beings). The basic assumption here is the equivalence of all human beings in the biology of their organs—we are all constructed from the same kit and from the same toolbox. Doesn't it seem a profound puzzle, then, how we manage to fight so much among ourselves about what supposedly divides us when underneath it all we are really the same?

Of course, the barriers and the hostility—the indignities (social and institutional)—faced by Jan Morris are not quite as formidable today as they were then. But we have a long way to go—especially in countries where, for instance, homosexuality still carries a death penalty. How can we be excellent human beings if fellow human beings refuse to accept who we are? And who are we, anyway? How do we know? Ultimately all we have is rough guesses based on comparison, one to another. If we were all of one colour, would we identify as "white," for instance? Well, no, probably not, because we would all be the same. *And yet we are all the same!* The differences we isolate as being definitive are not defining at all.

"The more I was treated as a woman," Morris has written of her experiences, "the more woman I became." It is an interesting and intriguing insight. "To me," she writes, "gender is not physical at all, but is altogether insubstantial. It is soul, perhaps, it is talent, it is taste, it is environment, it is how one feels, it is light and shade, it is inner music."

Light and shade? Inner music? Well, why not! To be honest, I can hardly think of a better definition of identity.

Chapter 17

Oxford: My Humanity Is Bound Up in Yours

My humanity is bound up in yours, for we can only be human together.

— Bishop Desmond Tutu

Doing research at Oxford from 1979 to around 1984 was very different from the types of research I was doing earlier. Initially I had wanted to study the spleen, about which surprisingly little was known at the time. But I went off that idea when I realized just how many little newborn mice I would have to kill. I have since then become an advocate of the three *R*s regarding the use of animals for research: replacement, reduction, and refinement. These are now accepted ethical principles in experimental research; the number of animals being used for research has dropped significantly. Instead I chose to work on cell surface membrane molecules of white cells and my DPhil thesis was titled "Studies with monoclonal antibodies on the potential clinical value of human cell membrane differentiation antigens." This was pure laboratory work in the Nuffield Department of Surgery. I found lab work to be quite challenging in the first weeks when I was spending hours mixing things in flasks, taking small aliquots in different tubes, spinning them in centrifuges, studying thin sections of human tissues (most of which I had collected previously while doing surgery), always on the lookout for new techniques to refine the research, and so on. Laboratory research of this type can be boring to start with but once you are "in the groove" and are producing exciting results, some of which add to the fundamental knowledge of science, it becomes your whole life, often seven days a week.

In the very first week I was in the labs, I wanted to know about everything and this nearly cost me my life. On the shelf in front of my desk space was a small bottle containing a white powder labelled sodium azide. It was used in the lab as a preservative. Curious, I opened the bottle, put a small amount on my finger, and was about to put it on my tongue to taste it when Rosie Hutchinson shouted "Stop!" from across the room.

I did, but looked puzzled. She let out a huge sigh and shook her head in disbelief.

"That is very toxic and probably would have killed you. For Christ's sake, be more careful."

"Okay," I said, more matter of fact than I actually felt. Indeed, when I looked it up later I found that, like cyanide, it can be absorbed through the skin either by inhalation or by ingestion—and like cyanide, it interferes with cellular oxygen utilization. Death can occur quite quickly when ingested in even relatively small doses.

I became much more careful after that. In fact, one of the biggest lessons in life I ever learned is that we all make mistakes; the important part is never making the same mistake *twice*.

My DPhil supervisor and friend John Fabre had an office across from my lab bench, and I could see him surreptitiously sneaking a look at me every now and then to make sure I didn't kill myself!

My research was at the intersection of immunology and genetics. Both subjects were also important to tissue typing, which was an essential element of clinical transplantation. In my research I was using newly discovered techniques, particularly monoclonal antibodies and powerful tissue staining techniques that led to one discovery after another. I described the presence of interstitial dendritic cells that had not yet been demonstrated in human tissues; I used double-staining techniques as a method to distinguish these cells from small blood capillaries; I used novel techniques to demonstrate the widespread existence of (self-directed) auto-antibodies; I mapped the distribution throughout the human body of important antigens coded for on the short arm of chromosome 6; and did the same for several other antigens, including those originally found on white cells and to which we had made monoclonal antibodies. All this work was published in prestigious peer-reviewed journals; some of the papers were cited several hundred times in the scientific literature and are still being cited today.

From world-renowned Oxford physician Sidney Truelove I learned about ulcerative colitis and Crohn's disease, and from others about diabetes and the management of cancer patients and all the cutting-edge research they were doing. Great Oxford surgeons helped me learn advanced surgery in so many subdisciplines: general, pancreatico-biliary, paediatric, endocrine, urological, and thoracic. Among these were Michael Kettlewell, Julian Britton, John Collin, Robert Wood, Nicholas Dudley, Joe Smith, and Alfred Gunning, and a kind, gentle surgeon's surgeon called Howard Steer. But the story I want to tell next happened when I was working with Peter Morris and the cancer physician Dr. Alastair Laing.

It was during the time when I was lecturer in charge of lymphoma surgery that a very sad event happened. In those days the accepted way to "stage," that is, to map the extent of the disease known as Hodgkin's lymphoma, was truly aggressive and intrusive: you had to do a laparotomy—open the patient's abdomen through a large incision, examine the whole abdomen and the retro-peritoneum, remove the spleen, take lymph nodes from several sites, and do a liver biopsy. The exact treatment that followed depended on the stage, but each of these bits of surgery carried its own risk. This was especially so for the splenectomy, which was a fairly large procedure, and removing this large and important (we know now) repository of lymphoid tissue, which is related to the immune system, left the patient exposed to certain types of infections, requiring in some cases lifelong antibiotics. To reduce the complications rate, one person usually performed the staging laparotomy, so that that person could gain the most experience and at the end of her/his term, usually a year, would teach the next person how to do it safely. Since our teaching hospital was a regional referral centre for many conditions, including lymphoma, I did several of these procedures a week. One of my patients, Katie, was a beautiful, auburn-haired, generally hearty and healthy teenager with a slightly freckled face; she had come with her family all the way from Scotland to see us.

I performed her staging laparotomy and that went without incident; findings from other investigations suggested she had Hodgkin's lymphoma in her central nervous system that required radiotherapy to her spine, in addition to the chemotherapy. Radiation and where it is directed in the body is a highly specialized science. The work is done by highly trained specialists who aim to protect the patient from the harmful effects of radiation. However, in Katie's case something went drastically wrong in the system, and she was left paralyzed and in a wheelchair for the rest of her life. Her parents, Joanna and Robert Spenser-Nairn, were devastated, as was Katie, of course. They were confused; they could not get all the answers they were looking for and had to find a way to cope with the tragedy. They were wonderful people and we became friends. Shahina and I helped to provide some of the answers they were seeking. They bought a small house in Oxford so that Joanna could stay with and support Katie while she continued to have long-term care in Oxford. Katie bore the whole process with unbelievable fortitude and made many friends of her own age in Oxford. Shahina and I remained friends with them for a long time and even after they had moved back to Scotland we visited with them.

A few years ago I called them from Toronto to have a chat. The memories were, of course, mixed, but what came through was not sadness or bitterness but the abundance and dignity of their lives, the number of activities, charities, and neighbourhood events they were all involved in, and the birthday celebrations of Katie's nieces and nephews.

I laughed with them, but afterwards I gently cried to myself in frustration. What was the point? We have our successes but we so often have failures. To caregivers, those failures can simply be part of the morbidity and mortality statistics we collect and discuss every week so we can learn and improve, but for the people affected it is not about statistics, it is about people and their lives and hopes and feelings and pain and suffering. Those errors can be bigger than life, bigger than death, for they alter lives, too much at times.

But when our patients suffer so, what happens inside of us? How do we react? How do we cope? We are human and we vary, but for many, tragedies like these touch us deeply. They do not go unnoticed, faces are not forgotten. You share in the sadness and the intense moments because all your patients are your friends. You pray a day doesn't come when you are inured and anaesthetized. Because if that happens, you diminish your patients and in the process you diminish yourself, and everyone is less human. You want to cry with them when they ask "Why me?" and if they die, you are left with a small empty space deep inside and that space grows with each death. Yes, you have to go on with the doctoring and with your other patients and with your own life, but that previous shared pain—that sympathy—makes you a better and better human.

Meanwhile, in a tale of triumph and tragedy, another emotionally significant event in my medical career was about to unfold in Oxford. In the laboratory, provided you supply them with nutrients, cancer cells will go on dividing indefinitely. This is what scientists mean when they say that the cells are "immortal." Normal cells stop dividing quite quickly.

The monoclonal antibodies I used for my research were made by manipulations that "immortalized" the cells so they could continue to produce antibodies continuously except when they were frozen. My doctoral thesis and my first book, on tumour markers, were largely based on studies using such monoclonal antibodies. One day, again while I was looking after patients with cancer, I was called to the emergency department. A young woman in her late twenties or early thirties was lying in bed, in great distress, short of breath, the veins in her neck very distended. She rolled around but couldn't find a comfortable position, because her abdomen was distended and tight as a drum skin. What she had was ovarian cancer, and the cancer cells had spread in her abdomen and were producing fluid unstoppably. This ascitic fluid kept building up, and every now and then she would come into the emergency department to have the fluid aspirated or drained through a needle or a catheter. But now this was not controlling the situation, the fluid was building up too fast, she was getting weaker and weaker and losing a lot of protein, and she was becoming exhausted and emaciated. She told me she knew she was dying, said she didn't want to have to come to the hospital so frequently, and asked if there was anything else that could be done that would give her relief.

As I recall now, I took her to the operating theatre and performed a palliative procedure called a peritoneo-venous shunt, which would divert the fluid from her abdomen, via a catheter placed beneath her skin, into the subclavian vein behind her clavicle. The ascitic fluid would now flow into her bloodstream and, provided we didn't push her into heart failure with fluid overload, she would have relief and wouldn't need to come into the hospital so often. After she recovered from anaesthesia and rested, I asked her permission to draw some of her circulating blood to see if I could grow the malignant cells from there for research purposes. Although she knew this would not help her personally in any way, she gave consent. In what was likely the first successful attempt under these circumstances, I was able to grow and propagate the malignant cells in the lab over the coming days and weeks. The patient was discharged home.

But my joy at the research success was marred by the fact that we could do no more for her. Her condition was terminal. I obtained her phone number from the social workers and called her at home to see how she was doing and if she needed any further help. I was shocked to learn that she lived alone and had no one to talk to or care for her at home. Social services arranged "meals on wheels" and hospital appointments and transport and checked in on her every now and then. She lived in an apartment on a street that was quite close to Linton Road, at the end of which was Wolfson College. I visited her at home a few times to comfort her, basically to hold her hand and just listen to her talk. She died soon after. It was a difficult experience. Her usual oncologist had been abroad; when he returned I explained what had transpired. As far as I know, her cells may well still be in a lab freezer somewhere in Oxford, an invaluable resource for research scientists attempting to cure cancer and other diseases.

The oldest immortalized cell line—known as HeLa—was derived in 1951 from a cervical cancer biopsy on a woman named Henrietta Lacks. HeLa cells were used to develop the first polio vaccine and for many, many other medical research and development purposes. No one knows how many of her cells are living in various labs around the world; estimates are that if you could pile all the HeLa cells that were ever grown onto to a scale they would weigh more than fifty million metric tons; they would wrap around the world at least three times, more than 350 million feet.

Controversially, the cells were extracted from Henrietta Lacks without her permission at Johns Hopkins Hospital in Baltimore, which, unfortunately, was not at all unusual at that time. The cells, in fact, became part of a famous 1990 Supreme Court of California case: *Moore vs. Regents of the University of California* (the remarkable story of Henrietta Lacks was told in 2010 in the bestselling book *The Immortal Life of Henrietta Lacks* by Rebecca Skloot). The court ruled that a person's discarded tissue and cells are not his or her property, and that they can be commercialized. I first heard about the case when I was working at Stanford University in 1998 (a law professor colleague of mine there had written about it). It was an important case, especially for me, as it dealt with the crucial subject of the ethics of race and class in scientific research. Many years later when I had moved to the University of Toronto and was working in the area of biotechnology for global health at the McLaughlin-Rotman Centre for Molecular Medicine I made *Moore vs. Regents* an important case study for my graduate students.

There was another reason why the case—why Henrietta Lacks—is so important to me. Henrietta Lacks, of course, was a black woman and her story reminded me of Dr. Christiaan Barnard's famous heart transplant back in 1968 between a coloured man and a white man. Here was a black woman, whose family was so poor they could not afford to see a doctor, having her cells harvested for the benefit of millions of mostly white patients.

* * *

It is often said that in surgery "you watch one, do one, teach one," but in many cases that is a gross exaggeration. Nevertheless, one does go from being a student or trainee to being a tutor or teacher. This happens all the time in the setting of a ward round, where students and junior doctors do rounds with more senior colleagues and in the process much knowledge is transmitted from generation to generation. Every six weeks or so, another batch of medical students starts their "surgical rotation" and you really don't know what they are going to be like. But every now and then, an exceptional student with a lot of potential comes through.

One such student was John Bell, a tall, slim Canadian with a strong Alberta accent. He was on a Rhodes Scholarship to study medicine in Oxford, planning to return to Canada after finishing. He was so bright you could confidently tell he was going on to greater things, and everyone who came across him noticed this. All our predictions came true, for he became at Oxford, successively, the Nuffield and then the Regius Professor of Medicine, following in the footsteps of his great mentor, David Weatherall. He also became a powerful figure in British academia and research funding, a key advisor to the British prime minister, and a champion of biotechnology. Our paths crossed many times. Shahina spent some time doing research in the Wellcome Trust

Centre for Human Genetics at Oxford, which John had co-founded with Peter Morris. I worked with John later when I was leading the study on grand challenges in chronic non-communicable diseases, a study that led to the creation of the Global Alliance for Chronic Diseases, which I headed for two and a half years. He has always been confident but not arrogant and has a very dry sense of humour. When we were being introduced at meetings he would often say, "Abdul taught me all the surgery I know. And that's very little!"

* * *

Oxford is renowned for its bad weather. Many people had colds that seemed to never go away. We were all victims but the ones that suffered most, it seemed to me, were people writing their DPhil theses. This was usually during the last year of their work. They went around in a daze, their clothes were wrinkled, they had a particular stooping gait, and it was obvious they were losing weight because of undernourishment. They were miserable and would hardly be able to hold a conversation if you stopped them along the hospital or college corridors or in the library. I had a bit of this syndrome when I was writing my thesis, and a friend of ours, Mary, whose future husband, Ken Lakin, was doing his DPhil about the same time as I, took pity on me and said she had a special Scottish porridge that was sure to help me gain weight. So several days a week, on my way to work, I would stop at her place and be fed this special nutritious porridge, with limited effect, just as the tonsillectomy I'd had as a kid in Dar es Salaam had little effect. But the cure for this thesis wasting disease really happens spontaneously at the very moment you submit your thesis to the university and you can no longer torture yourself by making changes to it. If I am asked what was the greatest day of my life, I would often say it was the day I submitted my DPhil thesis. It was certainly the day of the greatest relief!

Then the thesis had to be defended. An external examiner and internal university examiner were arranged, and on the set day I attended, wearing my gown and white bow tie, as was the tradition. It was held at Merton College Oxford where the internal examiner, a pathologist, was a Fellow. It might have been preceded by tea and scones (probably my imagination!). It took about four hours; I enjoyed it thoroughly and passed without difficulty. And from that moment, my name changed again from the surgical "mister" to the scientist "doctor."

* * *

My research had potential applications in immunology, transplantation, and even cancer. In fact, one of the studies I carried out on breast cancer won the Patey Prize of the Surgical Research Society of Great Britain. On one occasion towards the end of my time in Oxford I gave a research seminar on potential cancer applications of my work. Blackwell Scientific Publications was looking to publish a book on cancer markers and they asked one of the Oxford professors for the name of someone who might be able to write such a book; they were pointed to me because that professor had attended my seminar. The result was a book I edited and wrote many of the chapters for; it was published in 1987 and titled *Tumour Markers in Clinical Practice: Concepts and Applications.* I dedicated that book to my mentor: "To Peter J Morris, Nuffield Professor of Surgery, Oxford University 'for enabling the penny to drop, and allowing the ripples to define their own shores.'" This was just a small tribute to the man who, more than any other human being, taught me that medicine can be practised at the very highest level when the patient comes first, and when we pay attention to medical ethics. More than any other, he inspired me to become an academic surgeon-scientist. When faced with a difficult situation, I would often ask myself: "What would Peter Morris do?" He was that influential in my life. No one was more important in my professional life than Peter Morris. His very position as the pre-eminent surgeon-scientist of his generation cast him in the mould of a hero, someone to look up to. But I was encouraged not just to look up but also within and ask, "Can I emulate him?" He was a leader nonpareil in Oxford. I studied him, watching him, trying to understand why the people he led loved to follow and support him. I tried hard to understand charisma, which he had in larger measure than most people I have met, and learned that it was mostly innate, but was nurtured continuously by good leadership, sensible decisions, care for juniors, and attention to detail. I learned to distinguish between power and influence, and when necessary how to bring them together for good ends. I learned that caring for the people meant writing letters to the wives of your juniors when a kid is born, remembering birthdays, and sending flowers on special occasions. I learned of uncompromising high standards, where the patient always comes first, where the transmission of knowledge is accompanied by transmission of attitudes, and where acting ethically is second nature. I learned about being lucky.

* * *

My office in Oxford was very messy. I had an archaeological filing system, which meant no filing at all: papers, mostly copies of scientific publications that I had made on old machines that still used toxic chemicals (I think acetone was one of them, making me wheeze as I was copying), were placed one on top of another as they accumulated. If I were looking for a specific paper, I would first have to recall when I had copied it and then guess where it might be in the pile.

There was another oddity about my office. There was a short, stocky Zoroastrian surgeon who was very bright; he was studying for an advanced Oxford degree called Master of Surgery (ChM) that almost no one ever took or passed. He was very poor and had nowhere to stay and asked me if he could sleep in my office. I couldn't refuse, and we had to coordinate our arrivals and departures so we wouldn't get in each other's way. This was at times difficult because I was using a research technique called immuno-fluorescence, whereby I had to look at my tissue slides in the dark, so I had to stay in late to do that. In the morning he would sometimes still be asleep when I arrived, looking exhausted from all the studying he had put in during the night, perhaps kept awake by all the chemicals in my piles of photocopies. I think he spent most of the day in libraries, where I would occasionally spot him, half-asleep with a book in front of him, looking very unhappy. What was driving him? Why was he aiming so high and yet was so miserable?

I have often pondered on what might be the most frightening word in the world. I think it is *anhedonia*. At first I understood this to mean just the inability to experience joy and happiness and other positive emotions. More recently the definition seems to have expanded and I have to rethink. Now I understand anhedonia in a very nuanced way, for to me it encompasses the inability to experience suffering, too. Maybe joy and suffering are the same thing, or one leads to the other. But mostly, I think, they co-exist and we don't know.

I think my poor Zoroastrian friend was depressed. I don't remember ever seeing him smile.

Chapter 18

A Call Out of the Blue: Transcending Borders to Build Medical Schools in the Middle East

The best way to find yourself is to lose yourself in the service of others.

— Mahatma Gandhi

Luck is a matter of preparation meeting opportunity.

— Seneca

Not long after we returned to Oxford from Gloucester in 1979, Shahina gave birth to our daughter Lamees and had to stop work for a while as she really had her hands full with the newborn and with our boisterous son, Marwan, who was born in 1977. Our daughter Nadia was born in 1982. (All three were born in the same ward at the John Radcliffe Hospital 2, our main Oxford teaching hospital.)

I am ashamed and saddened to say that I was not much help with Lamees. I would be away all day, returning late at night, and working weekends to boot. We stayed for about a year in Cumnor, a suburb of Oxford, and then moved to Wolfson College, where I was a resident graduate student. Here we were lucky that there was an ingenious system of child monitoring: you could agree with a couple in the same quadrangle to "babysit" your kids when you went out and by throwing a switch that other couple could hear everything in your apartment.

We did this for each other all the time and it allowed us to go out with some friends—usually for drinks and dinner. Among these friends were Sue and Roland Fuggle and Rosie and Eric Hutchinson; Sue and Rosie were doing their DPhils about the same time as I. Our next-door neighbours were William Makgoba and his wife and kids; William had been a student of Bill Hoffenberg in Birmingham, and he went on to become head of the South African Medical Research Council and then the vice-chancellor of the University of KwaZulu-Natal. Shahina had a group of close friends, including Pat (who was by then married to Richard Phipps), as well as new friends Rosemary Eshel and her Israeli anthropologist husband Itzak; their children were born at about the same time as ours and they played together.

Our children were born into a different world, in England, not Africa. Was that an advantage for them? Are they as resilient as we were? Or were we better at covering up our insecurities? Their parents are both doctors. Did that make them better informed about health matters and endow them with better mental health than their peers? From childhood, they have had opportunities we lacked. Did that make them better prepared for a life of happiness and fulfilment, or did we just confuse them with their many identities? And if that's what we did, is that a good thing or a bad thing?

All that busyness in Oxford resulted in what for me became the biggest regret in life: that I didn't spend more time with our young kids as they were growing up. I have a big empty space in my soul, and even today I get tearful when I think of the harm

I might have done. I mentioned this at the convocation speech I gave at the University of Toronto in June 2010; Marwan, our son, was in the audience. Afterwards he jokingly said to me, "Dad, I don't know why you go on about this. We didn't even notice you weren't there!"

The kids were growing up, they had lots of friends both at home at Wolfson College and from outside, and they had a super-mum. Shahina kept them fed and happy, and took the brunt of bringing them up in a loving environment. I still don't know how she managed to do all that on her own.

Over the years I have tried hard to make up for my delinquency. We are as close a family now as is possible. Still, one pays a price. Today I cannot help but think of my own son and wonder if he ever thought about me as I thought about my own father. *We do the best we can.*

Of course, in my festering guilt the question I have to ask myself today is whether what I thought was "my best" was really best for me or best for them. I never really told my son that his remark at the graduation ceremony could be read in different ways and, in one sense, had painful resonances for me thinking about my own father—that my father, too, was all too often absent from us to the extent we didn't notice the absence. I had vowed never to be like my father and instead I had become exactly like him.

My hectic and self-absorbed insular life in Oxford had another deleterious effect. I lost contact with many of my friends, key among them my childhood friend Ajmal, who had moved to Mauritius and later to Canada. I kept in touch with my brothers and sisters, some of whom were living in Britain but also with others who had emigrated elsewhere. Keeping track of them while I was in Oxford and later was like pushing pins into a huge map of the world.

For instance, my older surviving sister lived for a long time in Morogoro before moving to Sana'a; my brother Said studied automobile engineering in California and returned to Tanzania where he followed in Father's footsteps in the cattle and butchery business; Fawzia trained to be a nurse and midwife in Nairobi and Edinburgh and became the head of nursing of the military health services in Oman; Ghaniya and her diplomat husband Abdulkhalique, both of whom had studied in Oxford while I was there, were posted in Vienna and then in many other capitals, with Abdulkhalique ending as ambassador of the United Arab Emirates to Argentina. Ghaniya had her Oxford Master's degree in chemistry and worked on and off for a long time with the Abu Dhabi National Oil Company; Latifa married a Saudi-Yemeni surgeon and moved to Riyadh; Zahra, who did a master's degree in research management, married a great nephrologist, Taher Yahya, and moved to Pennsylvania; and Fareeda, who became a dental surgeon, married a half-Arab half-Kurdish Iraqi surgeon. (I often think of her husband in Shakespearean terms, à la Romeo and Juliet: his mother was Sunni and his father was Shia!) Of my younger sisters, Nasra studied engineering at the University of Reading and went to work in Sana'a; next in line, my younger brother Mohammed studied to be a pilot in Oklahoma and worked as one in Tanzania until he became a businessman and also moved to Sana'a; and the youngest, Naima, who had stayed with us at Wolfson College, went to the University of London to study computer sciences and then to the United States to do an MBA and became the finance officer for a major multinational company based in Sana'a.

I often wonder what my mother would have thought of all this: a smart and talented woman who never had the opportunity to go to school, knowing that so many of her children—the girls especially—had earned advanced degrees and were working professionally in intellectually demanding jobs while raising the next generation. She must also have derived great satisfaction seeing that her grandchildren (some Sunni and some Shia, jokingly calling themselves "Sushi") were also studying and living all around the world! Our world is changing so fast that I think we can forget so much of the change is for the good.

By now we had another beat-up old car, a large brown Citroën that I named Desmondina, in honour of Bishop Desmond Tutu, who was very much on my mind at that time because of his activism against apartheid (which he compared to Nazism), his outspokenness on human rights issues generally, and his emphasis on reconciliation. He later co-founded and chaired the Truth and Reconciliation Commission of South Africa. It was from him that I first learned about *ubuntu*, the African humanistic philosophical term whose meaning is still evolving but is probably best explained as "the belief in a universal bond of sharing that connects all humanity." It's also been used to say, "I exist because you exist." He was an inspiration to me in so many ways, including through his advice that we just need to do our "little bit of good" wherever we are, because all those bits put together can overwhelm the world.

He was awarded the Nobel Peace Prize in 1984 and his honours include both the Albert Schweitzer Prize for Humanitarianism and the Gandhi Peace Prize. At the time I was really proud that the four greatest leaders from whom I could draw moral lessons and who inspired me were black: Bishop Tutu, Nelson Mandela, Martin Luther King Jr., and Julius Nyerere. (Nyerere visited Oxford in 1975 while on a state visit to give a lecture about the struggle for independence in South Africa. Shahina and I went to listen to him in the Sheldonian Theatre. It was a moving experience.)

In the final year before leaving Oxford, around 1983, I was appointed Fellow in Transplantation and went back to almost full-time clinical transplant work. The unit was still based at the Churchill Hospital but it had grown a great deal and there were now several young Senior House Officers sharing duty time and all the chores I used to do when I first came to Oxford in 1975. As a Fellow, I once had to go to retrieve kidneys at Harefield Hospital, not very far from Oxford, where the great Egyptian cardiac surgeon Magdi Yacoub had established his renowned heart transplant unit.

As I was dissecting the abdominal aorta and its branches to get to the kidneys, a memory came to me of the days in Houston and the other great cardiac surgeons there, Michael DeBakey and Denton Cooley. I was now an established surgeon and transplant specialist but had no idea yet where I was heading. I knew that my work in transplantation and bioethics would become an important part of my life and work, but where? How?

One day around 1984 I was in the theatre at the John Radcliffe Hospital operating on a child when a nurse came to tell me I had a long-distance call. I asked her to tell the person to call back in thirty minutes.

"Hello, is that Doctor Daar?" The accent was a mixture of American and Middle Eastern.

"Yes, it is. Can I help you?"

"This is Dr. Abdul Rahim Jaffer, undersecretary in the ministry of health of the UAE."

"Oh, thank you for calling me. What can I do for you?"

"I wonder if you would consider coming to Abu Dhabi for a few days?"

"I will look into it, but what is this about?" I was weary of entanglements that would take me away from my work.

"We need some advice on starting a kidney transplant centre

at our new hospital and also about medical education at our university. Can you come?"

Just as I would later have a conversation with the new dean of the not-yet formed medical school in Oman, I was being stealthily recruited without really knowing what was happening.

"Dr. Jaffer, let me give this some thought. Please call me again early next week."

And just like that, at that very moment, my life was being changed. Looking back over my career, this has happened so many times, usually while I was minding my own business. I was fortunate throughout my career that I have not really applied formally for any job. The closest was when I first came to see Peter Morris in Oxford, and even then I didn't formally write an application. And here again my life's trajectory was being shaped without my specific directed instigation. It happened again when I moved from the UAE to Oman in 1988, and again when I moved from Oman to Canada in 2000.

I am astounded by this inability to definitively tell *ab initio* where we are going to end up in life. Luck plays a big role. When I reflect on my life, I see clearly that what has worked for me was being open to opportunities, to quickly see their potentialities, to be open to exploring them, and to be open to taking risks. I have come to realize that life has a gloss that, with good food and good wine and travel to exotic places and having lovely kids, is nevertheless, as the Buddhists have taught us all along, full of existential pain and suffering largely caused by attachment to material things—and being constantly open to change in this life may be a way to reduce that pain.

Eventually I transitioned from surgery and organ transplantation to global health. I know that from my teenage years, I had begun to think about poverty and inequities. It is those thoughts that would one day lead me to working in global health. So why did I choose a career specializing in organ transplantation in the earlier part of my professional life? As I reflect on this, I begin to tease out the threads connecting these two domains. I was lucky never to accept silos and walls between the knowledge and skill sets of different medical disciplines, and I had the confidence to transition from one to another easily. The bigger truth that "it is not about you" was a constant refrain that—for me—translated into "I gotta do something impactful," not for the few but for the many. That was one push towards global health. The fateful trigger to actually transition to global health was the death of my sister from malaria, which continues to be one of the most important concerns of global health.

When now I think about transplantation, I see it was what brought me close to bioethics, which for me is about fairness and reducing inequities—a large part of global health. Transplantation is about saving and improving lives by means that involve sacrifice, altruism, and a focus on the welfare of others; these are mirrored by the concern for others that is fundamental to global health. The transcending of borders in global health is reflected in the crossing of the immunity barrier and transcending the "me" in the "you" in organ transplantation. Both are in their ways about the garment of destiny: the recognition that ultimately we are one.

Much of global health, of course, is focused on the so-called social determinants of health: the conditions under which people are born, grow up, live, work, and age. Thinking back to the Tanzania of my childhood, I know that almost all African children were born under unhygienic conditions at home. Most mothers were malnourished; their infants were born programmed for chronic diseases later in life. What kind of a future is that?

Destined for failure? They went hungry when their mothers ran out of breast milk. Huge numbers died before the age of five. The majority did not go to school, wasting their childhoods in a grubbing existence that did not prepare them for a future.

Prior to independence, the British authorities who ruled Tanzania cared little for the welfare of the native Africans. Healthy, vibrant people with an education who dream "big dreams" are a terrible threat to a ruling status quo that benefits from a helpless subsistent population that believes it lacks authority over its own destiny: much easier to keep the harnessed oxen turning in slow circles round and round. Prior to independence, for instance, there were three educational systems established along racial lines in Tanzania for Europeans, Asians (Indians), and Africans. An infuriating and not at all isolated example of the appalling inequality of the system was the disbursement of funds that were realized from the sale of confiscated enemy property after the Second World War. European students were allocated 760 Tsh (Tanganyika shillings) each; Asian students received about 200 Tsh each. An African student was allocated 2 Tsh. (St. Michael's and St. George's School, in fact, was built in 1959 in Iringa, using these particular funds, for the education of white European children only; no comparable educational facilities were built for African children. Given the funding disparities, how would that have been possible? It is a reminder to me every day that when we hear about "children failing" we need to ask ourselves if it is not we who have failed them.) Schooling for the African majority was therefore abysmal, as was health care and water and sanitation. It is not surprising therefore that water-borne diseases were a constant threat. Millions died young, in poor heath, and in poverty. And the despair, hopelessness, and fatigue was passed on to the following generations.

"Not so very long ago," wrote Frantz Fanon in *The Wretched of the Earth,* his seminal autopsy of the dehumanizing effects of colonization, "the earth numbered two thousand million inhabitants: five hundred million men, and one thousand five hundred million natives. The former had the Word; the others had the use of it. Between the two there were hired kinglets, overlords, and a bourgeoisie, sham from beginning to end, which served as go-betweens."

My friend and colleague Omari at the Aswan Butchery who died of kidney disease was one of Fanon's ghosts—the living dead. I can still see his face today: despite the loss of protein through his ailing kidneys, the massive swelling of his body that made it difficult for him to move, the accompanying conditions for which he could not afford proper medications—despite all these—my memory of him is that he was always smiling. In the end he was too ill to ride his bicycle to get to work. All he could do was wait. Death came as a welcome relief.

I wonder what became of Omari's wife and children. One day I will go to Tanzania and look for them.

Chapter 19

An Ethical Frontier: Crossing a Personal Rubicon

Isn't it amazing that we are all made in God's image, and yet there is so much diversity among his people?

— Desmond Tutu

In 1994 a young Dutch woman, Gea De Wilt, was admitted to Sultan Qaboos University (SQU) Hospital in Muscat, Oman, where I worked. There she delivered a baby boy whom they named Wisse. He was born premature at just over thirty-three weeks' gestation and was immediately taken to the Pediatric Intensive Care Unit (PICU). Gea and her husband, Wim, asked me if I would consider transplanting Wisse's kidneys into an Omani child. I asked Gea to tell me about her son. She explained that she and her husband were working in Oman in the petroleum industry. For ten years they had been trying to conceive, and finally with the help of in-vitro fertilization (IVF) she had conceived. At thirty-three weeks, however, she went into premature labour and delivered what externally appeared a healthy boy. Unfortunately, the infant had serious medical issues, the most critical being hypotonia, meaning that his muscles were not working. He was so floppy he could not breathe on his own and had to be placed on a ventilator. He was also put on antibiotics but his condition continued to deteriorate. Further tests established that the problem was not the muscles themselves but a problem centralized in the brain; tests confirmed widespread pathological abnormalities indicating that recovery was not possible. A scan showed absence (agenesis) of the corpus callosum (ACC), the part of the brain that connects the left to the right hemispheres.

Omani and Dutch experts who were consulted agreed that the child's life could not be saved and advised the parents to allow the ventilator to be switched off. The parents were informed, and the excruciatingly difficult decision was made. However, the mother was determined that despite her terrible grief her doomed son's life might have some meaning. Was there anything that could be done? she asked.

A seventeen-month-old Omani boy, Ahmed, had been admitted to the nearby Royal Hospital under the care of Dr. Nabil al Lawati. Ahmed had a genetic condition that caused him to develop end-stage kidney failure at a very early age, and without a new kidney he would die. Would I consider performing a kidney transplant? The odds of success were extremely low—virtually no chance at all.

I stayed up all night thinking about the circumstances, drawing on almost everything I had learned during my training and experience as a surgeon, physician, scientist, transplantologist, and bioethicist. No kidney had ever been transplanted at thirty-three weeks. If we went ahead, we would be in no man's land. My paediatric nephrology colleague at the ministry of health's Royal Hospital, Dr. al Lawati, had no relevant experience. I had never transplanted or even assisted at a transplant where the kidneys were from such a small baby. To be honest, I was not sure such an operation was even possible. The kidneys, after all, were about the size of a pair of kidney beans. It was madness!

The mother insisted we try. Here at least was a small chance that parents of another child might be spared the grief and pain she and her husband were dealing with. Their strength, courage, and generosity were incredible and I find myself moved by it even now, all these years later.

We transferred Ahmed from the Royal Hospital to SQU Hospital, and ten days after Wisse was born we performed the operation to remove his kidneys. I was assisted by Drs. Qassim al Busaidi, Elijah Kehinde, and Mohan Rangaswamy. At this point, I recalled the struggles that a physician named Bill Hoffenberg, whom we will soon meet, had to deal with in diagnosing brain death in Cape Town back in 1968. That was during the pioneering days of heart surgery and Hoffenberg had to declare the potential donor, Clive Haupt, dead before the heart could be transplanted. That had been a hugely controversial decision, and not just for racial but ethical reasons. My case here was different. Hoffenberg had to deal with brain death in an adult. I now would have to deal with brain death in a pre-term infant, and there were no guidelines then on how to do this. It was perhaps the biggest and most delicate ethical issue I had faced up to that point in my career. I had to improvise.

Since there was no way of ascertaining brain death, I had agreed with the anaesthetist that at 10 A.M. he would switch off the ventilator and I would not start surgery until the heart had stopped, which it did a few minutes later. I waited a further five minutes after that and then asked the anaesthetist to try to resuscitate the baby, and only when that failed, and all the staff were convinced that the baby had died, did I start the surgery to remove the kidneys, beginning at 10:25 A.M.

Forty-five minutes later we had removed the two kidneys, which were attached to short segments of the aorta and vena cava.

We perfused them with cold solutions and put them on ice in a kidney dish. We carefully sutured the wound and Wisse was respectfully wheeled to the morgue. I remember wondering what the parents of this poor child must have been thinking. By this time Ahmed had been prepped and anaesthetized by Dr. Andre Luon and his team in an adjacent operating theatre and was waiting to receive the kidneys I had just removed from Wisse.

Because of the small size of the blood vessels, I needed magnifying optical loops to anastomose (join together) the aorta to an artery in Ahmed's pelvis called the iliac artery, and the vena cava to his iliac vein. I had to work relatively quickly since Ahmed was not in a good physical state to tolerate anaesthesia for long, and also because the donor kidneys, although now perfused and chilled, would continue to deteriorate somewhat until they were supplied with warm oxygenated blood from Ahmed's own body. When the vascular clamps that I had applied while performing the anastomoses were released, Ahmed's pink oxygenated blood immediately filled the kidneys, warming them and turning them into beautiful little bean-shaped and bean-sized organs. Wanting to reduce the likelihood of failure caused by twisting and kinking of the blood vessels, I pulled the kidneys up into the right side of the abdomen so the vessels would be fully straightened out, stitched their capsules together, and then stitched them both to the under-surface of the gall bladder to reduce the chances of them twisting round each other.

In normal transplant operations, once the vascular clamps are released, the kidneys immediately start producing urine. To me this is one of the most beautiful sights imaginable! In this case, that did not happen because the ethical demands to establish death and prolonging the period when the kidneys were not perfused with oxygenated blood meant that they had very likely suffered some damage.

The next big challenge was now looking after Ahmed post-transplant. Nabil and I shared this task, pooling our knowledge of critical care of patients, immunosuppression, metabolic care, and nephrology. All went well, and we soon transferred the recipient back to the Royal Hospital where, miracle of miracles, about a week after the transplant operation, the kidneys began to work, producing increasing amounts of more concentrated urine and keeping the little boy alive without dialysis.

The transplant entered the record book that is kept in the University of California, Los Angeles Paul Terasaki Laboratory as the youngest successful functionally enduring deceased-donor kidney transplant in history: the recipient, at seventeen months of age, had been the second-youngest recipient of a deceased-donor kidney transplant.

Despite the tradition of never bringing the donor's family together with the recipient's, we brought the two mothers together to celebrate. In fact, we have a beautiful photograph of the two mothers—looking very happy—with the smiling infant boy. It was a very proud day for me, but that is not what I remember most—not what I cherish.

"I would have given my life for his life," Gea wrote me many years later, "but it was not an option. It was so sad and tremendously difficult to give him up. We had tried about ten years to get children, finally he was there and he could be with us only a few days. What was the meaning of his life?"

For me this story is significant at several levels. It is about two families with completely different backgrounds, means, customs, cultures, and identities who were brought together under unbearably difficult circumstances; they connected on the most basic level imaginable: life and death. It was about a change in identity brought about by medical means. It was also the story of two incredibly brave mothers, one a European who wanted to save the life of an Omani child; the other Ahmed's mother, who jumped into the unknown to save the life of one of her nine children. I will never forget them or their humanity.

It is also a remarkable moment for me, because it brought to mind the legendary Bill Hoffenberg, closing another open loop in my life: the past and the present as if one.

Chapter 20

A Warrior on the Front Lines of Apartheid: Bill Hoffenberg

If a man hasn't discovered something that
he will die for, he isn't fit to live.
— Martin Luther King Jr.

One of the earliest poems I memorized when I was at high school in Iringa was by Edna St. Vincent Millay. It starts:

What's this of death, from you who never will die?
Think you the wrist that fashioned you in clay,
The thumb that set the hollow just that way
In your full throat and lidded the long eye
So roundly from the forehead, will let lie
Broken, forgotten, under foot some day
Your unimpeachable body, and so slay
The work he most had been remembered by?

Even now as an adult, when I am in the shower or on a flight, these lines come to me unbidden. The poem and its theme of immortality are linked in my mind to transplantation. What could be simpler than life and death? We exist, and one day the Grim Reaper arrives and we are pushed into the next dimension. But it isn't that simple, not now and not then. Many a night as a young doctor in Oxford, I would remove organs from brain-dead patients in nearby hospitals for transplantation. For one human being it is the end; for another it is an extension: the precious medical gift of borrowed time. None of us is unaware of what awaits us eventually. I imagine we all have a way of creating leeway, however, when it comes to how we define "eventually." "Well, later rather than sooner!" we joke. What we mean is *Not now and can we just change the topic, please?* Most of us in our professional lives, of course, never have an opportunity to determine the *now* of death. Bill Hoffenberg was among the very few—the first—who did.

I first met Bill face to face in Kuala Lumpur towards the end of the 1980s. It was at a meeting of the Royal College of Physicians of London. He gave the presidential address, looking sartorially posh and official in his college gown, academic hat, ribbons, and medals. The Brits love pomp and circumstance, as obviously did the Malaysian hosts. He looked very distinguished. I asked to talk to him.

"Professor Hoffenberg, my name is Abdallah Daar."

He looked at me. "You the transplant surgeon and bioethicist?" The accent had distinct but distant South African elements.

"Yes, and I went to Wolfson College, Oxford, so we have something in common!" It was a cheeky attempt at fraternity; he had actually served as president of Wolfson from 1985 (just after I left Oxford) to 1993, while all I had been was a mere graduate student. I was deeply flattered, however, that he not only had heard of me but also knew of my work in depth—especially in the area of transplant ethics. We talked shop for a bit.

"My work, of course, hasn't generated the headlines yours did," I joked. But he waved away my modesty.

"There is so much to be done in transplant ethics, so many vexing issues. Maybe we should pool resources and study these difficult issues some day?" In fact, that is exactly what we went on to do when we created together an entity called the International Forum for Transplant Ethics (IFTE).

It was an honour for me that in addition to that IFTE work, and despite our age difference, we became close friends; he became another hugely important and influential mentor to me, for there was much to admire and learn from Bill. He was one of the most gifted physicians I ever met, but in many ways it is Bill "the man" whom I admired most; it was his basic decency and his commitment to social and racial justice that was a model for me as I progressed through my life and career.

In his work developing standards for ethical treatment of patients and in defining brain death, Bill had chaired a group of the Royal Medical Colleges of the UK to consider problems for determining death in children. The recommendations they came up with, however, had not covered infants born at thirty-three weeks' gestation who would become potential cadaveric (i.e., dead) donors ten days after birth—a situation I encountered and have described in the previous chapter.

I recall now a long conversation with Bill at dinner in the Cotswolds near Oxford. We had been discussing all day the ins and outs of brain death but never touched on the religious aspects because most of our IFTE group were skeptics about religion, if not outright professed atheists, like Bill himself.

"Have you ever thought about what happens to the person after death?" I asked Bill.

"Nothing. No continuation of any sort. The body decomposes and is recycled. That's it."

For someone like me, who entertained at least the possibility of transcendence in the sense of experience beyond the physical world alone, his characteristically blunt and honest dismissal of an afterlife was a sobering splash of cold water. Did I agree?

I wasn't sure. Many of my colleagues believe as Bill did, but I have never been able myself to discount the fact that something—some would call it the soul, or some form of the individual's memory—persists in an identifiable form. As I understand it, some Buddhist traditions that believe in reincarnation/rebirth call this the *avacya* (inexpressible) self, which migrates from one life to another; most Buddhist traditions hold that *Vijnana* (a person's consciousness) exists as an evolving continuum and is the mechanistic basis of what undergoes rebirth.

Even as science resolves one mystery after another, I am not sure it is capable of resolving the ultimate mystery. Science is an incomparable tool for answering the question *how*. But what about the *why*? For me, the notion of death as the final act is simply too bleak and too unfulfilling to serve as an explanation; is it really so clear-cut that there is nothing there, there? I have heard my friends say, "You are only saying that because you fear death." I disagree. Fear of death and a wonder at the possibility of transcendence are not necessarily equivalent. And to be honest, I accept my "I don't know" as a beautiful and even thrilling tribute to the magisterial wonder of the universe. "Where a man's metaphysics comes to an end," wrote Étienne Gilson, "his religion begins." It is of course one of the greatest existential unknowns, and it doesn't seem that we will ever be able to get confirmatory messages from across that ultimate barrier between life and death.

And isn't the simple fact of transplanting organs from the dead to the living not a practical form of transcendence? What do I mean, for instance, when I talk about *Clive Haupt's* heart (see below)—in the possessive: *his* heart and not someone else's? The recipient's, for instance? When the pathologist was examining the cold body of Philip Blaiberg, who had died with Clive

Haupt's heart in his chest, whose heart was being examined in the post mortem room—Clive's or Philip's? Is it really purely a semantic distinction? Meaning, in short, no real distinction at all?

We have digressed a bit. Let's go back to the sixties during the pioneering early days of heart transplantation. Bill was working as a consultant physician at the world-renowned Groote Schuur Hospital in Cape Town, where the colourful, controversial Christiaan Barnard had performed the first heart transplant in the world. In 1967—the year Barnard performed the first heart transplant—Bill was served a banning order by the South African government for his opposition to the apartheid regime.

The banning order essentially destroyed his career in South Africa; he was forbidden to see patients, teach, do research, or write, and there were many other curtailments of his human rights. These orders were used by the regime to silence and destroy the careers of those who were banned. There was a huge public outcry in support of Bill by students, academics, and others, including some from the then-racist Stellenbosch University, and from Harry Oppenheimer, chancellor of the University of Cape Town (UCT), who was a long-time chairman of De Beers, a legacy of Cecil Rhodes. Oppenheimer was born Jewish but later converted to Christianity. None of these protests changed the banning order. It was to come into effect on January 2, 1968.

But before then, Bill was to enter the annals of medical history. On the night of January 2, 1968, the surgeons who would perform the second heart transplant in history were anxious to get on with removing donor Clive Haupt's heart for its transplantation to the patient. From the surgeon's standpoint, any delay could seriously impair the viability of the heart. They needed the heart while it was still beating. The minutes ticked by, and members of the transplant team paced restlessly up and down the corridor, glaring at Bill through the ICU window.

"God!" roared the head of the surgery department impatiently. "What sort of a heart are you going to give us, Bill?" Large numbers of reporters and photographers from around the world were waiting outside the hospital for news as well. The pressure and urgency for Bill to declare Clive Haupt clinically dead was intense and palpable.

Bill was in a state of extreme and almost exquisite anguish. He recalls having almost a complete sense of helplessness and inadequacy; the science of diagnosing brain death under these conditions did not exist; he was essentially flying blind. "There were no accepted scientific criteria that allowed one to pronounce as dead a patient whose heart was still beating," he wrote in a memoir. The media was in a frenzy, of course, and the reputations of not a few surgeons—as well as the hospital—were at stake. By no means was public opinion unanimous even about the idea of transplantation. What if he was premature in his declaration? Who was he to literally play God? "After a sleepless night and three visits to the bedside [of Clive Haupt] to satisfy myself that there were no signs (other than a beating heart) I acceded to the request."

Bill Hoffenberg entered history as the first person to diagnose brain death under such conditions. (I found myself facing this complex and complicated ethical dilemma many times in my own career as a transplant surgeon.) Barnard went on to perform the transplant, which was covered in the media all over the world as a huge success, but was in fact premature, for the field was not yet ready and much research needed to be done. The recipient survived and was seen to be swimming in a carefully staged photograph two weeks later. He died not long after that, just as the first transplant recipient had. Many other surgeons around the world tried to do heart transplants the following year; they all failed and heart transplantation was set back by about a decade. It took off again partly because of research at Stanford by Norman Shumway. (I was honoured in 1995 to introduce Shumway at a Jewish Medical Ethics conference in San Francisco.)

On the day of Bill's forced departure from South Africa, March 28, 1968, twenty thousand people came to say goodbye to him and his wife, Margaret, at Cape Town airport. They were heading for London, England, and a life of glory. At the airport, Clive McBride, a black clergyman who was a friend of the Hoffenbergs, shouted, "Bill, we shall overcome!" followed by the crowd singing the great civil rights anthem of the same name.

Martin Luther King Jr., of course, had used "We Shall Overcome" many times; he recited the words from it in his final sermon delivered in Memphis before he died. In an earlier speech King had said:

> We shall overcome. We shall overcome. Deep in my heart I do believe we shall overcome. And I believe it because somehow the arc of the moral universe is long, but it bends towards justice.

Reverend King's quote always reminds me of a saying by the great Islamic scholar Seyyed Hossein Nasr: "Justice is inseparable from truth in human life."

* * *

In 1965 Bill had written to King inviting him to come to South Africa to give the annual TB Davie Memorial Lecture. King accepted the invitation but the apartheid government refused to grant him a visa and he was unable to go to South Africa at all before he himself was gunned down by a white racist, James Earl Ray, on Sunday, April 4, 1968, in Memphis.

Bill did not return to South Africa again for twenty-four years. His banning order in fact forbade him from returning. He did not witness first-hand the era of Nelson Mandela, who became the international public symbol of the freedom struggle against the police state and its brutality and violence. He missed seeing Mandela freed in 1990 after being incarcerated on Robben Island for eighteen of his twenty-seven years in prison. The redefinition of Bill's life trajectory later led to his and my paths crossing, although because of his early interest in organ transplantation and therefore in transplant ethics, I am convinced our paths would have crossed anyway.

Many years later, Bill and I became founding members of the International Forum for Transplant Ethics (IFTE), a group initiated in the 1990s by transplant surgeon Robert Sells of Liverpool. IFTE was a unique, dogma-challenging group of seven scholars from surgery, philosophy, law, ethics, and anthropology.

Bill was born in South Africa in 1923. His parents were Jewish but Bill was an atheist all his adult life. Interestingly, his father at one time had owned a pig farm, a fact of biography not dissimilar to my own and something I felt we shared. Bill was a tall, handsome, athletic, and very smart boy who got into medical school at UCT at the age of sixteen. At seventeen he forged his father's signature to pretend he was older so he could get into the army during the Second World War. He served in Italy as a paramedic and was later stationed in Algeria, where he led a rather dissolute life playing poker, drinking, and visiting the Casbah. After the bombing of Hiroshima and Nagasaki, he returned to South Africa, was demobilized, and went on to complete medical school.

From early on Bill crusaded to right the wrongs of the apartheid regime. He worked in hospitals caring for black patients, dared to call them "Mister," and fought to increase the numbers and improve the conditions of black medical students. In 1951 he went to London, England, to train for the MRCP exams, during which time he worked with the brother of novelist Graham Greene, Raymond, who was a consultant endocrinologist. He returned to South Africa in 1953 and over the next decades continued to fight for the rights of black people, championing educational equity and helping to provide legal aid to prisoners of conscience. He set up the first medical nuclear physics unit in South Africa to study thyroid diseases and malnutrition, especially kwashiorkor, a condition I later encountered frequently as a medical student in Uganda.

Bill's wife, Margaret, launched charity organizations to provide food for starving black kids in Cape Town (talk of scarcity in the face of plenty!) and Bill was working hard to empower the vulnerable and the forgotten. But he was now coming under the surveillance of the apartheid regime. His mail was opened and he was watched all the time, even at home at 1 Exeter Avenue, Bishopscourt. Their home became one of the very few places where whites could be found mingling with black Africans. It was the focus of many social occasions and visits by figures opposed to the apartheid regime, including author Alan Paton, who wrote the best-selling book *Cry, the Beloved Country.*

The whites wanted the juiciest riches of that beautiful and bountiful country, which they considered their Canaan. They feared that the Africans might ultimately deprive them of their God-given right to those riches, but the Africans didn't, largely because at the brink a black knight in shining armour called Mandela came to make a difference. As for Christianity, the Dutch Reformed Church, to which much of the white population belonged, reading and misreading John Calvin, actually supported and condoned the system of apartheid. Much later they recanted.

When he moved to London in 1968, Bill worked with another hero of mine, Peter Medawar, who like Michael DeBakey was of Lebanese origin. Medawar won the Nobel Prize in Physiology or Medicine in 1960 for his immunology work that set the scene for organ transplantation. Medawar (Mudawwar in Arabic), like DeBakey (Dabaghi), was an inspiration to me also because his ethnic background did not hold him back at all and I kept asking myself: *Then why would mine?* Bill took up the Chair of Medicine at the University of Birmingham in 1972, where he taught and mentored so many African students, including Babatunde Osotimehin, future minister of health of Nigeria and later the executive director of the United Nations Population Fund. Another was William Makgoba, the controversial, brilliant scientist who had been our neighbour at Wolfson College, Oxford, and who went on to head the South African Medical Research Council before becoming vice-chancellor of the University of KwaZulu-Natal. William did his DPhil laboratory work at Oxford down the corridor from where I was doing research for my own DPhil.

During his time in the United Kingdom, Bill continued to fight for the rights of South Africans and other oppressed peoples, including raising funds to investigate and bring to justice the perpetrators of the horrendous killing on September 12, 1977, of anti-apartheid activist Steve Biko while in police detention in South Africa. He also helped establish, among several others, a medical foundation for the care of victims of torture.

The one issue that truly brought him and me to work together was transplant ethics. We had both become disillusioned with the groupthink prevalent among many of our colleagues and established IFTE. Robert Sells and I had previously been commissioned by The Transplantation Society to go to India to do a study of the very complex and difficult issue of buying and selling kidneys for transplantation, and we learned a huge amount about transplant ethics. Our intense, probing working method in IFTE led to conclusions that made IFTE controversial from the very beginning. We worked on many subjects and published several papers, often in *The Lancet*. We worked on brain death and the persistent vegetative state; on presumed consent laws; and on commerce in organs. We dealt with other complex issues related to race, ethnicity, and culture in organ transplantation. We condemned the UK's political stance that government-appointed agents should inspect the motives of living donors to exclude commercial or other gain. (The UK law was subsequently revised to allow voluntary organ donation to be steered by doctors along conventional ethical rules.)

I found Bill to be always pleasant, thoughtful, well informed, thorough, and uncompromising when important principles were concerned. He was never overbearing, he was fun to be with, and the evening dinners after our intense IFTE working sessions were occasions to look forward to. Shahina met Bill several times and, like almost everyone else, especially women, was charmed by him. The one constant in Bill's outlook was his sensitivity to inequities and injustice. He understood instinctively the need to cross thresholds and the oneness of our species, although we are beset by our inability to listen to one another with humility.

"There is something curious that happens to some people," he wrote. "They have to cross a certain area, a line in their lives. Until then they tend to live contented quiet lives without concerning themselves about broader issues. But at some stage they do cross the line, and then all sorts of things fall into place and they begin to concern themselves more in the health or welfare of communities."

The task is to get people to cross that line. Bill showed us over and over again how to cross that line, boldly and humanely. The poet Longfellow wrote that "when a great man dies / For years beyond our ken, / The light he leaves behind him lies / Upon the paths of men."

Bill Hoffenberg transcended his own final threshold on April 22, 2007. I miss him still.

Chapter 21

Finding My Calling: A Global Health Commitment

I think what everyone should be doing, before it's too late, is committing themselves to what they really want to do with their lives.

— MATTHIEU RICARD, *The Quantum and the Lotus*

You have begun to hearken to that call, but for most people it is an unnoticed voice in the innermost recesses of their hearts.

— SHAYKH NAZIM ADIL AL-HAQQANI

In 1994 I was still working happily at Sultan Qaboos University in Oman as professor of surgery and head of the transplant program, with no specific plans to move into the field of global health. By then, I had developed a major interest in bioethics, especially the ethics of organ transplantation. As a result I was invited to a conference in Bangkok that year, and while there an event occurred that would radically alter my career and life trajectory. But before I discuss that, we need to travel back in time about thirty years.

As a medical student in the late 1960s and early 1970s at Makerere University in Kampala, Uganda, I was, as I have said, riveted to news of pioneering developments in heart surgery by the likes of Christiaan Barnard, Denton Cooley, Michael DeBakey, and others around the world. One of those "others" was a Japanese surgeon by the name of Juro Wada. What came to be known as the Wada case, will be my entry point for a topic that has become of great interest: science and faith.

On August 7, 1968, Dr. Wada performed the first heart transplant in Japan. Heart transplantation was at that point still very much a pioneering effort. Successes had been few. In fact, Dr. Wada's patient survived for eighty-three days before dying. The case, however, turned out to be very controversial for other reasons as well, and it would be those other reasons that had both practical and philosophical importance for me in the years to come.

Bill Hoffenberg had been forced to confront a very difficult decision in the Clive Haupt case, namely, how do we define death; what physiological conditions need to be met in order to declare a patient dead. And most important, what if we are wrong? Waiting too long to declare a patient dead was a huge problem for transplant surgeons like Christiaan Barnard with regard to organ viability. But the far bigger problem for Bill Hoffenberg was a premature declaration of death.

In Dr. Wada's case, he faced considerable backlash and uproar because of the way he applied the concept of brain death. Japanese culture was—and in many ways still is—culturally and religiously resistant to the idea of harvesting cadaveric organs for transplantation (I would confront the same resistance when working in Muslim Oman later). Secondly, Wada himself made the decision to declare the donor brain dead rather than leave the decision up to a disinterested third party. It was unethical then and would still be considered totally unethical today. He was derided as a cowboy, celebrity hound, a fortune hunter, and—most chillingly—a mere doctor playing God. He was criminally charged, and the scandal threatened to ruin not only Dr. Wada's career but also the cause of human organ transplantation in general. Charges were dropped eventually, but the deeply held bias among Japanese against the procedure endured. In fact, Japan to this day remains overwhelmingly skeptical and distrustful about transplantation. Compared to countries where organ transplantation is common and even routine, Japan still lags near the bottom in total number.

I was not much aware of these details in 1968, of course. For me it was simply an exciting new development in my chosen field of medicine, but not of direct consequence because I had not yet entered the field of transplantation. The issues confronted by Dr. Wada, however, would be the same that Bill Hoffenberg would have to confront and that I would be forced to deal with years later as well.

* * *

The weather in Bangkok in February 1994 was ideal, as long as your definition of ideal is hot. For me—a native African—I was in heaven. Temperatures ranged from 24°C to 33°C. I had been invited to address the first International Congress of the International Medical Parliamentarians Organization. Organ transplantation was one of the five themes of the congress. My talk was entitled "Forty Years of Organ Transplantation: Successes and Challenges."

Bangkok was overcrowded, and the traffic was an impassable snarl of honking cars and buses, small lorries, and bicycles. About thirty of us were in a coach slowly wending its way from our hotel in central Bangkok to a big conference centre in another part of the city. Despite the interminable coach journey, we made it on time and gathered in a large conference hall. At the appointed time, I stepped to the stage carrying my carousel of slides (this was before the widespread use of PowerPoint!).

The lights had been dimmed, and I could just make out faces of people in the audience.

After reviewing the history of transplantation, I embarked on a discussion outlining the role of religion and culture in the field of organ transplantation. I focused on Japan and its Shinto religion, as this was the most apt example of the interaction between religion and transplantation.

Shinto is as old as Japanese culture and is an important part of its ethnic identity. In Japan, Buddhism itself has been influenced by the native Shinto tradition and by other folk beliefs, which are different from those of China or Korea. A foundational element of Shintoism is reverence for purity: all gods are pleased with purity and angered by impurity and pollution. A corpse is the ultimate polluted matter, hence the requirement that purification rites be performed prior to burial. The dead human body is so impure, in fact, that Shinto has been reluctant to address it and has not even developed rites to handle it, but Buddhism, with which Shinto co-exists in Japan, has developed rituals and ceremonies for the dead and it is these that are used in Shinto.

The upshot is that in Japan it is very difficult to obtain consent from bereaved families for organ donation, dissection, or diagnostic post mortem examinations. In fact, even if a person has requested his remains be donated to a medical school for dissection, the family often will bar access.

Dr. Wada, as I mentioned earlier, was accused of inappropriately using brain death criteria to diagnose death in his donor's beating heart. The donor had been brought into hospital after having been involved in a drowning accident. Subsequent to the transplant operation, doubts were raised about the level of care the patient had received prior to being declared dead. Questions were raised as well regarding the severity of the recipient's condition. Had his condition *truly* warranted the radical decision to transplant?

Accusations were levelled that medical records germane to the case had been altered. Wada himself emerged from under the cloud and went on to have an internationally distinguished career. However, at least in Japan, public trust for cadaveric organ transplantation remained low. In fact, in the aftermath of the Wada controversy, cadaveric donation was declared illegal and the transplant field was set back by three decades. As mentioned above, the rate of cadaveric donation in Japan is significantly lower than in the West. I read recently that as many as 14,000 people in Japan are on the waiting list for an organ—kidneys mostly. The cultural distrust of transplantation is so high even now that very few doctors enter the field. The result, of course, is that most patients awaiting transplants survive only by dialysis or obtain organs illegally. Currently there is less than one transplant per million population in Japan, the lowest rate in the world for an industrialized country; in the United States, by contrast, there are twenty-six transplants. When I was growing up in Africa, the most common causes of death were related to poverty, poor nutrition and hygiene, and inadequate medical treatment. Japan is one of the richest and most sophisticated countries in the world; the conundrum I faced was very different from what I knew from my childhood. The issue in Japan was, and continues to be, religion.

I wonder, is there ever a reason for a human being to die unnecessarily? Should religious or cultural beliefs and attitudes be allowed to cause unnecessary death?

At any rate, at the end of my presentation I went back to my seat in the front row. After a little while, a middle-aged European approached me and asked if I would come with her to be introduced to someone at the back of the hall.

"Of course," I said, and followed her. The man I met was a tall, bespectacled, distinguished-looking Japanese who introduced himself as Dr. Hiroshi Nakajima, director-general of the World Health Organization.

"It is indeed an honour!" I responded.

He flattered me with enthusiastic comments about my presentation. He said he especially was impressed with my knowledge of Japanese culture. We talked for a few minutes. I thanked him and we parted. I still had no sense of why it had been so important for him to meet me. No worries! I felt great that I had made such a good impression. About two weeks later, I received a letter from Dr. Nakajima asking me if I would come to meet him at WHO headquarters in Geneva.

"Geneva!" I exclaimed with a grin. "Absolutely!" I still had no clue what he had in mind. But who would refuse a trip to the headquarters of global health?

I didn't have long to wait until his intentions became clear. I was ushered into his office at WHO headquarters. He wondered if I would be willing to assist the organization?

"With what kind of issues?" I asked.

"Difficult ethical issues," he answered.

I hardly needed further coaxing. We talked a few more minutes, and it became clear from what Dr. Nakajima was outlining that this was indeed an opportunity not only that I could not resist but one that had dropped from the sky like an answer to a prayer.

First, I would be appointed chair of an expert working group at WHO looking at potential infectious disease risks of xenotransplantation (the transplantation of organs from one species to another, such as from pig to human—there may be huge infectious disease risks). Over the years I became involved in a number of different projects including non-communicable diseases and mental health. My work with WHO, often indirectly, led to work with other United Nations agencies, including UNESCO, where I was appointed to its International Bioethics Committee. Much of our discussions there were predicated on the Universal Declaration on Human Rights. The latest substantive appointment was by the UN secretary-general himself, as a member of his Scientific Advisory Board.

One project in particular had crucial implications for me. In July 1996 scientists from the Roslin Institute at the University of Edinburgh stunned the world with the announcement that for the first time a sheep ("Dolly," named for Dolly Parton's breasts because the original cell that was cloned came from a mammary gland!) had been cloned in the laboratory from DNA extracted from an adult mammary cell. Not surprisingly, the announcement ignited a typhoon of controversy between those for cloning and those against. Dr. Nakajima wanted someone who could do a wide-ranging review of the field, examine its implications for public health, and come up with some recommendations.

When he asked me to undertake this task in 1998, I was still grieving for my sister Alwiya, who had died a few months before. I had taken a sabbatical leave to reflect on what I wanted to do in the future, and to teach and do research at Stanford Center for Biomedical Ethics. It was a good time for me to take on the research for the WHO work, and at Nakajima's request, I collaborated with the brilliant French medical geneticist François Mattei to write the WHO report that came to be known as the Daar–Mattei report (Mattei went on to become France's minister of health).

Bernard Dickens, a colleague I had met at WHO headquarters in Geneva, had heard that I was working on this report and invited me to take up an appointment as visiting professor at the University of Toronto's Faculty of Law, where I would teach a course on medical law with him and have some quiet time to work on the report. Our son Marwan and daughter Lamees were already studying in Canada, near Toronto, and I absolutely relished the idea of being that close to my children for six months. That made me decide to accept Bernard's invitation and I relocated to Toronto.

It was yet another of a series of moves that changed my life. The research for WHO revealed to me that almost no one was paying serious attention to the huge potential of the new scientific developments in biotechnology (genomics and other life sciences) to solving health problems affecting millions in the developing world. Once I understood this critical missing link between cutting-edge biotechnology and global health, I knew I had found a way to enter the field of global health.

In the way that life trajectories cross and intersect in meaningful ways, it was also the occasion for one of the happiest meetings I have ever had. Peter Singer would become not only an esteemed colleague with whom I would work for two wonderful decades but also a dear friend. This was the beginning of my actual move from surgery to global health. I was invited by the dean of the University of Toronto medical school, David Naylor, to come and take up a position as professor of public health sciences. It was the knowledge of that missing link and its implications that I would build upon to initiate a research, capacity-building, and innovation program with Peter Singer in Toronto. It truly was an opportunity for me to start thinking about positive change on a big scale—well, bigger than I had been accustomed to.

Chapter 22

The Next Einstein Will Be African

An imbalance between rich and poor is the oldest and most fatal ailment of all republics.

— Plutarch

But being an optimist isn't about knowing that life used to be worse. It's about knowing how life can get better. And that's what really fuels our optimism.

— Bill and Melinda Gates

When I switched career paths from surgery to global health and moved permanently to the University of Toronto in the year 2000, I hoped that in some admittedly small but not negligible way I could help to change the health and social circumstances brought on by poverty and discriminatory colonial policies in developing countries, particularly in African countries like my country of birth, Tanzania.

The health and social needs of the majority Africans were great when I was growing up in Tanzania. Children and adults, for instance, could go through life without adequate sight simply because they had no access to eyeglasses. Children were dying from type 1 diabetes because their families could not afford insulin or, worse, they just died because there was no one to diagnose the condition. Women would develop cancers that led them to early, painful deaths, sometimes lingering for years without access to analgesia. In some cases it wasn't just lack of access to health care: basic food stored for a while at home would become contaminated with fungi that caused liver cancer.

Frequent droughts meant no food security. Infant and maternal mortality rates are incredibly high in the absence of even basic health care. My mother delivered nine children without one death and she survived to tell the story: that would be an impossible achievement among our fellow poor citizens in Tanzania. Our lives (and we were not the most privileged) were so very different from theirs.

While we at least had some form of toilets and access to clean water when growing up, the majority of Tanzanians in the villages that we did not see were dying from water-borne diseases like cholera, typhoid, worm infestations, and so much dysentery that suffering from gastrointestinal symptoms was the norm. Millions of children in the developing world died from diarrhoea and pneumonia, and while the numbers have dropped by now, these are still common causes of death in children under the age of five years. Intestinal parasites like roundworm and hookworm were the norm rather than the exception (hookworm was—and continues to be—a very common cause of anaemia). Malaria killed children by the millions in poor countries and, again, while the total number of malaria fatalities has dropped over the years, the mosquitoes are still around and malaria deaths may rise again. Contaminated water caused then, and continues to cause now, many forms of diarrhoeal and other diseases, accounting for more than three million deaths a year, mostly in developing countries.

All the poverty, all the desperation, all the poor health I could discern as a teenager in Tanzania was preparing me, mostly subconsciously, for the work I was to do in global health beginning from around the year 2000. I could see direct links from the very poor health care for the majority African Tanzanians to the efforts to improve those conditions on a large scale once I embarked on global health.

As we began our work in global health in the year 2000, we were faced with grim statistics, thinking it cannot be right that every second of every day four women around the world give birth, but about every minute one of those women dies from complications of pregnancy and childbirth, mostly in the developing world. In Sweden, the risk of a woman dying during pregnancy and childbirth is 1 in 17,400; in Afghanistan, it is 1 in 8. But incredibly such disparities exist even in the United States today. In New York City, black women are twelve times more likely to die from childbirth-related causes than are white women—these higher rates of death and complications are not only a result of long-standing disparities in wealth and access to good facilities, but also compounded by racism and unconscious biases in health care.

Such disparities are wrong, plain and simple, so I wanted to play a part in the global effort to reduce them. It was a deep moral issue for both Peter Singer and me. Both of us believe deeply in the simple but profound motto of the Bill and Melinda Gates Foundation: Every life has equal value. And we both were touched by Dr. Martin Luther King Jr.'s famous "Letter from Birmingham Jail" in which he wrote: "We are caught in an inescapable network of mutuality, tied in a single garment of destiny. Whatever affects one directly, affects all indirectly."

If we succeeded in our mission, the result could be thrilling. Imagine what the world would be like if we could improve health in the developing world. What if a child in poverty had the food she needed to grow up healthy and strong? What if the child suffering from a deadly but easily cured infection had the vaccine he needed? Or if his family could afford something as simple as a mosquito net? Or a pair of eyeglasses? What if these unlucky children—and there are still millions of them around the world—had a chance instead of little or no chance? Who might they become? A path-breaking scientist who solves the problem of Third World droughts, perhaps, or a world leader who brokers lasting peace in the Middle East, or a philanthropist who funds schools and universities for deserving students—boys and girls—in poor areas of the world.

Peter and I have now been working for over two decades to achieve these goals (some of our work is described in our 2011 book *The Grandest Challenge: Taking Life-Saving Science from Lab to Village*). We have worked with the Gates Foundation and others to deliver the latest scientific advances in the lab to the villages, towns, and cities in developing countries. In 2010 we launched Grand Challenges Canada (GCC), a not-for-profit organization supported largely by the Government of Canada for funding global health science, technology, and social innovation; Peter has served as the CEO and I as its chief scientific and ethics officer and chair of its International Scientific Advisory Board—and we were, of course, both members of its governing board. As we had hoped, our efforts attracted the attention of many wonderful global health advocates. What was most gratifying, though, was the support that came from Microsoft founder Bill Gates. I know better than most that the generous commitments of organizations like the Bill and Melinda Gates Foundation have undoubtedly changed the face of global health, but not just by pouring in vast sums of money for research, innovation, health systems improvement, purchase of vaccines and medicines, and many other areas, but also because of the thoughtfulness with which Bill and

Melinda do all this. They work very hard at what they do; giving away money is not as easy as it sounds! I have not met Melinda, but have met Bill a few times, and what impressed me most about him is his vast knowledge about the subjects with which he engages. On one occasion I was talking with him about malaria—a disease whose eradication is very close to my heart—and he turned to me and said, "You know, a day will come when we will defeat this scourge of malaria. We are funding people to develop incredible tools for this, and others are coming up with some crazy ways of dealing with malaria." He was referring, among others, to his colleague and former Microsoft executive Nathan Myhrvold, who founded a company, Intellectual Ventures LLC, that buys and aggregates patents; their own labs have developed a tool called the Photonic Fence that uses low-cost sensor and laser technology to identify, track, and kill mosquitoes.

GCC funds mostly young people with outstanding ideas on how to solve grand challenges in global health. We have three major targeted research and innovation funding programs: Saving Lives at Birth, Saving Brains, and Global Mental Health. Some of these were in partnerships with organizations like the Bill and Melinda Gates Foundation, USAID, the UK's DFID (Department for International Development), the US National Institute of Mental Health, and the government of Norway. GCC became the world's largest funder of global mental health innovation and made significant contributions to reducing maternal mortality and saving the lives of young children and helping ensure they grow up healthy and without mental impairment. With our younger colleagues we also pioneered dealing with difficult ethical, legal, and social issues related to global health, and we have been working with the Gates Foundation on these kinds of issues since 2003.

In this way we, and many others, have contributed to the international effort to improve health in the developing world, and it's making a difference. For example, in the developing world not too long ago children born with cataracts or adults who developed cataracts often had no access to existing treatment options and would go blind. Increasingly now, they get access to a simple surgical procedure that corrects the problem and restores healthy sight for the rest of their lives. The question is how to increase the numbers of expert professionals who can deal with the huge existing backlogs of people with cataracts, and increase the facilities where they can perform these operations. About a decade ago, I had an opportunity to make a research trip to southern India to study the Aravind Eye Care System, accompanied by Gates Foundation members Fil Randazzo and Kristi Anthony. The Aravind Eye Care System has been described as the world's greatest business case for compassion. Harvard Business School uses its success story as a teaching case study. It is a remarkable system that treats the majority of its thousands of patients annually for free, but charges a reasonable fee to those who can afford to pay. Its outreach program to small villages, its patient-centred approach, its incredibly efficient logistics system, and its dedicated nurses and doctors have all become legendary. It has perhaps the lowest complication rate for cataract surgery in the world. And it's profitable, while charging 1/100th of what it would cost in Toronto to treat cataracts. I could see that such a system could make a huge difference in Africa, and I began planning with my esteemed colleague Dr. Kaushik Ramaiya, to introduce it in Tanzania. Recent government policy changes aimed at reducing corruption and increasing tax collection introduced by the president of Tanzania, John Magufuli, have resulted in a huge increase in government funding of health care, and it seems our dream of bringing the Aravind system and its efficiencies to the country, training more ophthalmologists and specialist paramedics, buying more equipment, and so forth will soon be realized without financial assistance from foreign donors.

The number of children dying before the age of five years has dropped from more than twelve million a year to less than six million in just over two decades, despite an increase in the world's population. In total the lives of more than 122 million children under the age of five years have been saved in the past twenty-five years. Maternal mortality has also dropped dramatically. Most major infectious diseases have come under control in most parts of the world, including in parts of Africa. Immunization with vaccines is the single most important public health measure to save children's lives, so it is gratifying to see that more than 86 percent of children worldwide now receive at least the basic vaccines. That saves lives but also for every dollar spent on childhood vaccines there is a return of $44 in economic benefits: a virtuous cycle that counteracts the vicious cycles of poverty.

The Grand Challenges approach/platform has a number of characteristics: ease of the grant application process; partnerships for generating ideas and funding; achieving rapid impact; a focus not just on science and technology innovation but also on social and business innovation; and moving rapidly from proven pilot projects to scaled-up solutions that are adopted by health care systems or require smart partnering with the private sector to develop and bring those solutions to market. This powerful platform has evolved into a global partnership, and a number of other countries have joined the network, including Peru, India, Israel, China, Japan, Thailand, and Ethiopia. This networked community meets every year to share best practices and listen to young scientists describe their global health innovations.

One of the more satisfying outcomes has been the launch last year of Grand Challenges Africa, on whose advisory board at the African Academy of Sciences I am proud to serve as chair.

We must understand one thing: although the speed of improvement of health in developing countries has itself been accelerating, the improvement itself is almost always incremental, taking time. Millions of children's lives have been saved, but there are still one million babies who die every year on the day they are born, and 2.5 million die in their first month of life.

We have made great progress against infectious diseases; for example, polio may be eradicated in the next few years (largely with the help of Rotary International and the Gates Foundation). However, there are emerging ones like the Ebola and Zika viruses that have come to haunt us. Large numbers of children still die from pneumonia and diarrhoea. And even old scourges like tuberculosis haven't yet been adequately controlled.

And although the focus, even in most developing countries, is shifting to chronic non-communicable diseases, which account for most premature deaths in the world, we seem to be losing the battle with some of them. These chronic diseases, which include type 2 diabetes, cardiovascular diseases (like heart disease and stroke), many types of cancers, and chronic lung diseases, take their largest toll in developing countries. The difficulty in controlling them is due to our inability to influence behaviour and address the social determinants of health, often in the face of unrelenting pressure from industries (such as beverage and tobacco) and poor government policies. So now from the vantage point of my membership on the board of the World Diabetes Foundation, I can see the magnitude and frightening rate of increase of the type 2 diabetes pandemic; with all its complications, including eye disease, kidney disease, and peripheral vascular disease often leading to gangrene and amputations, this pandemic will hugely strain the budgets and health care systems of most countries in the world, especially those of developing countries. Smoking tobacco alone is projected to kill one billion people this century if not checked; smoking, unfortunately, is increasing in poor countries, pushed by tobacco companies chasing profits over human health. Obesity is increasing throughout the world, not just in rich countries, and we don't really know how to stop that epidemic, especially among children and adolescents. Or rather we know what works in theory but fail to implement the solutions. The interplay between behaviour and genes is complex in most cases. When I was on the board of directors of Genome Canada, another major Government of Canada–funded research and innovation funding organization, I tried hard to ensure the interests of developing countries were taken into account whenever we were funding large research projects.

In Africa recently, an initiative has been brought about largely through the efforts of the US National Institutes of Health (NIH) and the Wellcome Trust of the UK. A specific African consortium called H3Africa (Human Heredity and Health) is already making a huge difference in research, capacity building, scientific training, and biobanking. An African post-doctoral program funded by the African Academy of Sciences, the US NIH, and the Bill and Melinda Gates Foundation has already been established and this too will make a large difference in Africa.

There is another huge global health challenge: mental health. When I was head of the Global Alliance for Chronic Diseases (GACD) I got my colleagues on the board to agree to add mental health as one of our priorities, with the result that last year GACD came up with a more-than-$60-million (the largest in history) call for proposals to fund innovation and research in mental health for the benefit of patients in the developing world and the poor and underserved in the rich world.

And then there are disasters, some human-made as in Syria, and some from natural phenomena like earthquakes, floods, and drought (some made worse by climate change). The consequences can be devastating for the innocent civilians. Women and children take the brunt. And yet much of the humanitarian response system is uncoordinated, inefficient, territorial, and lacking when it comes to seeking and applying innovative solutions. This is why last year at GCC we started the Humanitarian Grand Challenges initiative that I described at the beginning of this book.

Over the past two decades, there has been a lot of learning. What once seemed impossible now attracts the statement "It's not rocket science!" One of the lessons is that improving global health and reducing inequities is not expensive. A package of basic mental health care tools costs only a few dollars per person per year, but the economic cost of not attending to basic mental health needs is enormous. Rwanda has shown us that you can reduce newborn mortality by 30 percent in only seven years by seriously encouraging mothers to exclusively breastfeed in the first hour and for the first six months; by cutting the umbilical cord cleanly (GCC and its partners have funded a program of using topical antiseptics in Nepal for this purpose); and by kangaroo-style skin-to-skin contact between the infant and the mother (actually, you would get much better results if the father also did this in the first hour of the infant's life). No high tech, just simple measures than can save millions of lives. GCC has funded the development of intranasal oxytocin to stop post-partum haemorrhage in patients in poor countries—this has the potential to save thousands of maternal lives.

A few years ago I was funded by the visionary Gates Foundation, through GCC, to work with a team developing a drought-resistant breed of maize for Africa. Is this global health? Absolutely! Many parts of Africa are beset with frequent droughts. Forty-five percent of childhood deaths are somehow linked to malnutrition, and so agriculture and nutrition are vital to health.

What we have also learned from much scientific evidence is that improving the future for African children requires efforts directed at improving early childhood development, especially during the first one thousand days of life (including the nine months of pregnancy). This field is now called Developmental Origins of Health and Disease (DOHaD). According to DOHaD scientific evidence, a malnourished pregnant mother will program her child to develop chronic diseases like diabetes, heart disease, hypertension, and so on when that child grows up—and that risk is transmitted to the next generation because the programmed child becomes the parent. It is this area that I am now focusing on with my mostly African colleagues at the Stellenbosch Institute for Advanced Study (STIAS) in South Africa, where I am a permanent Fellow and convenor of the Health in Transition strategic theme. I am also involved with building African scientific and economic capacity through my work with the African Union and the African Academy of Sciences, and most recently through my position as chair of the External Advisory Group of the Tackling Infections to Benefit Africa (TIBA) Partnership.

And another piece of great news: extreme poverty has been cut in half since 1990. Since extreme poverty is a key social determinant of health, we can expect health to keep improving over the next few decades.

Among our biggest successes at GCC was the introduction of a program called Stars in Global Health, a revolutionary innovation- and research-funding program that allowed mostly young applicants to apply for a grant of $100,000 for an idea they may have by sending in a two-minute video instead of applying through the traditional cumbersome process. If they achieve proof of principle of their global health idea, they could go on to receive up to a million dollars for scaling up. These wonderful videos are publicly available on the GCC website. Innovators from poor countries, including a huge number from Africa, had not previously received research and innovation grants at this scale. Thousands of lives have already been saved and many thousands more have been touch by the resulting innovative solutions. Equally important is that the innovators have been very successful in shaping health policies by engaging government officials and decision-makers in their countries. And they have already created thousands of jobs and strengthened livelihoods. But in the long run, the greatest benefits have been in building the capacity of these young innovators to continue innovating for global health. For me, two young Africans we funded through GCC illustrate the progress that has been made and will continue to be made. Dr. Dixon Chibanda of Zambia and his colleagues have pioneered the "Friendship Bench," a brief, clinically proven cognitive behavioural therapy intervention for depression delivered by community "grandmothers" on simple wooden seats located on the grounds of health clinics. And in Tanzania, Fredros Okumu has developed amazing ways of studying "the most dangerous animal on earth: the mosquito" (as his TED Talk was titled), with huge potential to manage malaria in the future. Fredros obtained his PhD through these studies at the Ifakara Health Institute.

These young scientists will one day make their mark on the whole of humanity and be the driving force for Africa's scientific renaissance. In 2003 the African Institute for Mathematical Sciences and the Robert Bosch Stiftung, a German foundation, created a platform for engaging and encouraging young African scientists. It is called the Next Einstein Forum (NEF)—so named because of the idea that the next Einstein will be an African woman or man. It recognizes NEF Fellows from among the best of scientists and technologists, among them being Evelyn Gitau, a cellular immunologist from Kenya with whom I have worked to launch Grand Challenges Africa, a research and innovation funding program modelled on Grand Challenges Canada.

Africa is no longer the "dark continent." It has huge potential. There has been tremendous progress in improving health and building scientific capacity, mostly achieved by collaborations and partnerships among many people and institutions. As in many developing countries, there have been many lost opportunities. Yet there *is* now hope that the next Einstein will come from Africa.

Chapter 23

A Profile in the Courage of Idealism: Izzeldin Abuelaish and the Four Semites

> I refuse to accept the view that mankind is so tragically bound to the starless midnight of racism and war that the bright daybreak of peace and brotherhood can never become a reality. . . . I believe that unarmed truth and unconditional love will have the final word.
>
> — MARTIN LUTHER KING JR.

> The opposite of love is not hate, it's indifference.
>
> —ELIE WIESEL

To this day I continue to be mentored and influenced and inspired by people I meet, and not necessarily by elders (an increasingly smaller and smaller club, I am afraid to admit!) but by energetic and idealistic contemporaries as well. Throughout my career in medicine—and now as a crusader in the fight for improved health for needy people around the world—I have experienced more than my share of setbacks, frustrations, and even failures. The first lesson a young doctor learns is that despite her best efforts, patients will die. It is a hard lesson but it is learned; we cannot do our job otherwise. What is more difficult to accept—what I did not accept then and what I refuse to accept even today—is that as a society we can continue to allow death to occur *unnecessarily.*

In a previous chapter I reflected on Julius Nyerere and his profound impact on me in my awakening social consciousness. Hegel wrote that the history of the world is in essence the "progress of the consciousness of freedom." To me freedom and opportunity cannot be separated. No human being can truly be free if he or she is denied opportunity; as a global health advocate I see children in too many countries around the world living in conditions that I can only describe as cruel and barbaric. Poverty is a form of bondage, as is injustice, lack of proper medical care, and sexual or economic exploitation.

I often find myself wondering why it is that our governments seem so reluctant to act, why they seem so inadequate to the task. It is so frustrating that I am often seized by anger so intense it is blinding—impotent rage! Why do we allow so much death and violence to continue? Why are so many still so poor and unhealthy? As I related in another chapter, as a teenager I was politicized by the Palestinian–Israeli conflict—a conflict that sadly remains *even today* a deeply sorrowful blight on humanity's sorry legacy of senseless death and violence.

How could this conflict be going on still? Will there never be peace between Israelis and Palestinians? How many more innocent victims do we need before we wake up to the reality that we must find ways to live in peace? And yet, it seems so hopeless. When the weight of hopelessness overwhelms me, I think of a very special friend of mine and realize that we are never without the resources needed to solve even the most daunting problem or obstacle.

In 1967, when I was at high school listening to BBC broadcasts about the 1967 Six-Day War, a Palestinian boy about my age was living through a war that he would later describe as "looking like the end of the world."

Izzeldin Abuelaish and I crossed paths in 2009 in the aftermath of an almost unspeakable personal tragedy that would have very likely destroyed any other man.

Of course, back then in high school I had no idea that Izzeldin and I had so much in common: he too was from a large family; he woke at 3 A.M. to help earn money for his family as I had; he was a voracious reader who excelled academically; he had a strong mother who pushed him and his siblings hard to obtain education. He was the first to attend university, and so was I. He too was the first of his family to win a scholarship to medical school and become a doctor. We both ended up studying in England and subsequently at one of the best universities in the world (Oxford, for me; in his case, Harvard). Our families both had had land confiscated—for his family that was a very real form of exile: Izzeldin's family's property had been expropriated by the Israeli government and resettled by members of the Sharon family (the same Sharon who would command Israeli forces in the Six-Day War). As a result, Izzeldin and his family were forced into poverty among fellow Palestinian refugees in the heavily militarized area of the Gaza Strip, often referred to as one of the most hopeless, dismal, and overcrowded ghettos in the world.

In December 2009 I had already been at the University of Toronto for nine years when Israel invaded the Gaza Strip in a twenty-two-day military assault known as Operation Cast Lead. I was aware of what was happening from the news, of course. Both sides were pointing fingers, not a surprising feature in what had become a six-decades-old conflict. Still, the reports of casualties were alarming. According to a UN report, as many as fourteen hundred Palestinians were killed, a majority of whom were civilians. As many as twenty thousand were made homeless, and basic services like electricity, water, and access to emergency medical services had either been disrupted or destroyed.

Very shortly thereafter I received a letter from a man named Michael Dan, addressed to Peter Singer and me. "I have a serious proposition for you," the letter began. Dan went on to describe an individual by the name of Izzeldin Abuelaish. He "is a Palestinian Ob/Gyn who holds a postgraduate diploma in fetal medicine from King's College Hospital, London, and a MPH from Harvard. He is stuck in Gaza (where he lives) with his eight children." Izzeldin's story was about to become both horrifying and heartbreaking.

After a week of severe bombardment, some of it on densely populated areas in crowded neighbourhoods, Israeli troops began a ground incursion into Gaza. Tragically—and for reasons that remain inexplicable to this day—an Israeli tank opened fire on the apartment owned by Dr. Izzeldin Abuelaish, only a few minutes after he and his children had finally decided to move to Canada. There were two explosions. Izzeldin's daughters Bessan, aged twenty-one, Mayar, fifteen, and Aya, thirteen, and their cousin Noor were dead. Two other daughters were badly injured.

"They killed my daughters," Izzeldin wrote in his unforgettable book *I Shall Not Hate: A Gaza Doctor's Journey*. "All I could think was: This is the end. This is the end."

In the letter to Peter and me, Michael Dan had come right to the point: "If you can offer him a position, e.g., a research fellowship, then I will pay his salary for three years. Please read over his CV. I think you will be impressed. My checkbook is open. Time is of the essence."

Even more heartbreaking, only three months earlier Izzeldin had lost his beloved wife to leukemia. He was absolutely and utterly bereft. Remarkably, instead of surrendering to despair and embracing hate, he made a vow to himself and to his murdered daughters and niece: "If I could know that [they would be] the last sacrifice on the road to peace between Palestinians and Israelis, then I would accept their loss."

After receiving Michael's letter and before the tragedy had struck, we sprang into action. We pulled out all the stops. Peter and I immediately contacted Michael to organize and coordinate a campaign to bring Izzeldin and his family to Toronto. Peter would focus on dealing with the university, Michael on diplomatic issues and logistics, and I would concentrate on communicating directly with Izzeldin and his family to address their needs upon arrival in Toronto. I had to make the first call, however, and I admit I was very nervous. To this day it is difficult for me to even imagine what he was going through emotionally. The connection between Toronto and Gaza was quite poor.

"Hello, Dr. Izzeldin? My name is Abdallah Daar."

"Dr. Daar, yes. Thank you." The voice on the line was strong—courteous—but betrayed spidering seams of fatigue. "Why are you calling at this terrible time in our lives?"

"I am calling from the University of Toronto," I explained quickly. "Before the line is cut, yes, let me tell you quickly why I am calling."

"Okay."

"We have heard a lot about you, your family, and your work building peace with Israelis. We want to help to get you and your family safely out of Gaza and bring you to work as a researcher at our University of Toronto."

He sounded relieved. "That's very kind." He said he would have to ask his children. "They are doing very well at school here." He said he had received an offer from the University of Haifa in Israel, but I had the sense that he believed the children, especially, might benefit from a dramatic change of scenery. Wouldn't relocating only a short distance to a university inside Israel fester raw wounds?

Of course I told him to take whatever time he needed to decide. I also told him, however, that I was quite well known for my persistence. Was that a problem? "I will keep calling every day," I said in as upbeat a tone as I could manage, "until you have made up your minds!"

He laughed warmly. He said that was fine, and we hung up.

Meanwhile the pummelling bombardment of Gaza continued. The building adjacent to the Abuelaish home was reduced to rubble. On January 14, an Israeli tank aimed its gun directly at their house but rumbled away only after Izzeldin identified himself as someone well-known by the Israeli authorities because of his work caring for Israeli and Palestinian patients across the border at Soroka Hospital of Beersheba University, where for years he had worked five days a week, returning to Gaza over the weekend to look after poor Palestinian refugee patients.

And then the tragedy struck and his daughters and niece were killed.

I continued to call Izzeldin in Gaza. We talked about what was happening and how the situation seemed to be deteriorating. Luckily, the condition of his two daughters still in hospital had improved. He said that he had talked again with his family about a move to Toronto.

"Yes, it is time." He thanked me again and I said we would take care of the arrangements.

On March 3, 2009, Peter and I were at Toronto's International Pearson Airport to greet Izzeldin. A large contingent of print and TV reporters had also appeared. We had made arrangements for the terribly traumatized surviving children to follow, and a short while later Peter, Michael, Izzeldin, and I were celebrating their safe arrival.

"Welcome to Canada!"

It was a wonderful but bittersweet moment; I could not imagine what they were going through. I still cannot. What struck me most about Izzeldin was his infectious smile and his contagious courtesy. He is a deeply intelligent and thoughtful man, of course, but what overwhelms anyone in his presence is his quiet but indomitable strength and purpose. Time and time again in my life I have been deeply moved by exactly that quality. I imagine it was true of Jesus and the Prophet, of Gandhi, and Nelson Mandela and Martin Luther King Jr. and Mother Teresa.

At the same time, none of these leaders could be accused of starry-eyed idealism or naïveté. King understood the threat he confronted; he understood the risk he took walking unarmed into what might have seemed a fight he could not win. But he did win the fight—not permanently perhaps—for there will always be new battles. Izzeldin to me is a true and formidable idealist because he is a hard-nosed pragmatist. His enemies are no match for his commitment to justice.

H.G. Wells once wrote that a "great nation suffers but does not die." I believe that to be true of great people as well. Confronting and overcoming adversity is what prepares people for great and spectacular challenges. It makes for great copy for politicians to bellow about making a country "great again," for instance, but a nation is not great because of its geography or its politicians. It is great because its people are. It is with each and every one of us that we must begin. If we ask nothing of people but everything from a country, it is a hollow and meaningless accomplishment.

Are we great? Are *we* great? The distinction is profoundly meaningful, I think. It is important to remember that by the time of the attack in which his daughters and niece were killed, Izzeldin had already won awards for his bridge-building work between Palestinians and Jews. Peace was a path to which he was committed. What happened to him was a direct challenge to his commitment to peace. He easily could have surrendered and demanded revenge and no one would have been surprised. But he did not demand revenge and in doing so he becomes an enactment of the peace process itself. If I can do it—I who have lost so much—why not you?

Twice he has been nominated for the Nobel Peace Prize. He continues to speak around the world and his "I Will Not Hate" campaign reminds me very much of my childhood hero, Gandhi.

Then and now Izzeldin Abuelaish is asked—again and again—*why* he does not hate the Israelis who killed his daughters and niece. He answers by asking which Israelis exactly he is supposed to hate. The Israeli doctors who worked tirelessly to save the life of one injured daughter and the eyesight of another? Should he hate them? Or his many Israeli colleagues? And what about the many Israelis babies he had delivered over the years—should he hate them, too?

What he demands is not revenge but justice—and not for himself but for his daughters and niece. Hate solves nothing.

In fact, in memory of his daughters and niece, he founded the Daughters for Life Foundation to provide financial support for education for girls from Palestine, Israel, Jordan, Lebanon, and Syria as well as scholarships to study in Canada, the United

States, and the United Kingdom. He continues to work tirelessly on behalf of peace between Israelis and Palestinians.

A difficult challenge? "Yes!" No one has more of a right to speak authoritatively about the challenges of peace than Izzeldin. He is the first to acknowledge how steep the incline is—how formidable the obstacles that block the path to peace. But hopeless? "No! Never." Izzeldin believes that there exists no problem created by human beings that cannot also be solved by human beings. We do not lack the resources; what we lack is the will and the commitment.

Nobel Peace Prize–winner and author Elie Wiesel noted that Izzeldin's story "is a necessary lesson against hatred and revenge." President Barack Obama referred to the book in glowing terms in a major speech, and former president Jimmy Carter praised Izzeldin for "remarkable commitment to forgiveness and reconciliation that describes the foundation of a permanent peace in the Holy Land."

Peter Singer (who is of Jewish ancestry—his parents had fled from Hungary), Michael Dan, Izzeldin, and I—so different in so many ways—remain the best of friends and respected colleagues. In fact, you could say we have become Toronto's own "Four Semites"!

Izzeldin became an associate professor at the University of Toronto, working in the same Dalla Lana School of Public Health (DLSPH) where I am working. He is now being considered for a full professorship position for his research, teaching, and creative professional activities. One of his contributions is the study of the harmful effects of hate on health. His older surviving children have graduated from the University of Toronto and are working while the younger ones continue doing very well at school. Not too long ago they celebrated their new lives by becoming Canadian citizens! They may be in exile, but now they have another, new identity.

Thinking back to how Izzeldin came to Toronto and the small part I was so happy to play in making that happen, I reflect not only on the similarities between us but also the similarities between the work of his Daughters for Life Foundation and the work I am now doing in Africa with the Developmental Origins of Health and Disease initiative: we are both trying to build a better and healthier future for young people.

Einstein said that problems cannot be solved using the same techniques that created them. Izzeldin reminds me constantly that we cannot look to others—governments, for instance—to solve our problems if they are mostly responsible for creating the problems. What can each one of us do? We must each of us become agents of change.

There is another hero in this story, of course, and that is Michael Dan. I admire him profoundly for his extraordinary generosity and humanity. Michael is proudly Jewish. He is a shy, warm, incredibly intelligent human being. His humility is humbling. He wanted no recognition whatsoever for his efforts—both financial and humanitarian—in helping Izzeldin and his family. A Jew reaching out across a divide to help a Palestinian? Yes! That is how bridges are built! That is how humanity learns how to walk hand in hand. And let's not be naïve. Both Michael and Izzeldin (especially) have been the targets of much hateful rhetoric from those on both sides who are adamantly and militantly opposed to peace. *Why?* I wonder.

"We are addicted to our egotism," writes the brilliant and popular historian of world religions Karen Armstrong, to "our likes and dislikes and prejudices, and depend upon them for our own sense of identity." Like her, I—and others like Izzeldin—consider religion a potentially powerful instrument in helping human beings realize their full potential. It isn't about blind obedience to rules and antiquated orthodoxies; it's about exploring the richness of our humanity. Armstrong herself is a former nun who has written dozens of books about the nature of religion and its effect on human beings. In fact, she has created her own movement based on what she called the Charter for Compassion. I met her at the Chautauqua Institution, where I go every year and where she has been a regular speaker. What she urges is that peoples and religions around the world embrace compassion as a "core value." What a beautiful and beautifully simple idea!

Albert Camus said that we all carry within us "our places of exile"—"our crimes and our ravages." Our task, he said, is "not to unleash them on the world" but to "fight them in ourselves and in others." Camus was an Algerian and a French citizen who witnessed first-hand the brutal cruelties and indignities of colonialism. In fact, he fell out with his intellectual soulmate Jean-Paul Sartre for refusing unilaterally to condemn the French for their violence against Algerians in their brutal and protracted war. Instead, he condemned the violence on *both sides*. I think Camus would agree with Izzeldin and Karen Armstrong that we all need to think less about who is right and more about what is the right thing to do. It might start with compassion. It absolutely requires humility.

Michael Dan was Peter Singer's classmate at medical school in Toronto. He trained to be a neurosurgeon, worked in the United States, and with money inherited from his father Leslie Dan (a philanthropist who supports Jewish causes in both Canada and Israel), Michael dropped surgery to become a philanthropist and ethical entrepreneur focusing mainly on helping First Nations Canadians. He cares deeply about human rights and how to bridge the divide between Jews and Palestinians, supporting, for example, the University of Haifa in northern Israel, where 25 percent of the student body is Arab.

In Canada Michael has helped about one hundred NGOs and funded major Indigenous projects. In April 2015 he and his wife, Amira, donated $10 million to establish the Waakebiness-Bryce Institute for Indigenous Health at the University of Toronto's Dalla Lana School of Public Health. It is the world's first privately endowed research institute dedicated to the health of Indigenous peoples.

Michael cares deeply about human rights and has strong views about Israel and the Palestinians that he is not shy to talk about. In a 2013 interview with Haroon Siddiqui in the *Toronto Star,* Michael said that he was disillusioned with Israeli policies against Palestinians and felt alienated from both Israel and established Canadian Jewish organizations. He added that Israel should have jumped on the 2002 Arab peace plan, "an absolutely paradigm-changing proposal—every Arab state would recognize Israel, have normal relations with Israel, so long as Israel returned to the 1967 borders. But Israel just completely dismissed it."

"We have become a xenophobic people," he went on to say. "The irony is that we have faced racism and xenophobia throughout our history. . . . And the Jewish DNA is practically the same as the Palestinian DNA. We are brothers. The Palestinian attachment to land is as deeply rooted as the Jewish attachment to the land."

We are indeed brothers and sisters. One species. We are all human. As I have said, there is no clash of civilizations because we have one human civilization. I often think of voices like that of Izzeldin's when I listen to news reports about tensions and violence, in the Middle East or elsewhere, and when I hear people talking about how "hopeless" is the prospect of peace.

It will never happen. Not too long ago, I asked Izzeldin if he ever became discouraged and how he dealt with the defeatists who insist peace will never happen.

"Of course," he said, amused. "I am human. I am discouraged—every day." He said there are many times when he feels he has hit a wall and is so overwhelmed with fatigue and frustration that it would be so easy to quit. He never does.

"No. I will never give up. Never!" His smile is, as I said, deeply infectious. I believe him. For one thing, he is one of the few who has actually earned a right to be confident. Who better to ask about prospects of peace than a man who has paid so steep a personal price in the quest for peace?

I too believe that peace will prevail against hate. Not today and not tomorrow, but someday. And that obligates us to think what we can do each and every day to make that *someday* happen one day sooner.

I have always been drawn not only to remarkable intelligence but also to the beacons of the ideal—to individuals with an extraordinary commitment and an enlightened faith in human potential. I feel it with people like Izzeldin Abuelaish and Michael Dan, just as I felt it back in Tanzania with Julius Nyerere.

Many remarkable men and women have mentored me in my life; my hope is that in my turn I have been as meaningful and influential a mentor to younger colleagues. A mentor, I am convinced, is like a compass that keeps us oriented on our path: keeping us true to what is best in all of us. And we all need mentors in our lives; after all, we never know when we will be called upon to be the best we can be.

"I must uphold my ideals," wrote a wise Anne Frank, "for perhaps the time will come when I shall be able to carry them out."

Final Word

Concluding in Toronto, Where Identity Is a Poem

If destructive technology amplifies violence, constructive technology amplifies compassion, and technological lessons are universal.

— Richard Rhodes, *Hell and Good Company*

[Rumi] is trying to get us to feel the vastness of our true identity . . . like the sense you might get walking into a cathedral.

— Coleman Barks, interpreter of Rumi

When the weather is fine in Toronto, two friends and I enjoy a long walk, often ending up at a restaurant called Death in Venice on Queen St. West.

Michael Mendelson, Murray Glow, and I talk all the way, including during brunch. The restaurant is a favourite of ours and happens to be owned by a University of Toronto Turkish engineering graduate who is so fond of Mahler that he has a huge tattoo of him on his forearm.

Today, we are talking about identity. I tell them of my encounter with the Brimos and of their experiences as Syrian refugees. We remark upon the fact that we live in one of the largest and most affluent cities in North America, where the population is more than 50 percent immigrant. Michael and Murray tell how almost every one of their friends, including Murray, has married a Gentile (a *goyim* if you want to be offensive). We agree that assimilation is a big thing nowadays. The rabbis are worried, Murray jokes, and we all laugh.

To be honest, however, I am feeling a bit blue. I have recently returned from an exhausting overseas trip on behalf of my global health commitments and, well, I am tired and not just a bit frustrated. *Are we doing enough? Are we making any difference at all?*

As is the custom here in Canada, more than two people cannot meet for any length of time before conversation swings like metal shavings to a magnet to the soap-opera melodrama south of the border. *Are we in trouble? Is there something we're missing? What is going on?* The news is relentlessly bad. But it isn't just the bad news: it's the ratcheting rhetoric of hostility and anger that characterizes so much of what we call social discourse today. *What are we doing? What are we actually talking about? Are we really this far off the rails? What the hell is everyone so pissed off about?*

Experts who should know tell us that the world has never been in better shape. At no time in history have we been more prosperous, healthier, or better educated. I know from my own work that amazing progress is being made in even the most remote areas of the world. Why does it seem then that our canoe is headed over the lip of the falls? "The myth," writes philosopher John Gray, "is that the progress achieved in science and technology can occur in ethics, politics, or more simply, civilization."

Is Gray right? Is his pessimism with regards to the human condition justified? Like many of my fellow human beings who take the time to consult the dismal record of human war and violence, I have to admit that the news is not encouraging. It also may be true that in our mechanical culture we rely too much upon technology as a remedy to the seemingly intractable problems of human nature. "We can imagine," writes Oxford philosopher and historian Leszek Kolakowski, "a universal brotherhood of wolves but not of humans." His explanation being that unlike human needs that are boundless, the needs of wolves "are limited and definable and therefore conceivably satisfied." Human needs, he asserts, "have no boundaries we could delineate."

I certainly agree that an appeal of a scientific or technical problem is that it creates the context of its own solution (it is achievable), but does that mean we are doomed to stumble as if blind in the darkness of irresolvable ethical, political, or religious conflicts? My answer is this: a change of heart is not the kind of technological achievement that we can hold out at a distance and admire. A change of heart is a way of learning how to exist and flourish in the world in ways that are different from before. I will say this, however, to the pessimists: it is true that ethical or political innovation lags behind—often very far behind—other kinds of change, but that is to be expected.

There will always be a huge difference between what we know and what we believe. I think of people like Bill Hoffenberg, Julius Nyerere, Abdus Salam, Jan Morris, and Izzeldin Abuelaish, and so many others—each are pioneers of the heart. It isn't easy being the first. The important lesson for us who are not among the first is to make sure they are not the last.

Recently I had the great fortune to meet Matthieu Ricard at the home of a good friend, Umesh Khimji, in Muscat, Oman. Matthieu is the son of French philosopher Jean-François Revel and was raised in a highly charged intellectual environment. Himself an esteemed scientist with a PhD in molecular genetics from the Pasteur Institute, Matthieu stunned his father and family by abandoning a career in science to train as a Buddhist monk in Tibet. In fact, his decision to exile himself from his former life to pursue a spiritually centred life in the Himalayas was chronicled in a remarkable best-selling book entitled *The Monk and the Philosopher*, co-written with his atheist philosopher father. Besides being one of the most ferociously intelligent individuals I have ever met, Matthieu is also among the most humble, the most unassuming, and the most sincere.

In the book Jean-François asks his son why—with so much invested in his scientific profession and being surround by so many brilliant professionals—he would literally turn his back on such a promising career. Matthieu of course smiled when I asked a somewhat similar question: Why, Matthieu? Why? He obviously had heard the same question many times!

"I couldn't help noticing," he answered, "that the mastery such people possessed in their particular field was often not matched by even the simplest human perfections—like altruism, goodness, or sincerity." He should know, for he had recently written a book of a thousand pages on altruism!

At my first meeting with Matthieu (called "the happiest man in the world," a description that he is not at all fond of), I was discussing with him the issue of how we cope with repeated suffering and loss. I assumed he thought I was referring to doctors like myself, or nurses, who are at risk of burnout because we see our patients suffer and often die. But I was really thinking back to people like Katie and her parents, and of my friend Izzeldin. Matthieu said something I will never forget. "With empathy there *is* a limit, and too much can cause burnout; but not so with compassion, which is unlimited."

* * *

On the way back, Michael, Murray, and I go along Kensington Market and at the southwest corner of Oxford Street (always notes of Oxford!) and Augusta Avenue, opposite a vegan shop called Urban Herbivore, I see an apparition. Sitting on a small metal chair and typing on a very, very old Smith Corona is a tired-looking, thin woman in her early twenties, wearing sunglasses, a ring in her right nostril, and a colourful unicorn pinned to her light-grey sweater. A small, cheap, rickety metal table, covered with an off-white rough cloth, supports her typewriter. On the top right of the cloth is drawn a dark-blue sky with some stars and a sign of the zodiac; on the left is a yellow sun with radiating rays. The writing and the style and colours on the cloth call to mind a Gypsy woman wearing huge earrings with a glass ball in front of her. (Now there's a people who are being persecuted in Europe. What are they? Hungarians? Indians?)

We stop talking, approach her, and I ask if I could take a photo. She says yes, but only if you commission a poem. I say, sure, and she asks what is my topic, and I immediately say "Identity."

This is the poem she writes for me:

identity
it takes some time to see your eyes
for they ask questions in the morning
choosing who you'd like to be
within the day, but there is something
in the way, that you are one within
a place, surrounded by so many other
stories. your identity is written in
the things you bring to fruition,
your creations working back to
create yourself in understandings
of how you see yourself in time
who you are inside
and how you touch what is
outside.
P.S.
THE SPONTANEOUS PROSE STORE@PSEUDONYMSAYS

I donate some money, take a photo with her, and ask her name. "Leah. What is yours?"

"Abdallah."

In Hebrew, "Leah" means tired, but in Gaelic it means sunshine.

* * *

I started this book with a quote from Martin Luther King Jr. Without having planned to do so, I have ended it today, on April 4, 2018, exactly fifty years after King's assassination. And as I look back, I realize much of his work—his dreams—remain unfulfilled. A dream.

Racism, terrorism, extreme nationalism, Islamophobia, anti-Semitism, demagoguery, fear mongering, and indeed fear of the future seem to characterize our world today. Politicians and terrorists alike abuse religion and culture. It seems as if the world is coming apart and all the good promises of globalization are in retreat. We reach our hands out across the divide but instead of an embrace we experience a cold rebuke. We need to talk about what we all have in common yet find ourselves in noisy and often ugly conflict over trivial superficialities regarding what makes us different. We occupy isolated communities and nations instead of thinking of ourselves as members of one species who share a common human destiny.

In this age of growing fear of "the other," it is time to talk about our common humanity not as a cliché but as a fact of life that needs to be not only reckoned with but also applied. We all need to come to terms with our human universality; we need a deeper understanding of people and their histories, cultures, traditions, persuasions, and religions. We need a movement in which millions of people gather in their small social communities to tell their origin stories to their neighbours. It is not walls we need, nor suspicion, but increased understanding and appreciation of all the wonderful and enriching differences that make us what we are. "We are all caught in an inescapable network of mutuality," wrote King, "tied into a single garment of destiny."

I was born in an Arab household in Tanzania and attended university in Kampala. I was forced to become a refugee for having the wrong identity. I landed in London and studied at the University of Oxford. I have built medical schools and worked in Oman for ten years before moving to the University of Toronto nearly two decades ago. Along the way I have been lucky to have so many wonderful mentors and role models to help illuminate my way. My work keeps me travelling around the world more than two hundred days of every year, where I continue to observe and learn.

ACKNOWLEDGEMENTS

At Barlow Books, I am very grateful to Sarah Scott for her vision, wisdom, encouragement, and personal attention throughout the publishing process. She has been a tower of strength. She has also put me in touch with some outstanding professionals, including Debby de Groot, Tracy Bordian, Wendy Thomas, and the very talented cover designer Paul Hodgson. Her greatest contribution, however, was to introduce me to my admirable editor, Jonathan Schmidt. Jonathan's insights encouraged me to see myself differently. He taught me to take writing risks, and to rethink the thrust of the book. I have come to really value his guidance, searching, probing, and guiding me through many rounds of revisions, each of which enriched the manuscript. Thank you, Jonathan.

A few years ago I was fortunate to have been offered a Fellowship at the Stellenbosch Institute for Advanced Study (STIAS) so that I could begin work on this book. I thank Hendrik Geyer, Bernard Lategan, Christoff Pauw, Maria Mouton, Nel Marie Van der Merwe, and all the remarkable people I have met at STIAS over the years.

The process of writing this book reminded me of events, people, institutions, and places. They have merged to shape my several identities.

Tanzania nurtured my growth, educated me, sent me to medical school, and taught me the evils of colonialism. Many of the people in the drama of childhood and adolescence are mentioned in the book. In my adult life I have been honoured to work with many great Tanzanians, including Peter Msolla, Burton Mwamila, Hassan Mshinda, Mwele Malecela, and Kaushik Ramaya.

I spent some of the happiest times of my life in Uganda, until Idi Amin's madness made me a displaced person. I have returned many times to that beautiful country, which produced a truly outstanding research scientist, educator, and compassionate human being: Nelson Sewankambo. To meet him is to know how high a person can rise in the scale of humanness.

I landed penniless in London but with a supporting cast of friends. The United Kingdom enabled me to complete medical school and begin to earn enough money to survive and thrive. Once I got to Oxford, life changed dramatically, and mentors, role models, great teachers, colleagues, and patients played leading roles in shaping my life. I have mentioned most of these important people in the book, but one was so incredibly influential that I take my hat off again to say how grateful I continue to be for all that I learned from Peter J. Morris. He continues to be an inspiration to this day.

The Sultanate of Oman was, and continues to be, a land of beauty and grace and generous, open-minded people, led by HM Sultan Qaboos, the most enlightened of Middle Eastern leaders. At Sultan Qaboos University, Sheikh Amur al Marhubi and Dr. Yahya al Mandheri were vice-chancellors who welcomed me with open arms, as did Dr. Nasser al Lemki, the director of the university hospital. The late Chris Grant, my colleague in the department of surgery, was not just a great surgeon, but a wonderful friend. We were all energized and renewed by generations of younger colleagues, residents, nurses, and medical students—many of whom are now professors and medical leaders.

The University of Toronto made it possible for me to merge my biomedical interests seamlessly with global health, and to innovate and build impactful programs. I am grateful to David Naylor, Catharine Whiteside, Harvey Skinner, Howard Hu, and Ross Upshur. Peter Singer has been, for two decades, a very valued colleague and friend. We were truly fortunate when at the beginning of our work the late, great Harvard professor of Kenyan origin, Calestous Juma, introduced us to Elizabeth Dowdeswell, who is now Lieutenant Governor of Ontario. As our work evolved, many of our graduate students have ended up working with us in our various initiatives. These include Jim Lavery, Karlee Silver, Jocelyn Mackie, Andrew Taylor, David Brook, Claudia Emerson, Shane Green, Obidimma Ezekia, Ken Simiyu, Dominique McMahon, Fabio Salamanca-Buentello, Kristen Yee, Billie-Jo Hardy, and Sarah Ali-Khan. In 2010, Peter and I co-founded Grand Challenges Canada (GCC). We were very fortunate to have had the visionary businessman and philanthropist Joseph Rotman as GCC's founding board chair.

Over the past two decades I have worked in various capacities with the Bill and Melinda Gates Foundation. I thank all the people there who have supported our work, directly or indirectly, including, of course, Bill and Melinda Gates themselves, Carol Dahl, Tachi Yamada, Trevor Mundel, William Foege, Jeff Raikes, Susan Desmond-Hellmann, Chris Alias, Steven Buchsbaum, Kedest Hancock, Fil Randazzo, Kristy Anthony, and many others.

Internationally I have worked with great leaders, scientists, and clinicians, including Betsy Nabel, Alain Beaudet, John Bell, and Celina Gorre in my work with the Global Alliance for Chronic Diseases; Shekhar Saxena, Vikram Patel, and Pamella Collins in global mental health; Romain Murenzi and Mohammed Hassan at the Third World Academy of Sciences; Irina Bokova,

Flavia Schlegel, Henk ten Haave, and Dafna Feinholz at UNESCO; and on UNESCO's International Bioethics Committee, Alireza Bagheri, Jonathan Moreno, and Christiane Druml, amongst many distinguished bioethicists. I applaud my many extraordinary colleagues on the UN Secretary General's Scientific Advisory Board, including Hayat Sindi, Wole Soboyejo, Ada Yonath, Dong Pil Min, Maria Ivanova, Jorg Hacker, Gabisa Ejeta, Joji Carino, and Tanya Abrahamse.

At the African Academy of Sciences I had the honour of working with professors Berhanu Abegaz, Tom Kariuki, Nelson Torto, and Kevin Marsh. At the African Union's New Program for Africa's Development, I had the honour of working with professor Aggrey Ambali.

My sincere thanks to everyone.

Index

Note: AD = Abdallah Daar

Friends at medical school: Dr. Naphtali Agata (on Dr. Daar's right) is now Chair of the Kenya Medical Research Institute. Dr. Zeph Gaya is a distinguished surgeon in Eldoret, Kenya.

About the Author

Abdallah Daar, OC, FRS (C), D.Phil (Oxon), FRCP (Lon), FRCS, FRCSC, is Professor of Clinical Public Health; Global Health; and Surgery at the University of Toronto; and Permanent Fellow of the Stellenbosch Institute for Advanced Study.

Born in Tanzania, Dr. Daar was educated at Oxford University. He taught and worked as a transplant surgeon at Oxford before going to the Middle East, where he helped to build two new medical schools.

Dr. Daar was a member of the UN Secretary General's Scientific Advisory Board and UNESCO's International Bioethics Committee, and was the founding Chair of the Global Alliance of Chronic Diseases. He has been an advisor to the World Health Organization and the Bill and Melinda Gates Foundation. He is also a Fellow of the Royal Society of Canada and the African Academy of Sciences, and is a member of the board of the World Diabetes Foundation.

His numerous international awards include the Hunterian Professorship of the Royal College of Surgeons of England and the UNESCO Avicenna Prize for Ethics of Science. In 2017, Dr. Daar was made an Officer of the Order of Canada for his contributions to global health and for co-founding Grand Challenges Canada. Dr. Daar works extensively in Africa, where his main focus of work is on building scientific capacity, and leading a research team working on developmental origins of health and disease.